WHAT IS GLOBAL STUDIES?

What is global studies, and how does it relate to globalization? Responding to this frequently asked question, Manfred B. Steger and Amentahru Wahlrab provide the first comprehensive overview of this emerging field.

Authoritative and accessible, this primer speaks to students and instructors interested not only in key theories but also in applied teaching and learning programs designed to educate 'global citizens' to meet the concrete challenges of the twenty-first century. Linking the influential arguments of major thinkers in global studies to their own framework, the authors discuss the 'Four Pillars of Global Studies': globalization, transdisciplinarity, space and time, and critical thinking.

The book, with instructive appendix materials, will appeal to readers seeking a deeper understanding of global studies—one of the most popular fields of study in major universities around the world.

Manfred B. Steger is Professor of Sociology at the University of Hawai'i-Mānoa, Honorary Professor of Global Studies at RMIT University, and a globalization consultant for the US State Department.

Amentahru Wahlrab is Assistant Professor of Political Science at the University of Texas at Tyler.

Praise for *What is Global Studies?*

With the astounding success of the emerging field of global studies in universities around the world, questions arise about what it is, and whether there are central intellectual issues at its core. This book provides those answers by tracing the historical development of the field and showing that there are central pillars in the study of the "global imaginary." This thoughtful book provides the roadmap for what global studies is and what it promises to become, and is required reading for anyone interested in this flourishing field.

Mark Juergensmeyer, *University of California, Santa Barbara; Author of* Thinking Globally: A Global Studies Reader

Manfred Steger and Amentahru Wahlrab have given us the most comprehensive discussion about the multiple origins of global thought and research that I know of. It sets a new standard for what it means to analyze the very diverse theorizations and debates that have generated this field.

Saskia Sassen, *Columbia University; Author of* Expulsions: Brutality and Complexity in the Global Economy

This is a very exciting book. It is a major discussion of the field of global studies, an arena that is rapidly becoming a crucial domain of academic work. The authors are enviably fair, address the most vital themes in the discourse of global studies, and express their views with admirable clarity. Of particular interest to readers will be the exploration of disciplinarity, the relationship between the study of globalization and global studies, the exploration of global studies as a mode of critical inquiry, and the general organization of the field.

Roland Robertson, *University of Pittsburgh and University of Aberdeen*

Steger and Wahlrab have produced a book that simultaneously introduces, describes, and interprets the new field of global studies in relation to its theories, concepts, and research methods. *What is Global Studies?* is thus a masterful survey of the global mentalité or "imaginary" that informs the field, including the "significations and articulations" that have enabled it to escape the gravitational pull of more familiar, local imaginaries. The writing is everywhere inclusive, balanced, and clear, and the structure of the whole designed to satisfy—and this is no mean feat—both the beginning student and the seasoned scholar.

Giles Gunn, *University of California, Santa Barbara*

WHAT IS GLOBAL STUDIES?

Theory and Practice

Manfred B. Steger and Amentahru Wahlrab

Routledge
Taylor & Francis Group

NEW YORK AND LONDON

Please visit the e-resource website at
www.routledge.com/9780415684835

Published 2017
by Routledge
711 Third Avenue, New York, NY 10017

and by Routledge
2 Park Square, Milton Park, Abingdon, Oxon, OX14 4RN

Routledge is an imprint of the Taylor & Francis Group, an Informa business

© 2017 Taylor & Francis

First edition published by Pearson Education, Inc. 2004
Second edition published by Pearson Education, Inc. 2007
Third edition published by Pearson Education, Inc. 2009
Fourth edition published by Pearson Education, Inc. 2011
Fifth edition published by Pearson Education, Inc. 2014

Library of Congress Cataloging in Publication Data
Names: Steger, Manfred B., 1961- author. | Wahlrab, Amentahru, author.
Title: What is global studies? : theory & practice / Manfred B. Steger,
    Amentahru Wahlrab.
Description: New York, NY : Routledge, 2016. | Includes bibliographical references.
Identifiers: LCCN 2016017577 | ISBN 9780415684842 (hardback) |
    ISBN 9780415684835 (pbk.) | ISBN 9781315459332 (ebook)
Subjects: LCSH: International education. | Globalization—Study and teaching.
Classification: LCC LC1090 .S75 2016 | DDC 370.116—dc23LC record available at
    https://lccn.loc.gov/2016017577

ISBN: 978-0-415-68484-2 (hbk)
ISBN: 978-0-415-68483-5 (pbk)
ISBN: 978-1-315-45933-2 (ebk)

Typeset in Bembo
by RefineCatch Limited, Bungay, Suffolk

For Perle and Sarah

CONTENTS

Images   *ix*
Figures   *xi*
Acknowledgments   *xiii*

Introduction: Global Studies and the Global Imaginary   1

1 The Intellectual Origins and Evolution of Global Studies   25

2 The First Pillar of Global Studies: Globalization   53

3 The Second Pillar of Global Studies: Transdisciplinarity   86

4 The Third Pillar of Global Studies: Space and Time   114

5 The Fourth Pillar of Global Studies: Critical Thinking   145

Appendix: Global Studies Resources   *181*
Bibliography   *191*
Index   *204*

IMAGES

I.1 The *Daily News* Globe, 1930s   5
I.2 'Earthrise', taken from Apollo 8, 1968   6
2.1 World Economic Forum Meeting in Davos, Switzerland, 2016   75
2.2 Anti–ISIS Demonstration in India, 2015   79
4.1 'Glocal' Dynamics, reflected in the Cityscape of Shanghai   131
4.2 'Glocal' Dynamics, reflected in the Cityscape of Seoul   131
4.3 'Blue Marble Shot', taken from Apollo 17, 1972   139
5.1 Anti-WTO Protests in Seattle, 1999   150
5.2 Global Citizenship Poster at RMIT University, 2015   160
5.3 'Occupy Wall Street' Camp in Washington, DC, 2012   162
5.4 Zapatista Gathering in Chiapas, Mexico, 1994   164

FIGURES

I.1 International Studies, Area Studies, or Global Studies? 11
I.2 The Four Pillars of Global Studies 19
1.1 The Use of 'Globalization', 1930–2008 26
1.2 Genealogy of 'Globalization': Early Evolution of
    the Four Meaning Branches 32
2.1 Databases Listing Number of Articles and
    Publications on Globalization, 2015 54
2.2 The Explosion of 'Globalization', 1990–2000 58
2.3 Academic Globalization Debates: Four Intellectual Camps 72
2.4 Ideologies, Imaginaries, and Ontologies 74
2.5 Public Globalization Debates: Three Ideological Perspectives 80
3.1 Interdisciplinarity, Multidisciplinarity, and Transdisciplinarity 94
3.2 Dimensions of Globalization 98
4.1 Giddens vs. Albrow: Globalization as Continuity or Change? 123
4.2 Deterritorialization Absolutists and Relativists 128
5.1 Two Interrelated Stages of Critical Thinking 147
5.2 Pluralization of Critical Theory 149
5.3 Characteristics and Outcomes of Critical Global Studies 156
5.4 Hans Schattle's Typology of Global Civic Engagement 161

ACKNOWLEDGMENTS

It is a pleasant duty to record our debts of gratitude. First, we want to thank our colleagues, students, and friends at the University of Hawai'i-Mānoa, the University of Texas at Tyler, and the Royal Melbourne Institute of Technology (RMIT) University. Nothing is more important for the development of a new field than stimulating discussions with interested faculty and students.

Manfred wants to extend his special thanks to the faculty in the Department of Global Studies at the University of California Santa Barbara for their tremendous support, assistance, and kindness over nearly a decade of close contact and cooperation. This book would not have been written without Manfred's close intellectual and personal friendship with Paul James, the visionary Director of the Institute for Culture and Society at Western Sydney University. A number of crucial arguments made in this book originally emerged and were refined during many years of stimulating discussions of globalization matters between Manfred and Paul that also resulted in a number of co-authored publications.

Amentahru would like to thank Isaac Kamola for years of engaging him in discussions on globalization and global education. His critical insights have sharpened Amentahru's arguments for the better.

We appreciate the engagement of colleagues from around the world who have channeled much of their enthusiasm for the study of globalization into the development of the Global Studies Consortium, a transcontinental professional organization dedicated to strengthening the new transdisciplinary field of global studies. We also want to express our deep appreciation to numerous readers, reviewers, and audiences around the world, who, for nearly two decades, have made insightful comments in response to our public lectures and publications on the subject of globalization. Jennifer Knerr, Lydia de Cruz and the other editors at Routledge have been shining examples of professionalism and competence. We especially appreciate the persistence and patience shown by Craig Fowlie, the innovative Editorial Director at Routledge, who was willing to wait for the completion of this long overdue book. Finally, we want to thank our families—especially our partners Perle and Sarah—for their love and support. Many people have contributed to improving the quality of this book; its remaining flaws are our own responsibility.

what do we become? specified in smth or general?
as global scholars
to read the literature of the field

to read/think/write rigilously

INTRODUCTION

Global Studies and the Global Imaginary

how does GS position themselves with globalization?
Models from different positions of knowledge

Global studies emerged in the late 1990s as a transdisciplinary field of academic inquiry exploring the many dimensions of globalization. 'What is there is also here and what is here is also there' is probably the most succinct and uncontroversial summary of globalization's central dynamics of inter-connectivity, reconfiguration of space and time, and enhanced mobility. Although it has been extensively studied in sociology, economics, anthropology, geography, history, political science, and other fields, globalization falls outside the established disciplinary framework. It is only of secondary concern in these traditional fields organized around different master concepts: 'society' in sociology; 'resources' and 'scarcity' in economics; 'culture' in anthropology; 'space' in geography; 'the past' in history; 'power' and 'governance' in political science, and so on. By contrast, global studies has placed 'globalization'—a contested keyword without a firm disciplinary home—at the core of its intellectual enterprise. The rise of global studies represents, therefore, a clear sign of the proper recognition of a new kind of social dynamic. But it also demonstrates that the nineteenth-century realities that gave birth to the conventional disciplinary architecture are no longer ours.[1] Although global studies has open transdisciplinary ambitions, it is not hermetic. It welcomes various approaches and methods that contribute to a transnational analysis of the world as a single interactive system.

Calling for a special academic context for the study of globalization, the new field has become increasingly institutionalized in the academy. Yet, global studies does not see itself as just another cog in the disciplinary machine of contemporary higher education. In spite of today's trendy talk about 'globalizing knowledge' and 'systematic internationalization'—which often seems to be more about the neoliberal reinvention of the academy as big business than creating new spaces of epistemological diversity—the traditional Western academic framework of knowledge specialization has survived largely intact into the twenty-first century. Often forced to make compromises and find less than desirable accommodations with the dominant academic order, global studies challenges a fractured mindset that encourages the division of knowledge into sharply demarcated areas populated by disciplinary 'insiders'. Consequently, the new field is also critical of the parochial departmental structure of higher education that operates institutionally in most cases as an inward-looking defense mechanism against real and suspected threats from 'outsiders'. In the roughly two decades of its existence, global studies has thrived on the growing academic disaffection with this insular status quo. Although it seeks to blaze new trails of social inquiry, the newcomer is not afraid of presenting itself as a fluid and porous intellectual terrain rather than a novel, well-defined item on the dominant disciplinary menu. To use Fredric Jameson's apt characterization, global studies generates an academic 'space of tension' framed by multiple disagreements *and* agreements in which the very notion of globalization itself is being continuously produced and contested.[2] Thus, the evolving field has attracted scores of unorthodox faculty and unconventional students who share its sincere commitment to studying transnational processes, interactions, and flows from a perspective framed by broad research networks rather than narrow disciplinary communities.

Most importantly, global studies both embraces and exudes a certain *mentalité* we call the 'global imaginary'. It is a sense of the social whole that frames our age as one shaped by the intensifying forces of globalization.[3] Giving its objective and subjective aspects equal consideration, global studies suggests that enhanced interconnectivity does not merely happen in the world 'out there' but also operates through our consciousness 'in here'. To recognize the significance of global consciousness, however, does not support premature proclamations of the death of the nation-state. Conventional national and local frameworks have retained significant power. Although the nation-state is not disappearing, it is true that it has been forced by globalization to seek sometimes rather uneasy accommodations with a slowly evolving architecture of global governance—an embryonic form of global society that can no longer be derided as a utopian pipe dream. Indeed, people's growing recognition of their shrinking planet—and their precarious place in it—has played an important role in the destabilization of the traditional national and local settings in which humans have imagined their communal existence in modern times. Hence, it is not surprising that global studies shows great interest in transnational educational initiatives centered on the promotion of 'global citizenship' rooted in embedded cosmopolitan visions that link the local to the global and vice-versa.

While globalization processes have been unfolding for millennia, it is hard to deny that interconnectivity has kicked into a higher qualitative and quantitative gear since the 1980s. To acknowledge this global systemic shift is not to deny the obvious continuities between globalization's current phase and modernity's earlier forms of expansionism reflected in such powerful social dynamics as industrialism, capitalism, colonialism, imperialism, secularism, and the nation-state system.[4] But even with the benefit of privileged hindsight granted to early twenty-first century observers, it is hard to determine whether contemporary globalization—and thus global studies—should be considered the latest chapter in modernity or an irrevocable break with an era that started with the Industrial Revolution. As we discuss in Chapter 4, there are good arguments on both sides of this debate. Perhaps the best we can do from a global studies perspective is to generate new, critical interpretations of the complex relationship between modernity and globalization.

Let us make one more point in this introduction of our subject. Global studies responds to the specific opportunities and challenges of global interdependence as they unfold in the daily lives of billions and billions of sentient beings that call this wondrous planet home. The new field exhibits a strong interest in new public policy initiatives such as ecologically sustainable modes of cooperative problem-solving that frequently cross the academic/non-academic divide. Students of global studies realize that tackling the pressing 'global issues' of the twenty-first century requires sustained theoretical reflection on an academic level as much as enduring 'real-world' community engagement. This critical imperative to connect theoretical insights to practical matters—especially innovative public policy proposals—sits at the very core of global studies and thus frames the conception and organization of this book.

The Rise of the Global Imaginary

It makes sense to point to innovative mid-twentieth-century articulations of 'the global' as the early stirrings in a process that would eventually lead to the birth of a new star in the academic firmament. But how did these new significations and articulations of the global imaginary manage to escape the strong gravitational pull of more familiar concepts at the heart of the national imaginary? For example, the term 'inter-national' had long enjoyed a virtual monopoly over conceptualizations of social interactions that reached beyond the sharply delineated territory of the modern nation-state. As it turns out, the emergence of global studies corresponds to the rise and growing presence of the global. But ideas and images of the global and the globe were already becoming quite popular in the early twentieth century—at a time when the ascent of the buzzword 'globalization' that followed at the heels of the disintegrating Soviet bloc was still many decades away. One crucial factor for the early popularity of the 'global' relates to the development of the modern media and communications industries whose executives recognized the worldwide reach and power of their expanding networks serving mass audiences. A number of newspapers around the world—particularly in the United States, the United Kingdom, Canada, and Australia—started to use the word 'globe' as an identity marker, such as the *Boston Globe* or the *Globe and Mail*.

From the 1920s forward, some newly constituted commercial airlines featured globes in their advertising projections. Founded in 1927, Pan American World Airways flew under a blue globe logo until its economic collapse during a very different period of global competition in the early 1990s. The *Daily News*—later the inspiration for the *Daily Planet* of Superman movies' fame—proudly displayed a gigantic rotating globe in the lobby of its New York headquarters at its opening in 1930. Already in the 1910s, a number of Hollywood movie studios had seized upon globes as a vital component of their corporate image. The first logo for Universal Pictures from 1912 to 1919 incorporated a stylized Earth with a Saturn-like ring. It was called the 'Trans-Atlantic Globe' or 'Saturn Globe'. In the 1920s, its revised logo was planet Earth floating in space with a biplane flying around it and leaving in its wake a trail of white vapor. Built in 1926, Paramount Pictures' New York headquarters was topped by an illuminated glass globe, which was later blackened in response to anticipated perils linked to World War II. In the immediate aftermath of that war—and in the spirit of celebrating the global reach of the communications industry—the Hollywood Foreign Correspondents Association initiated a series of media presentations and receptions they called the Golden Globe Awards.

Indeed, World War II proved to be a watershed in the evolution of global consciousness. Just as the eighteenth-century revolutions and the ensuing two decades of Napoleonic warfare in Europe had ushered in the national age, the most destructive war of the twentieth century served as a crucial catalyst for the birth of the global era. Unlike World War I—at the time known as the Great War and largely confined to Europe and the Mediterranean region—World War II raged as a worldwide contest in

IMAGE I.1 The *Daily News* Globe, 1930s

Source: Wikipedia, https://commons.wikimedia.org/wiki/File:Lobby_and_Globe_in_
News_Building.jpg

multiple theaters from the Mediterranean and the Atlantic to the Pacific.
Military success depended more than ever on the effective formation of
trans- and multinational alliances. The three major Allied war conferences
of Teheran (1943), Bretton Woods (1944), and Yalta (1945) laid the foundation of a global political and economic order, which divided the planet into
expansive regions seeping across national borders. At the outset of the Cold
War, people started to use the terms 'global' or 'world' to characterize these
new geopolitical spheres: the First World comprised of Western democra-
cies; the Second World encompassing the communist bloc; and the Third
World consisting of colonial territories and newly independent countries in
Asia, Africa, and Latin America. Destabilizing the Eurocentric system of
Great Powers that had grown to maturity in the late nineteenth century,
World War II intensified the permeation of the dominant national imaginary by those ideas and practices that took the entire globe as their frame of
reference. Reflecting people's growing consciousness of belonging to a
global community connected across planetary space and time, the global
imaginary was nurtured along by the rapid development of more sophisticated transportation, information, and communication technologies with
strong roots in wartime innovations such as radar, basic computing machines,
shipping improvements, and jet engines. Ultimately, the civilian applications of wartime technologies culminated in the invention of the personal

computer and the Internet, thus dramatically multiplying the speed and intensity with which ideas, images, practices, people, and materials moved across national spaces.

Even the late eighteenth-century European yearnings for national liberation became globalized as decolonization movements in Africa and Asia generated new nation-states eager to assemble under the global umbrella of the United Nations. But nothing captured the rise of the global imaginary as starkly as the dawning space age. Most of all, the awesome picture of 'Earthrise'—first taken by Apollo 8 astronaut William Anders after the first-ever manned orbit around the moon on December 24, 1968— did much to enhance people's awareness of our collective journey on Spaceship Earth. Our world is endowed with magnificent yet finite resources suited to sustain life on our precious planet. The fragility of the blue globe suspended in the vast cosmos conveyed in these Apollo images loomed large in the emergence of transnational and countercultural 'new social movements' in the 1960s and 1970s that centered on categories of

IMAGE I.2 'Earthrise', taken from Apollo 8 in 1968

Source: NASA, http://www.nasa.gov/sites/default/files/images/297755main_GPN-2001-000009_full.jpg

ecology, indigeneity, race, gender, and sexuality. The ascent of the global imaginary reached another threshold when the Berlin Wall fell in 1989, which marked the compression of the three worlds of the Cold War period into the one world of globally integrating markets and digital technologies. Anticipated by prescient thinkers like Marshall McLuhan and Hannah Arendt as early as the 1950s, certain aspects of utopian-sounding social formations like the 'global village' and the 'global society' were already assuming material forms in the second half of the century.[5]

Though still a long way from the full-blown condition of globality, the world was clearly becoming more integrated. The growing presence of the adjective 'global' in the news, advertising, policy circles, and the entertainment industry reflected the remarkable rise of a global imaginary. It punctuated the binary language of nationalism and its exclusivist claims to the management of modern societies. It was in this transformative context of becoming worldwide—both in an objective and subjective sense—that the global ceased to be the accidental quality of the international and became something in itself—and the field of global studies was born.[6]

International Studies, Area Studies, or Global Studies?

As recently as three generations ago, notions of the social whole—including 'the market'—were rarely stretched across the borders of the nation-states. In other words, commonly held intuitions of community and belonging were reflected in a national imaginary that shaped people's sense of belonging as members of the national community. Twentieth-century social scientists used of the term 'inter*national* relations' only to refer to changing connections among territorial states and nationally bounded societies. Thus, when sociologists analyzed the international dimensions of 'societies' or political scientists theorized 'the balance of power', they remained within the conceptual limitations of a state-centric perspective that has been aptly characterized as 'methodological nationalism'.[7]

During World War II and its aftermath, this nation-state centered approach also dominated the relatively new academic disciplines of international studies (IS) and international relations (IR). Focusing on the international as a system comprising nation-states as discrete units operating within a condition of structural anarchy, IR in its realist iteration originated as a subfield within American political science. Early proponents included displaced European scholars like Hans Morgenthau, Ernst Haas, and Henry Kissinger who assumed dual roles as academics and government advisors in aiding their country's new role of superpower. Similarly, IS grew up in a national security environment. For example, the Association for Asian

Studies, the largest US institution dedicated to the study of Asia, was founded in 1941 when World War II government agencies such as the Office of War Information and the Office of Strategic Services turned to the social sciences to develop regional specializations that would aid the US war effort. Responding to these requests with two independent reports, the Social Science Research Council's (SSRC) Committee on World Regions and Columbia University's Committee on Area Studies recommended the use of social scientific methodologies to enhance the framework and quality of what came to be known as 'area studies' (AS) and 'development studies'.[8]

As these fields gained popularity and institutional support within the US academy during the Cold War era, IS and AS, too, mushroomed into largely autonomous fields. Their growth occurred in response to the perceived threat of Communism and the establishment of new nation-states—and potential clients of Moscow—in the wake of decolonization. Seeking to thwart the Soviet Union's involvement in Europe and the Third World, IR and IS pursued overlapping academic and political agendas that benefited from the generous support of US funding agencies linked to the powerful national security establishment headed by the Pentagon, the FBI, and the CIA as well as philanthropic organizations like the Carnegie, Ford, and Rockefeller Foundations. The same is true for AS. As John Lie notes, both the US government and many of the leading private foundations (like the Ford Foundation and the Rockefeller Foundation) promoted an area studies perspective that was linked to Western-centric notions of modernization and economic development. As a result of these new funding streams, AS was considered big business and became institutionalized in large research centers and academic departments at most major US universities.[9]

Similarly, the International Studies Association (ISA) arose as a national organization committed to the promotion of 'research and education in international affairs'.[10] Founded in 1959 largely by disaffected American political scientists, the ISA embraced a methodological nationalism that served the geopolitical strategies and priorities of the First World in general, and US hegemony in particular.[11] Mainstream IR scholars treated the state as the main actor—and thus _the_ central unit of analysis and the principal mover—of world politics. Traditional IR scholarship focused primarily on the self-interested actions of nation-states—especially with regard to security issues—and often at the expense of other crucial dimensions such as culture, ecology, and ideology. Attached to dominant behaviorist designs and rationalist modeling schemes, IR researchers sought to find generalizable analytical frameworks capable of explaining and predicting power dynamics in international affairs with the hope that such theories might contribute to the prevention of large-scale wars, especially a nuclear exchange between the West and the Soviet bloc.

Growing, in part, out of IR and IS, global studies still draws to some extent on international relations analysis. In particular, the new field has benefited from social constructivist IR scholars committed to deconstructing the unitary actor model of the state in favor of a more complex conception that emphasizes an amalgam of interests, identities, and contingency. Some of these revisionist tendencies in IR also appeared under the label 'institutionalism'. Perhaps the most serious challenges to the canonical status of the inter-national in IR came in the late 1980s and 1990s from a number of insiders who coined the phrase 'complex interdependence' to emphasize the changing dynamics of the international system and the part played in it by states *and* a growing variety of non-state actors. Recognizing the rapid transformation of the power and authority of national governments under globalizing conditions, Robert Keohane argued for a revision of IR's key concept of sovereignty from a territorially defined barrier to a bargaining resource for politics characterized by complex transnational networks.[12] As Barrie Axford notes, this new transnational theoretical orientation in IR partly corresponded with the more fluid approaches of 'international political economists' and 'regime theorists' who examined the workings of institutionalized systems of cooperation in global issue areas such as economic development, climate change, surveillance, and digital technology.[13]

However, the success of these new intellectual initiatives depended to a significant extent on the redirection of funding by US government and philanthropic organizations from IS and AS to the newcomer global studies. As Isaac Kamola's pioneering work on the subject has demonstrated, starting in the mid-1990s, a number of important funders announced plans to replace area structures with a global framework. For example, the SSRC recommended defunding 'discrete and separated area committees' that were reluctant to support scholars interested in global developments and policy-relevant 'global issues'. When conventional area studies experts realized that traditional sources of funding were quickly drying up, many joined the newly emerging global studies cohort of scholars centered on the study of globalization. Major universities, too, reduced the level of support for area studies teaching and research programs while developing new investment schemes and strategic plans that provided for the creation of new global studies or global affairs programs and centers. Kamola points out that major professional organizations like the National Association of State Universities and Land Grant Colleges and the American Association of Colleges and Universities eagerly joined these instrumental efforts to synchronize the initiatives of 'globalizing the curriculum' and 'recalibrating college learning' to the shifting economic landscape of the 'new global century'.[14]

As we discuss in more detail in Chapter 2, this reorientation of AS and IS toward global studies occurred in the ideological context of the rise of 'neoliberalism'—an economistic doctrine at the core of a comprehensive worldview we call 'market globalism'.[15] Expanding across the globe after the fall of Soviet communism, this extreme version of pro-market thinking was built on the classical liberal ideal of the self-regulating market. Politically engaged neoliberal academics like Friedrich Hayek and Milton Friedman advocated the creation of a single global free market, free trade, privatization of state ownership, deregulation of national economies, radical tax relief, and the spread of consumerist values around the world. Spearheading what became a burgeoning ideological movement, these two Nobel Prize-winning economists had seized upon the crisis of nation-state centered Keynesianism in the 1970s to pitch their doctrine to rising conservative politicians in the United States and United Kingdom. Still, it represented a remarkable ideological achievement for influential voices in the 1990s to harness the concept of 'globalization' to their neoliberal outlook. Corporate media associated with this market ideology saturated the global public sphere with the neoliberal credo of economic efficiency and prosperity coupled with unprecedented technological progress. In this context, some commentators have coined the term 'academic capitalism' as an overarching framework for understanding the profound ways in which neoliberal globalization and the knowledge economy have been transforming higher education around the world.[16]

Part and parcel of this changing higher education environment, global studies was nurtured by a solidifying neoliberal landscape that articulated the rising global imaginary in concrete pro-market political agendas and programs. The recipient of new material and ideational, market-oriented initiatives, global studies benefited from the shift toward globalization. Sensitive to the post-1989 imperatives of the 'new economy', global studies researchers began to move beyond old territorialist notions of the nation-state by emphasizing transnational processes and global transformations. Consequently, they considered the state as but one important actor in the thickening web of today's transnational interdependencies. Encouraging the development of multi-actor, interdependent models of world order, they paid equal attention to proliferating non-state entities such non-governmental organizations, transnational corporations, global social movements and networks, and other transnational social and political forces.

Moreover, its multicentric and multidimensional understanding of the dynamics shaping our globalizing world made global studies a field with strong 'applied' interests in public policy. Today, many global studies scholars engage topics often neglected in IR, such as ecology, social space, media and communication, ideology, history, gender, ethnicity, technology, and poverty—all of which are conceived in terms of linkages and flows across state boundaries. Finally, the problem-centered focus of global studies encourages the forging of strong links between theory and practice—and among the worlds of academia, political organizations, and social movements—that operate in various concrete settings in the daily lives of people around the globe.

As James Mittelman has emphasized, the rise of global studies has occurred in the context of an extended quarrel within the fields of IR and IS where innovative 'para-makers' have challenged the dominant 'para-keepers'.[17] Leading the defense of their 'international' paradigm against the latest wave of 'globalization theory', para-keepers have downplayed the significance of deterritorialization and other transnational dynamics for

FIGURE I.1 International Studies, Area Studies, or Global Studies?

Area Studies (AS): language, history, culture, national security, war, modernization development

Global Studies: culture, ecology, ideology, interests, identities, and contingency

International Relations (IR): borders, nations, states, war, societies, balance of power

International Studies (IS): international system, realism, structure, states, security their respective fields and reasserted the priority of politics over economics in world affairs. Para-makers, on the other hand, have been supportive of some features of the global studies paradigm. Indeed, they are increasingly willing to question even IR's holy grail: the centrality of the state as an actor in world politics. Since the late 1990s, such IR para-makers have endeavored to broaden their research agenda by incorporating analyses of international political economy and cultural aspects of relationships between states, as well as considering the growing significance of non-state actors and global governance problems. As a result of both the shifting material incentive structure favoring global approaches and the para-makers' intellectual efforts, a growing number of IR and IS researchers have become more engaged in the burgeoning academic efforts to establish new global studies programs and research centers. At a minimum, international studies experts in the social sciences and humanities have developed new 'global' repertoires. As Jan Nederveen Pieterse points out:

> In most cases this means upgrading previous international or comparative study programs and in some cases it includes regional studies. In the last 15 years, centers, programs, and courses under the heading of global studies have mushroomed across the world. They combine globalization studies in diverse disciplines and build on existing international relations and development studies programs.[18]

Lately, even the rather conventional International Studies Association has shown a new openness to discussing the impact of globalization on the conventional frameworks of IS and IR. For example, the overarching theme of its 2015 annual meeting was devoted to questions about the future of area studies in a globalizing world.

This auspicious tendency toward cooperation also exists in contemporary area studies whose advocates have increasingly moved away from the old Cold War rationales that once shaped the contours of their field. In addition, the Western-centric template of studying the various regions of the world as the 'other' has lost most of its legitimacy. Matthias Middell observes that to study the world's various regions under the global conditions of the twenty-first century implies rich opportunities for collaboration between global studies and area studies.[19] Under the impact of globalization, a growing number of area studies para-makers have embraced the new label 'transregional studies', which signifies a novel interest in the interconnectedness of world regions and the importance of neglected regions such as oceans, large lakes, and vast mountain chains that were previously not included among the conventional 'areas'. Middell aptly points to a 'spatial turn' in area studies that is of particular interest for the research agenda in global studies for it implies that areas or regions are not naturally given but socially constructed and as such are the result of conflict about the application of certain regimes of territorialization in the world. Like 'nations' and other socially constructed forms of bounded space, uncritical notions of areas nurture the legacies of former global inequalities and thus shape the ways in which we understand our contemporary world order.[20]

The Contours of the Field

While global studies has benefited from significant shifts in funding toward 'global' research and teaching on the macro-level of the university, government, and major philanthropic organizations, it also resonates with a new intellectual agenda focused on 'globalization'. It fosters a multireferential understanding of a social whole that is no longer exclusively normalized within a national framework, but equally applicable to local and global settings such as global cities and globally connected regional networks. Most importantly, global studies draws its core reason for being from the fact that we live today in an unprecedented age of interconnectivity brought about by globalization. As we demonstrated, the growing power of the global imaginary in the twenty-first century is reflected in language—especially the proliferation of such terms as 'glocalization', 'globality', 'globalism', 'globish', 'creolization', 'McDonaldization', 'McWorld', 'hybridity', 'outsourcing', 'texting', 'skyping', 'googling', 'tweeting', and so on. New digital technologies combine with new social media platforms to facilitate the movement of people, goods, services, money, ideas, and culture across political borders more easily and quickly than ever before.

Despite the obvious benefits associated with a growing mountain of digitalized 'information' and the results of 'big data' research readily accessible in real-time to billions of people around the world, globalization certainly has its downsides. Greater connectivity and mobility for the privileged few is often bought at the price of disconnection and immobility for the underprivileged multitude. New sources of insecurity and disruption are reflected in a public discourse that increasingly revolves around global problems that reach deeply into every aspect of social life: transnational terrorism, pandemics like AIDS and Ebola, global financial crises, growing disparities in wealth and wellbeing, increasing migration pressures, the planetary climate change crisis, and the food crisis in the global South. Responding to these global challenges quickly and effectively requires the generation and implementation of new ideas that go beyond the traditional academic framework of the bygone twentieth century dominated by the preoccupations and concerns of the global North. Still largely anchored in the ensconced disciplinary silos of an outdated European academic landscape, contemporary higher education struggles to provide students with a better understanding of how the local has become entangled with the global in myriad ways that profoundly shape how we live our daily lives in the twenty-first century.

The educational imperative to grasp these complex spatial and social dynamics of globalization animates global studies' transdisciplinary efforts to reorder human knowledge and create innovative learning environments. Relying on conceptual and analytic perspectives that are not anchored in a single discipline, the new field expands innovative interdisciplinary approaches pioneered in the 1970s and 1980s such as world-systems analysis, postcolonial studies, cultural studies, environmental and sustainability studies, and women's studies. The power of the rising global imaginary and its affiliated new globalisms—reflected in changing material and ideational support infrastructures—goes a long way in explaining why global studies programs, departments, research institutes, and professional organizations have sprung up in major universities around the world, including in the global South. Recognizing this trend, many existing programs have been renamed 'global studies'. Demand for courses and undergraduate and postgraduate degrees in global studies has dramatically risen. Increasingly, we see the inclusion of the terms 'global' or 'globalization' in course titles, textbooks, academic job postings, and extracurricular activities. Universities and colleges in the United States have supported the creation of new global studies initiatives that are often funded by major government institutions and philanthropists. For example, Northwestern University announced in 2015 it received a donation of $100 million—the largest single gift in its history—from the sister of the prominent investor Warren Buffett for the establishment of the Roberta Buffett Institute for Global Studies.

Drawing on thematic and methodological resources from the social sciences and humanities, global studies now encompasses about 300 undergraduate and graduate programs in the US alone.[21] Some pioneering universities like the University of California Santa Barbara or the University of North Carolina at Chapel Hill house programs that currently serve nearly 1,000 global studies undergraduate majors. The Division of Global Affairs at Rutgers University-Newark and RMIT University's (Melbourne, Australia) School of Global, Urban, and Social Studies, for example, accommodate hundreds of masters and doctoral students. In 2015, the University of California Santa Barbara launched the first doctoral program in global studies at a Tier-1 research university in the United States. In addition to the creation of these successful degree-granting programs, there has been a

· Where is GS field located in transnational educational system.

· place of language in GS/ Which language author writes

TABLE I.1 Undergraduate and Graduate Majors in Global Studies Programs

Institution	Undergraduate Majors	Graduate Majors	Total Undergraduate and Graduate Course Enrollment
University of California Santa Barbara: Department of Global Studies	900–1100	19 (MA & PHD)	20,238 undergraduate
University of North Carolina at Chapel Hill: Curriculum in Global Studies	800–850	20 (MA)	8,191 graduate and 18,421 undergraduate
RMIT University (Melbourne, Australia): School of Global, Urban, and Social Studies	331	212	800–1,000 undergraduate
Sophia University, Japan: Graduate Program in Global Studies (GPGS)	416	158 (MA and PHD)	13,435 (12,117 undergraduate and 1,153 graduate)
Middlebury College: International and Global Studies	100	N/A	2,526 undergraduate

Data supplied by James Farrer of Sophia University, Jodi Cutler of University of California at Santa Barbara, Jonathan D. Weiler of University of North Carolina at Chapel Hill, Tamar Mayer of Middlebury, and Paul Battersby at RMIT University

· How many people write books what address GS?
· infancy of the field

phenomenal growth of scholarly literature on globalization. New journals, book series, textbooks, academic conferences, and professional associations like the Global Studies Consortium or the Global Studies Association have embraced the novel umbrella designation of 'global studies'.[22]

No set definition of GS

A recent issue of the journal *Globalizations* contained a special exchange forum titled, 'What is Global Studies?' Featuring eight contributions—a lead article on the subject followed by six substantive reaction papers and a final response by the lead author—the forum provided a platform for debating the significance and scope of a transdisciplinary field that had been taking many universities around the world by storm. Promising to publish additional commentaries in subsequent issues—if such would indeed be received in the future—the journal editors affirmed their intent to keep the spotlight on the multiple dimensions and meanings of the evolving field:

> We hope others will explore new meanings of globalization in the context of the debate about similarities and differences between

· exploration / experimentalism
· 21st century
· trans disciplinary / inter disciplinary

· transnational
· globalization
· contested

'studies of globalization' and 'global studies', bring fresh ideas to the concept of globalization, broaden its scope, and contribute to shaping debates of the future. We are dedicated to opening the widest possible space for discussion of alternative understandings of globalization. We encourage the exploration and discussion of multiple interpretations and multiple processes that may constitute many possible globalizations, many possible alternatives.[23]

The strong response of the journal's readership exceeded even the editors' most optimistic expectations. As a result, three additional response essays were published in a subsequent issue, followed by a separate thematic volume on 'Globalization: The Career of a Concept', which included a lead article on the genealogy of globalization and twelve substantive interviews with academic pioneers of global studies hailing from a broad range of disciplinary and geographic backgrounds.[24] This lively 'global studies debate' continued in subsequent issues of the leading English-language globalization journal, the latest installment coming in the form of an insightful essay that raised critical questions about the power to define global studies and the considerable stakes involved in these kinds of delineating efforts.[25]

Clearly, the fledgling field and its associated imaginary have come a long way in a relatively short period of time. Institutional support for global studies scholarship has dramatically increased in leading universities around the world, and less research-oriented higher education outfits have embraced the new framework of global studies in their more applied teaching and learning missions. At the same time, however, many academics outside the field often complain about its lack of focus, which makes it appear to be the study of 'everything global'. Like other interdisciplinary programs that developed in the 1990s, global studies often invited the impression of a nebulous and rather confusing combination of widely different approaches operating on various levels of analysis. As Philip McCarty notes, 'In Global Studies there was, and remains, a strong tendency to revel in the mesmerizing complexity of it all'.[26]

Should there be a more coherent global studies framework? As we noted at the outset of this Introduction, its transdisciplinary DNA makes global studies a deliberately fluid and porous endeavor. As the heading of the *Globalizations* issue suggests, the persistence of the deceivingly simple question, 'What is Global Studies?' demonstrates that many students and faculty are still unclear about its scope and methods. Moreover, scores of global scholars still quarrel over what themes and approaches their field should or should not entail. Hence, it would be a mistake to close one's eyes to the equally legitimate demands of global studies students and faculty to map out the contours of the field by identifying the features of some emerging agreements. Convinced that global studies programs will earn a more prominent place within the quickly changing twenty-first-century landscape of higher education characterized by shrinking budgets and new modes of instruction, a growing number of thinkers like those featured in the *Globalizations* exchange forum—to whom we refer in this book loosely as 'global studies scholars'—have begun to synthesize various common theoretical perspectives and problem-oriented approaches. Their efforts have contributed to the necessary mapping exercise without falling prey to the fetish of disciplinary boundary making. While we applaud their willingness to take stock of what unites us, we also hope for the continuation of open-ended, critical exchanges on the nature of global studies.

Approaches and Rationales

In a transdisciplinary field as complex and multilayered as global studies, the mental openness to the unexpected and the willingness to constantly rethink basic claims and assumptions ought to count as both virtues and necessities. While it makes sense to avoid a rush to dogmatic closure fueled by the desire for definitive answers, the remarkable growth of the field has made it necessary to introduce pertinent contents and existing approaches to new audiences. What are some useful common approaches that global studies instructors and students should take? Offering both students and interested academics a general outline of the origins, evolution, and theoretical components of an academic 'space of tension' that still suffers from growing pains should be conducive to finding more common ground without closing down discussion or sweeping disagreements under the rug. Global studies scholars must be more concerned with conveying the value of their global imaginary beyond their inner circle of colleagues and students who are already sold on the endeavor. The challenge is to present global studies as a reasonably coherent transdisciplinary project dedicated to exploring processes of globalization with the aim of engaging the complex global problems the world is facing in the twenty-first century.[27]

Eve Darian-Smith notes perceptively that such a careful and inclusive exercise in delineation also serves valuable pragmatic goals:

> For bureaucratic and institutional purposes, it is important to arrive at some general consensus about what 'global studies' entails. This is necessary in order to formalize an intellectual community of scholars and students, and to garner resources and funding for research agendas. Having a general idea about what the field of global studies

encompasses is essential in order to hold conferences, submit grants, and to have one's work published, read, cited, and taught in classrooms. Moreover, articulating what constitutes 'global studies' today makes it possible to think about its future directions in the years ahead as an emerging field of inquiry.[28]

Indeed, growing demands from students and faculty for delineating the main contours and central features of global studies constitutes the first of four principal rationales for writing this book. Second, we are interested in providing insight into matters of institutional and curricular development in global studies. By giving consideration to both theoretical and practical concerns, this study aims to contribute to the ongoing efforts to find common ground in a field that is quickly outgrowing its academic childhood.

Our third motivation for producing this study relates to the fact that books with the signifier 'global studies' in their main title are still quite rare and usually attached to introductory textbooks and readers.[29] In addition to supplying a comprehensive conceptual delineation of the field, we seek to provide readers with a better understanding of the historical development of the field. As Jan Nederveen Pieterse has observed, global studies is a project in the making and its intellectual profile is just starting to develop.[30] Hence, there exists a real need for a substantive primer on the subject, which introduces a large and diverse audience to the basic features, historical evolution, and institutional infrastructure of global studies. We have endeavored to write such a book that speaks to both undergraduate and graduate students while satisfying the expectations of more advanced academics and informed readers. We always explain our key concepts and theoretical arguments and relate them to concrete examples and contexts. Although we have deliberately kept our discussion as accessible as possible, we have sought to expand beyond the conventional primer format by delving more deeply into the influential conceptual frameworks and historical developments of global studies. At the same time, we have attempted to show how theoretical and historical matters relate to the pressing pedagogical concerns of teaching and learning.

Our fourth and final motivation for writing this book is to introduce readers to the major thinkers in global studies and their influential literary contributions from the 1990s to today. Again, rather than providing our audience with an abstract survey of the theoretical frameworks of leading scholars, we present their perspectives in a lively historical narrative that integrates their arguments into our own conceptual framework configured around what we think of as the four pillars of global studies: globalization, transdisciplinarity, space and time, and critical thinking.

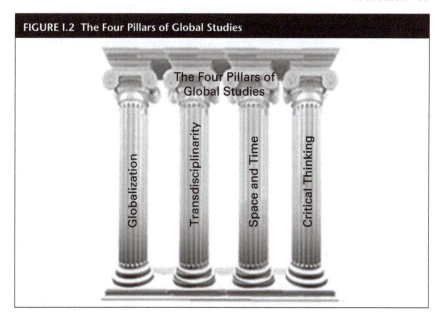

FIGURE I.2 The Four Pillars of Global Studies

Book Outline

To make our discussion as accessible as possible, we have organized the chapters of this book around frequently asked questions we encountered when presenting lectures about global studies to academic and general audiences around the world. Chapter 1 responds to two basic questions:

- What is the relationship between 'globalization' (the concept) and 'global studies' (the academic field of inquiry)?
- What are the historical origins and evolution of 'globalization' (the concept) and 'global studies' (the academic field of inquiry)?

Since the story of global studies is inextricably connected to the conceptual development of globalization, we start Chapter 1 with a genealogical account of the keyword and its major meaning trajectories from its earliest appearance in the 1930s to its explosion onto the public discourse of the Roaring Nineties. After examining the seminal contributions of three influential globalization pioneers in the 1990s, we show how the fates of an early version of 'globalization studies' and the new field of 'global studies' began to intertwine in concrete institutional settings. To that end, we narrate the success stories of two trailblazing global studies programs located in large research universities on two continents: the University of California Santa Barbara, United States, and RMIT University in Melbourne, Australia.

Forming the main portion of the book, Chapters 2 to 5 provide answers to the central question, 'What does global studies encompass?' In these chapters, we introduce readers to our basic conceptual framework: the four principal 'pillars' or 'framings' of global studies. Again, rather than presenting our outline of the main features of the field in abstraction, we locate our arguments within a historical framework that helps to contextualize the perspectives of some of its key thinkers.

Chapter 2 argues that *globalization* is the primary subject of global studies. Serving as the master concept of the field, 'globalization' constitutes its first pillar because it sits at the very core of global studies. The complex and uneven dynamics of contemporary globalization have provoked countless intellectual battles and disagreements over how to define the keyword and which of its many dimensions should be privileged. Still, there is little dispute over the significance of globalization processes for global studies. Building on the previously discussed evolution of the four major meaning trajectories of 'globalization', the chapter introduces readers to the seminal contributions of influential globalization pioneers that helped shape the contours of the emerging field. It also covers the major arguments and perspectives on the subject that have taken place over the last two decades in two separate but increasingly interrelated arenas. One discussion has proceeded mostly within the ivory tower of academia, while the other has unfolded in the more visible arena of public discourse. We end the chapter by arguing that the principal voices in the academic globalization debates can be divided into four distinct intellectual camps: globalizers, rejectionists, skeptics, and modifiers.

Chapter 3 explores how global studies applies a *transdisciplinary* framing to the study of globalization. This chapter reacts to questions of how global studies fits within the conventional disciplinary order of the modern university as well as how it integrates a variety of disciplinary approaches and insights into a new framework of understanding the transnational dynamics of our globalizing world. Challenging the Eurocentric disciplinary framework shaped by the national imaginary of the nineteenth and twentieth centuries, global studies embraces multiple forms of *inter-*, *multi-*, and *trans-*disciplinarity. These involve, for example, the formation of issue-driven teams of both academic and non-academic investigators focused on real-world problems like violence, inequality, and environmental degradation and dedicated to the integration of knowledge involving several disciplines such as sociology, urban studies, political science, geography, anthropology, history, biology, engineering, ecology, and economics.

We introduce the conceptual frameworks of influential global studies scholars by means of concrete illustrations that show how their work involves transdisciplinary projects. Focused on global complexity, they explore these growing forms of interdependence through domains, dimensions, networks, flows, fluids, and hybrids—the key concepts behind their transdisciplinary attempts to globalize our research imagination. However, their holistic desire to convey the big picture must be balanced against a towering intellectual challenge facing the field: finding new ways of integrating separate strands of knowledge that augment our understanding of the increasing complexity, fluidity, and connectivity of our globalizing world. In short, global studies must be sufficiently broad and transdisciplinary—without being grandiose or abstract—to encourage the revival of big-picture approaches yet remain open to discipline-specific efforts that make valuable contributions to the field.

Chapter 4 shows how the development of global studies has been framed by new conceptions of *space and time*. After all, global-scale dynamics such as 'deterritorialization' and 'denationalization' are the principal reason for why the term globalization was coined in the first place. However, this much-debated 'compression of space and time' should not be imagined as a top-heavy process starting with the global stratum and then running downward to the regional, national, and local layers. People's orientation toward what is explicitly global in scale does not mean that sub-global scales have lost significance. In fact, globalization processes create new and complex geographies that often emerge from deep inside spaces and places that do not necessarily scale at the global level. Globalization is not just about processes of deterritorialization—the transcending of traditional spatial boundaries—but also about processes of reterritorialization, that is, inscriptions and eruptions of the global *within* the national and the local. The local and the global are not mutually exclusive endpoints on a vertical spatial scale but an interlinked space of flows directed and redirected in digital real-time. In this chapter, we discuss a number of crucial spatio-temporal themes such as the ongoing debate on whether globalization represents the consequence of modernity or a postmodern break; the changing role of the nation-state; the changing relationship between territory and sovereignty; the growing significance of global cities; the increasing fluidity of spatial scales; new periodization efforts around time and space; and the emergence of global history as a transdisciplinary endeavor.

Chapter 5 argues that global studies both employs and encourages various forms of critical thinking. Going beyond the purely cognitive understanding of 'critical thinking' as balanced reasoning propagated by leading Anglo-American educators during the second half of the twentieth century, this fourth pillar reflects the field's receptivity to the activity of social criticism that problematizes unequal power relations and engages in ongoing social struggles to bring about a more just global society. Advancing various critical perspectives, global studies scholars from around the world draw on different currents and methods of 'critical theory'—an umbrella term for modes of thought committed to the reduction of exploitation, commodification, violence, and alienation. Such a critical global studies calls for methodological skepticism regarding positivistic dogmas and what are often presented as 'objective facts'; the recognition that all 'facts' are socially constructed and serve particular power interests; the public contestation of uncritical mainstream stories spun by corporate media; the decolonization of the (Western) imagination; and an understanding of the global as a multipolar dynamic reflecting the concerns of the marginalized global South even more than those of the privileged North.

Taking sides with the interest of social justice, critical global studies thinkers exercise what globalization scholar William Robinson calls a 'preferential option for the subordinate majority of global society'.[31] We offer some examples of such critical thinking as it relates to global political activism, global civil society, and global environmentalism. Moreover, such global activist thinking embraces the pedagogical mission of fostering 'global citizenship' as defined in the United Nations Secretary General's 2012 Global Education First Initiative and many other cosmopolitan visions anchored in values of justice, diversity, and solidarity. The chapter ends with a brief overview of some influential criticisms directed at the field itself.

The Appendix presents useful information about global studies journals, global studies programs and professional associations, and pertinent online resources. We also provide additional resources on the following website connected to the book: www.routledge.com/cw/steger. These e-resources include three examples of successful research projects recently undertaken in the field. Demonstrating the relevance of these four pillars of global studies for both theoretical and applied research, these concrete illustrations of cutting-edge inquiry produced by both seasoned scholars and doctoral students go a long way toward answering the frequently asked questions, 'What sort of research is being conducted in the field?' and 'What are some of the major analytical frameworks and methodological approaches utilized in global studies?' Although most global studies scholars favor qualitative methodologies anchored in the social sciences and humanities, a significant number of research projects adopt a mixed-methods approach that embraces the use of critical quantitative tools capable of adding empirical value to largely qualitative research designs. Indeed, many academics working in the field apply their theoretical inquiries to concrete policy issues. Second, our e-resources provide three global studies sample syllabi developed by the authors for two undergraduate courses (introductory and advanced) and one graduate seminar (for both MA and PhD students). Corresponding to the themes presented in the chapters, we hope that these additional materials will assist readers in their intellectual journey toward a deeper understanding of global studies as a fertile academic space of tension guided by a rising global imaginary prepared to meet the challenges of our interdependent world.

NOTES

1 Fredric Jameson, 'Preface', in Fredric Jameson and Masao Miyoshi, eds., *The Cultures of Globalization* (Durham and London: Duke University Press, 1998), p. xi.

2 Ibid., p. xvi.

3 For a book-length treatment of the 'global imaginary', see Manfred B. Steger, *The Rise of the Global Imaginary: Political Ideologies from the French Revolution to the Global War on Terror* (Oxford and New York: Oxford University Press, 2008). For an updated discussion, see Manfred B. Steger and Paul James, 'Levels of Subjective Globalization: Ideologies, Imaginaries, Ontologies', *Perspectives on Global Development and Technology* 12.1–2 (2013), pp. 17–40.

4 See Anthony Giddens, *The Consequences of Modernity* (Stanford: Stanford University Press, 1990). We discuss Giddens's theory of globalizing modernity in Chapter 4. For an excellent interpretation of 'global systemic shift', see Roland Benedikter, 'Understanding Contemporary Change. What is the "Global Systemic Shift" of our Days and How Does it Work? A Seven-Dimensional Approach of Reconstruction, Analysis, and Foresight to Address "Post-Ideological," "Post-9/11," and "Post-Empire" Complexity', *Transcience* 4.1 (2013), pp. 20–35.

5 Marshall McLuhan, *Understanding Media* (Cambridge, MA: MIT Press, 1994 [1964]); and Hannah Arendt, *The Human Condition* (Chicago: University of Chicago Press, 1958).

6 See also Martin Albrow, *The Global Age: State and Society Beyond Modernity* (Stanford: Stanford University Press, 1996), p. 81.

7 See, for example, Ulrich Beck, 'Toward a New Critical Theory with Cosmopolitan Intent', *Constellations* 10.4 (2003), pp. 453–68; and Paul James, *Nation Formation: Towards a Theory of Abstract Community* (London and Thousand Oaks: SAGE, 1996).

8 This section on area studies is greatly indebted to Isaac Kamola's insights on the subject. I have utilized some of the arguments that appear in his PhD dissertation, *Producing the Global Imaginary: Academic Knowledge, Globalization, and the Making of the World* (Minneapolis, MN: University of Minnesota, May 2010), especially Chapter 4: 'The U.S. Academy and the Production of the Global Imaginary'.

9 John Lie, 'Asian Studies/Global Studies: Transcending Area Studies in the Social Sciences', *Cross-Currents: East Asian History and Culture Review* 2 (March 2012), p. 9: https://cross-currents.berkeley.edu/e-journal/issue-2. Accessed 22 January 2016.

10 For a history of the first decades of the International Studies Association, see Henry Teune, 'The International Studies Association' (1982) at: http://www.isanet.org/Portals/0/Documents/Institutional/Henry_Teune_The_ISA_1982.pdf. Accessed 20 January 2015.

11 Stephen Rosow, 'Toward an Anti-Disciplinary Global Studies', *International Studies Perspectives* 4 (2003), p. 7.

12 Robert O. Keohane, *After Hegemony: Cooperation and Discord in the World Political Economy* (Princeton, NJ: Princeton University Press, 1984).

13 Barrie Axford, *Theories of Globalization* (Cambridge, UK: Polity Press, 2013), p. 38.

14 Kamola, *Producing the Global Imaginary,* Chapter 4: 'The U.S. Academy and the Production of the Global Imaginary'.

15 See Manfred B. Steger and Ravi K. Roy, *Neoliberalism: A Very Short Introduction* (Oxford: Oxford University Press, 2010); and Manfred B. Steger, *Globalisms: The Great Ideological Struggle of the Twenty-First Century,* 3rd ed. (Lanham, MD: Rowman & Littlefield Publishers, 2009).

16 See Brendan Cantwell, Ilkka Kauppinen, and Sheila Slaughter, eds., *Academic Capitalism in the Age of Globalization* (Baltimore, MD: John Hopkins University Press, 2014).

17 James Mittelman, 'Globalization: An Ascendant Paradigm?', *International Studies Perspectives* 3.1 (February 2002), p. 1.

18 Jan Nederveen Pieterse, 'What Is Global Studies?', *Globalizations* 10.4 (2013), p. 499.

19 Matthias Middell, 'What Is Global Studies All About?', *Basel Papers on Europe in a Global Perspective* 105 (2014), p. 45: https://europa.unibas.ch/fileadmin/europa/redaktion/PDF_Basler_Schriften/BS105.pdf. Accessed 16 February 2015.

20 Ibid.

21 For a listing of these colleges and universities, see: https://bigfuture.collegeboard.org/college-search.

22 For detailed information, see the appendix at the end of this book and the Companion Website at www.routledge.com/cw/steger.

23 Editorial, 'What is Global Studies?', *Globalizations* 10.4 (2013), p. 497.

24 Manfred B. Steger and Paul James, eds., 'Globalization: The Career of a Concept', Special Issue of *Globalizations* 11.4 (2014).

25 Eve Darian-Smith, 'Global Studies—The Handmaiden of Neoliberalism?', *Globalizations* 12.2 (2015), pp. 164–8.

26 Philip C. McCarty, 'Globalizing Legal History', *Rechtsgeschichte/Legal History* 22 (2014), p. 284.

27 See also Philip C. McCarty, 'Communicating Global Perspectives,' *Basel Papers in European Global Studies* 105 (2014), p. 34: https://europa.unibas.ch/fileadmin/europa/redaktion/PDF_Basler_Schriften/BS105.pdf. Accessed 16 February 2015.

28 Darian-Smith, 'Global Studies—The Handmaiden of Neoliberalism?', p. 165.

29 See, for example, Manfred B. Steger, *The Global Studies Reader* (Oxford: Oxford University Press, 2014); Mark Juergensmeyer, *Thinking Globally: A Global Studies Reader* (Berkeley, CA: University of California Press, 2014); Darren J. O'Byrne and Alexander Hensby, *Theorizing Global Studies* (Houndmills, UK: Palgrave Macmillan, 2011); and Patricia J. Campbell, Aran MacKinnon, and Christy R. Stevens, *Introduction to Global Studies* (Chichester, UK: John Wiley, 2010).

30 Pieterse, 'What Is Global Studies?', p. 500. Also see our discussion in the conclusion of Chapter 5.

31 William I. Robinson, 'What Is a Critical Globalization Studies? Intellectual Labor and Global Society', in Richard P. Applebaum and William I. Robinson, eds., *Critical Globalization Studies* (London and New York: Routledge, 2005), p. 14.

1

THE INTELLECTUAL ORIGINS AND EVOLUTION OF GLOBAL STUDIES

Let us remember that we started this book with a clear premise: the birth and rising fortunes of global studies as a relatively new transdisciplinary field of inquiry are inextricably linked to the emergence of globalization as a prominent theme in late twentieth-century discourse. The increasing visibility of worldwide integration favored the global as a new conceptual framework and unit of social analysis that enabled people to make better sense of their rapidly changing world and their place in it. Indeed, the growing awareness of the expansion and multiplication of worldwide inter-connections called out for a new keyword that captured the scale and inten-sity of changing forms of human contact. 'Globalization' filled this need perfectly because it emerged from the very process it referred to.[1] It also conveyed the sense of an unprecedented compression of space and time—mediated by new digital technologies—which many people experienced as both exhilarating and unsettling.

Given these tightly intertwined meaning trajectories of the concept globalization and global studies, we can best illuminate the origins and evolution of the field by acquiring a basic understanding of how the idea of globalization arose and developed over time. This is especially important since the origins and uses of the concept reach back much further than those of the field. While Chapter 2 discusses the significance of globalization as the subject of global studies in more detail, it is necessary to start our inquiry into the beginnings of the field by recounting—in broad strokes—its remarkable journey from obscurity to superstardom in the span of only seven decades. Hence, we open this chapter with a brief genealogy of

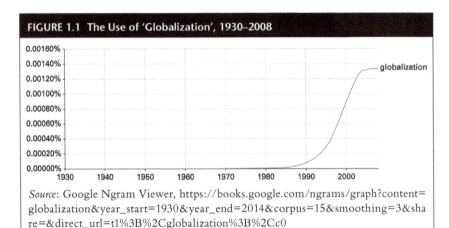

FIGURE 1.1 The Use of 'Globalization', 1930–2008

Source: Google Ngram Viewer, https://books.google.com/ngrams/graph?content=globalization&year_start=1930&year_end=2014&corpus=15&smoothing=3&share=&direct_url=t1%3B%2Cglobalization%3B%2Cc0

globalization—the concept, not the process—to explain the main circumstances leading up to its discursive explosion in the 1990s. The remarkable popularity of the buzzword at the end of the twentieth century is even more astonishing when considering that it only entered general English language dictionaries for the first time in the 1961 edition of the *Merriam-Webster Third New International Dictionary*.

But the suddenness of its emergence also contributed to the widespread erroneous assumption that there must have been a quick invention of a term whose time had come. When globalization took the world by storm in the Roaring Nineties, it carried meanings that related predominantly to the social spheres of *economics* and *business*. The normative articulation of these meanings occurred mostly in positive terms that celebrated the global spread of free-market capitalism facilitated by the information and communication technology revolution that swept the planet in the wake of the Cold War. But the concept was hardly new. 'Globalization' had already been in use for half a century and its associated meanings had actually been far broader and more varied than those foregrounded in the dominant neoliberal definitions of the 1990s. So let us begin our inquiry into the origins and evolution of global studies by first turning our attention to the genealogical trajectories of globalization—one of the most important concepts for understanding the passage of human societies into the third millennium.

A Genealogy of 'Globalization': The Four Meaning Branches

Recent research confirms that there was no single genius who self-consciously coined the term 'globalization'—which then, quickly or slowly, became part of the shared lexicon of our age.[2] Instead, the beginnings of the use of the concept are rather complicated and involve several intellectual codifiers and ideational currents. Surprisingly, some early uses of globalization go back to meaning trajectories that did not endure on the long road toward consistent academic (and public) language use. Like our species *homo sapiens*, which emerged over many millennia together with different kinds of hominids who thrived for a time before becoming extinct, some lineages of the concept turned out to be evolutionary dead ends. Likewise, the evolution of the concept was multibranched, and the shoots of its development were often discontinuous and intermittent—buffeted by ferocious winds of change and encountering unanticipated twists and reversals.

Engaging in a genealogical exploration of 'globalization' involves, first, tracing its use in written texts and then recording these sequences and patterns of use. Second, it entails reading pertinent texts for their meaning and discerning the extent to which their authors have a reflexive understanding at the time that they are using a particular term such as globalization to denote what is now the dominant meaning—the expansion and intensification of social relations and consciousness across world-space and world-time.[3] Third, it involves a contextually sensitive biographical search, which should include interviewing prominent authors to find out about how they came upon the concept. Finally, a genealogical exploration of globalization entails understanding the shifting nature of our increasingly interconnected world in which such a key term becomes both possible and necessary.

Early uses of globalization tended to involve a broad web of understandings. These variously signified universalizing processes such as interregional connections, the act of being systematic, an early childhood development phase, and the dynamics of linking the entire world together. Recent research efforts on the genealogy of globalization spearheaded by Paul James and Manfred Steger have revealed the existence of at least four distinct genealogical branches in the meaning formation of the keyword prior to its rapid take-off phase in the 1990s.[4] The first branch is rooted in the fields of education and psychology, the second in society and culture, the third in politics and international relations, and the fourth in economics and business.

Education & Psychology

The educational branch appears to be the oldest of the four and relates primarily to the universalization and integration of knowledge acquisition.

In 1930, the first use of globalization in the English language occurred in a pedagogical anthology co-edited by William Boyd, the author of *The History of Western Education*, a classic textbook that went through multiple editions over the next few decades.[5] For the Scottish educator, the term denoted not only a certain conceptual holism but also an entirely new approach to education: 'Wholeness . . . integration, globalization . . . would seem to be the keywords of the new education view of mind: suggesting negatively, antagonism to any conception of human experience, which over-emphasizes the constituent atoms, parts, elements'.[6] In other words, this educational meaning branch of globalization had hardly anything to do with 'whole worldness' since it addressed the issue of human learning processes running from the global to the particular.

Boyd and his collaborators originally acquired the term by translating the French term *globalisation* (not *mondialisation*!) as used by Ovide Decroly in the 1920s.[7] Referring to a 'globalization function stage' in early childhood development, the Belgian educational psychologist placed his new concept at the center of his early twentieth-century 'New Education' movement. It was connected to a holistic pedagogical system for teaching children to read—*la méthode globale* ('whole language teaching')—which is still used in some Belgian and French schools bearing Decroly's name. By the 1990s, however, this education and psychology meaning trajectory had either largely dried up or mutated into its more contemporary denotation of a 'globalization of education', that is, the study of the role played by globalization in the process of internationalizing and rejuvenating educational systems worldwide.[8] In recent years, globalization has become a keyword in pedagogical literature exploring the dramatic changes that impact higher education as a result of new forms of digital technology and increased student mobility.[9]

Society and Culture

Organized around cultural and sociological meanings, the second evolutionary branch of globalization originated in the 1940s. The first instance of this usage seems remarkable for both its unusual context and the form in which it was delivered. In 1944, Lucius Harper, an African-American editor of the *Chicago Defender*—which was at the time one of the most influential black newspapers in the United States, with an estimated readership of 100,000—published an article that quoted from a letter written by an African-American US soldier based in Australia. In the letter, the G.I. refers to the global impact of World War II in spreading certain American sociocultural views about 'negroes':

The American Negro and his problem are taking on a global significance. The world has begun to measure America by what she does to
us [the American Negro]. But—and this is the point—we stand in
danger . . . of losing the otherwise beneficial aspects of globalization
of our problems by allowing the 'Bilbos in uniform' with and without
brass hats to spread their version of us everywhere.[10]

'Bilbos in uniform' was a critical reference to Theodore G. Bilbo (1877–
1947), a mid-century Governor and US Senator from Mississippi renowned
for his avid advocacy of segregation and affinity for the racist practices of the
Ku Klux Klan (KKK). Bilbo echoed Hitler's *Mein Kampf* in asserting that
merely 'One drop of Negro blood placed in the veins of the purest Caucasian
destroys the inventive genius of his mind and strikes palsied his creative
faculties'.[11] At the time, the elected Congressional representatives of the
segregated South successfully blocked any federal legislative attempt to
clamp down on lynching. They insisted that such practices were something
that 'Northerners could never understand' and should, therefore, remain a
matter of state regulation. It is difficult to assess the wider impact of Harper's
use of globalization since no other article employing the keyword was
published in the *Chicago Defender* for decades.
    A second early instance of the concept's use in a socio-cultural sense is
not quite as compelling but more perplexing. In 1951, Paul Meadows, an
American sociologist whose name is strangely missing in the contemporary
pantheon of global studies pioneers, contributed an extraordinary article to
the prominent academic journal, *Annals of the American Academy of Political
and Social Science*. Meadows's essay stands out for reasons that will become
readily apparent:

The culture of any society is always unique, a fact which is dramatically described in Sumner's concept of *ethos*: 'the sum of the characteristic usages, ideas, standards and codes by which a group is
differentiated and individualized in character from other groups'.
With the advent of industrial technology, however, this tendency
toward cultural localization has been counteracted by a stronger
tendency towards cultural universalization. With industrialism, a
new cultural system has evolved in one national society after
another; its global spread is incipient and cuts across every local ethos.
Replacing the central mythos of the medieval Church, this new
culture pattern is in a process of 'globalization', after a period of
formation and formulation covering some three or four hundred years
of westernization.[12]

That passage is worth quoting at length, not just because it is one of the first pieces of writing to use 'globalization' in the contemporary sense of the term, but because Meadows's analysis employs the keyword in a *conductive* relation with terms such as 'localization', 'universalization', and 'Westernization'. Meadows's act of putting 'globalization' in inverted commas suggests that he was quite self-conscious about using the term relationally. The synergy formed among meaning clusters such as 'globalization', 'localization', and 'culture' suggests that Meadows was far ahead of his time. Another remarkable achievement of this article lies in its author's uncanny recognition of a strong link between 'globalization', 'ideology', and 'industrial technology'. As he notes at the end of his essay's introductory section, 'The rest of this paper will be devoted to a discussion of the technological, organizational, and ideological systems which comprise this new universalistic culture'.[13] Although Meadows's understanding of globalization probably comes closest to its contemporary meaning, this socio-cultural branch would remain dormant for decades until it reemerged in the 1980s and 1990s in the writings of globalization pioneers like Roland Robertson, Mike Featherstone, Anthony Giddens, John Tomlinson, and Arjun Appadurai.[14]

Politics and International Relations

The third branch of the formation of the keyword is rooted in the disciplines of politics and international relations (IR). In 1965, American political scientist Inis Claude published an article on the future of the United Nations. Treating universalization and globalization as the same phenomenon, he mentioned the latter only once in passing under the heading of 'The Movement Toward Universality'. Claude argued that, 'The United Nations has tended to reflect the steady globalization of international relations'.[15] Three years later, with no reference to Claude, an extraordinary article appeared in which author George Modelski linked 'globalization' to 'world politics' in general, thereby offering a remarkably robust and dynamic definition of the concept:

> A condition for the emergence of a multiple-autonomy form of world politics arguably is the development of a global layer of interaction substantial enough to support continuous and diversified institutionalization. We may define this process as globalization; it is the result of the increasing size, complexity and sophistication of world society.[16]

This passage reveals a remarkably sophisticated rendition of a complex process. In July 1968, Modelski led a team of researchers at the University of Washington in drafting an application to the US National Science Foundation, which, for the first time, used globalization in the title of a comprehensive research project: 'The Study of Globalization: A Preliminary Exploration'. Unfortunately, their project was soundly rejected. Over the next decades, this line of 'globalization research' was reinvented several times before it finally was recognized as worthy of study. Although Modelski's seminal contribution to the evolution of the keyword had the potential of changing the entire field of IR, it had surprisingly little impact other than prefiguring the vigorous and highly contested political debates of the 1990s on the impact of globalization on the nation-state, the rise of non-governmental organizations and transnational corporations, and the new political framework of 'global governance'.[17]

Economics & Business

The fourth genealogical branch favored meanings associated with economics, trade, and business. In the post-Cold War context, these aspects of globalization were usually discussed in conjunction with the ongoing information and communication technology revolution. The initial economic usage of the term, however, occurred in the late 1950s in connection with the extension of the European Common Market and a possible 'globalization of [trade] quotas'.[18] In 1962, François Perroux, a French political economist, used the keyword akin to the contemporary dominant understanding by relating it directly to the formation and spread of increasingly integrated economic markets on a planetary scale. As recent research shows, Perroux coined the influential phrase of the '*mondialisation de certains marches*' ('globalization of some markets').[19]

This expression, of course, was destined to become the title of a famous 1983 *Harvard Business Review* article penned by the Harvard Business School Dean, Theodore Levitt. His essay titled, 'The Globalization of Markets', imbued the concept with strong neoliberal economistic meanings, which ultimately leaked into the public discourse for good. For example, American globalization guru Thomas Friedman adopted one of Levitt's subheadings as the title of his bestseller, *The World Is Flat*.[20] Indeed, Levitt's seminal contribution laid the foundation for the popular depiction of globalization as an 'inevitable' economic process mediated by cutting-edge technology that was destined to give birth to a 'global market for standardized consumer products on a previously unimagined scale of magnitude'. But the description of what the business professor considered 'indisputable empirical trends' was inseparable from his neoliberal ideological prescriptions. For example, he insisted that multinational companies had no choice but to transform themselves into global corporations capable of operating in a more cost-effective way by standardizing their products. The necessary elimination of costly adjustments to various national markets depended, according to Levitt, on their swift adoption of a 'global approach'. What he had in mind was the willingness of CEOs to think and act 'as if the world were one large market—ignoring superficial regional and national differences. . . . It [the global corporation] sells the same things in the same way everywhere'.[21] Levitt's stated imperative of economic homogenization inspired hundreds of similar pieces in business magazines and journals that sought to convince leading companies to 'go global'. The advertising industry, in particular, set about creating 'global brands' by means of worldwide commercial campaigns. Hence, it is hardly surprising that the founder of the advertising giant Saatchi & Saatchi was one of Levitt's most fervent disciples.

With the collapse of Soviet communism and the transformation of communist countries in the global South into state capitalist one-party systems during the 1990s (as in the case of China or Vietnam), Levitt's mantra of the 'inevitable globalization of markets' merged seamlessly with an American triumphalism that celebrated the irrevocable relegation of Soviet-style communism to the 'dustbin of history'. Having escaped its academic business school context, the public interpretation of globalization as an economic-technological phenomenon was falling to global power elites who shared Levitt's ideological perspective. As we discuss in some detail in the next chapter, these influential commentators subscribed to a comprehensive worldview that presented globalization as a beneficial, inexorable process driven by the new technologies of the digital age and destined to lift millions out of poverty while furthering the spread of democracy and freedom around the globe.[22]

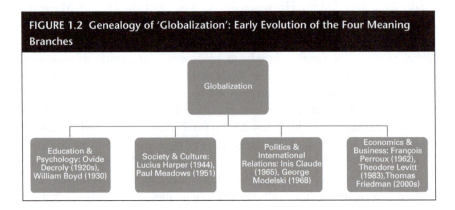

FIGURE 1.2 Genealogy of 'Globalization': Early Evolution of the Four Meaning Branches

Globalization

Education & Psychology: Ovide Decroly (1920s), William Boyd (1930)

Society & Culture: Lucius Harper (1944), Paul Meadows (1951)

Politics & International Relations: Inis Claude (1965), George Modelski (1968)

Economics & Business: François Perroux (1962), Theodore Levitt (1983),Thomas Friedman (2000s)

'Globalization Studies' in the 1990s

As we have seen, the rise of the concept 'globalization' can hardly be separated from the careers of numerous persons and collectivities—academic and non-academic—who endowed the concept with very specific meanings. Fascinatingly, recent interviews with trailblazing globalization researchers in the 1990s show that most of them do not remember a distinct eureka moment at which globalization took an axiomatic hold upon their minds. Whether these academics grabbed the concept out of the public debates they followed in the media, or whether they reached inside themselves and seemingly took it from their own evolving literary imagination, the concept somehow appeared to have been 'already there' and was now available to be developed in academic ways that related to their wide-ranging research interests.

Indeed, hardly anyone seemed to have encountered globalization in an academic context before the 1990s. For example, anthropologist Arjun Appadurai noted that he 'probably' came upon the concept 'in the very late 1980s—most likely sometime between 1989 and 1991. I would say it was after the fall of the Berlin Wall. The context? Most likely, I read about "globalization" in the press, rather than encountering the term through an academic route'. Religion scholar Mark Juergensmeyer concurred: 'I also remember a lot of talk about "globalization" in the immediate aftermath of the fall of the Berlin Wall. So that would put my encounter with the concept sometime around 1989 or 1990'. Likewise, Nobel Prize-winning economist Joseph Stiglitz confessed that, 'I don't remember the context or the first time I heard "globalization"'. Perhaps it was around the publication of Thomas Friedman's book, *The Lexus and the Olive Tree* [1999] or a bit earlier'. Similarly, anthropologist Jonathan Friedman found it hard to date his first encounter with the concept: 'The media were starting to use "globalization" and business got into the act as well. And I remember a lot of talk about the "end of the nation-state" [in the 1990s], which was very much linked to this new buzzword "globalization" '. The same goes for global historian Nayan Chanda: 'I don't recall exactly the first time I encountered "globalization," but it must have been in the early 1990s'. The prominent urban sociologist Saskia Sassen joined the chorus: 'I cannot remember the exact moment when it happened. All I know is that I found myself at some point using it'.[23]

Only a few years later, however, globalization scholars, hailing from a variety of disciplines, such as David Held, Anthony McGrew, Fredric Jameson, and James Mittelman had already assembled the first comprehensive anthologies and transdisciplinary mappings of their subject matter.[24] As we shall discuss in more detail in the next chapter, a number of seminal contributions in the 1990s framed this early phase in the evolution of global studies, which is sometimes referred to as the period of 'globalization studies'. From the beginning, globalization pioneers like Roland Robertson, David Harvey, Saskia Sassen, Manuel Castells, and Arjun Appadurai represent prominent examples in a long list of unorthodox scholars who had always been uncomfortable with tightly circumscribed disciplinary frameworks. Their strong transdisciplinary affinities combined with their desire to break away from disciplinary demarcations deeply influenced the evolution of global studies during this crucial decade.

Thus, the early period of globalization studies in the 1990s did not differ in significant ways from the more explicit phase of global studies that unfolded in the 2000s and beyond. Often emerging as a pragmatic consensus designation, the label 'global studies' did not solidify until the late 1990s and 2000s. As we discuss in Chapter 5, globalization researchers used the related terms 'global studies' and 'globalization studies' loosely and without much system-building ambition. Some might have used global studies in the pursuit of their transdisciplinary research projects or to name new programs and centers at their respective universities. Others experimented with the designations 'critical globalization studies', 'transnational studies', and 'globalism research' interchangeably with global studies. Indeed, some of these designations are still in use today. Looking back, Paul James notes perceptively that, 'Studies of globalization and, more generally, studies in the broad and loosely defined field of "global studies" did not become conscious of themselves as such until the 1990s'.[25]

The final section of this chapter illustrates this fluid transition from 'globalization studies' to 'global studies' by focusing on the formation and evolution of two trailblazing global studies programs. Linking their interest in globalization dynamics to the reconfiguration of various existing international agendas and initiatives, scholars at the University of California Santa Barbara (UCSB) and the Royal Melbourne Institute of Technology (RMIT University) took the lead in a process that turned the general phrase 'global studies' into a recognized designation for a budding field of inquiry anchored in new institutional arrangements. But the confinement of our narrative to these two institutions is not meant to detract from the efforts of other scholars immersed in similar programs that emerged roughly at the same time at other universities around the world such as Sophia University and Hitotsubashi University in Japan, the University of Leipzig in Germany, Stellenbosch University in South Africa, Lomonosov Moscow State University in Russia, and Rutgers University Newark in New Jersey.

A Tale of Two Trailblazing Global Studies Programs

The Global & International Studies Program at UCSB

In most cases, the translation of a new intellectual vision into viable academic courses, programs, and institutions requires both a dedicated team effort and good luck in the sense of connecting to an existing constellation of engaged people who share the vision. The successful founding and evolution of global studies at UCSB is no exception to this rule. While it is impossible for the ensuing summary to do justice to the contributions of all the faculty and staff involved in the initial formative years of what would eventually become the Global & International Studies Program, it is nonetheless crucial to keep in mind that it was a collective endeavor that depended on the active engagement of dozens of people. At the same time, it would be disingenuous not to highlight the leadership roles of some key individuals such as Richard Appelbaum, Giles Gunn, Mark Juergensmeyer, Sucheng Chan, and others who guided global studies at UCSB through these difficult early years.

In late 1994, the noted sociologist Richard Appelbaum accepted an appointment to chair his Provost's Ad Hoc Planning Committee to study the feasibility of creating a common administrative home to several international programs located in various colleges and research units at UCSB. But his acceptance had been somewhat hesitant and cautious given that only two years earlier he had served on a similar taskforce whose recommendation in favor of establishing a new 'School of Global Issues' had ultimately been rejected by the UCSB Chancellor. A member of UCSB's sociology department since 1971, Appelbaum was a firm believer in the virtues of multidisplinarity as reflected in his own broad academic training that included formal coursework and degrees in such diverse fields as public law, political science, economics, philosophy, communications, sociology, anthropology, urban studies, labor studies, international studies, and foreign languages. Deeply rooted in the humanist Marxist tradition reflected in the 'critical theory' approach of the Frankfurt School of Social Research, Appelbaum had long advocated a more systematic integration of critical and interdisciplinary methods in the social sciences. In addition to his intellectual breadth, he had gained a university-wide reputation for both his pragmatic approach and his proven institution-building capabilities. Committed to the 'international perspective' he had acquired as a Ford Foundation-sponsored field researcher in Peru, his research in the Guatemalan highlands, and a frequent visiting scholar in Asia, Appelbaum had been attuned to the growing impact of globalization dynamics on the international system in the changing post-Cold War environment. His recognition of the significance of global processes was further enhanced after encountering the work of globalization pioneers such as Roland Robertson and Anthony Giddens, both of whom confirmed his own understanding of the global dimensions of social change.[26]

Opportunities for the successful establishment of an overarching 'global studies' unit at UCSB had dramatically increased not only with the ongoing support and leadership of the religious studies and comparative literature scholar Giles Gunn but also with the recent arrival of Mark Juergensmeyer. A seasoned political scientist and prominent South Asia area specialist, Juergensmeyer had gained an international reputation as a sociologist of religion exploring cultural tensions, which political theorist Benjamin Barber had recently described as the 'dialectic of Jihad versus McWorld'.[27] In his comprehensive study on a new wave of religious revolutions altering the political landscapes in the Middle East, South Asia, Central Asia, and Eastern Europe, Juergensmeyer had reconfigured his intellectual approach around the central analytical category of 'the global'.[28] Like Appelbaum, he was a skilled academic entrepreneur with significant institution-building experience and committed to designing new academic programs anchored in transdisciplinary approaches to a rapidly globalizing world. Advocating a more explicitly 'global orientation' toward the study of international affairs, Juergensmeyer had previously served as Head of School of Hawaiian, Asian, and Pacific Studies at the University of Hawai'i-Mānoa. However, when he continued to encounter what appeared to be intractable bureaucratic resistance to his vision of developing a new graduate program in international studies especially designed to engage 'global issues', Juergensmeyer decided to leave Hawai'i and take his ideas elsewhere. He accepted a professorial appointment in UCSB's sociology department where he found not only a more conducive academic environment but also ideal intellectual partners in Richard Appelbaum, Giles Gunn, the religion scholar Richard Hecht, the eminent political economist Benjamin C. Cohen, and other 'globalists' committed to advancing this new framework at their university.

Serving together on Appelbaum's committee, these scholars agreed that UCSB's new international unit should primarily address the globalization dynamics that were shaping the world now and into the future. Emphasizing the contemporary transition into a 'transnational era' in which global issues were the signature elements, they embraced the label 'global studies', by which they meant paying primary attention to transnational events, processes, and flows rather than maintaining the conventional IR focus on relations between nation-states. At the same time, however, Juergensmeyer, Gunn, and Appelbaum insisted that such a global studies framework ought to acknowledge in explicit ways the continued relevance of nationalisms and nationhood and, therefore, should be assembled around the dialectic tensions between the 'global' and the 'international'. They offered two additional pragmatic reasons for why they thought it would be prudent not to dispose of the conventional 'international' label altogether. First, as their extensive research on the subject had revealed, no other academic institution in the US was using the designation 'global studies'. In short, global studies programs simply didn't exist in the country. Second, they pointed out that some influential colleagues at UCSB had reacted negatively to 'global studies', complaining that it sounded like a rather hazy concept and thus seemed a poor substitute for the familiar term 'international'. As Juergensmeyer recalled, 'They said, "You might as well call it 'stratospheric studies' or 'hemispheric studies' ". In other words, they were convinced that global studies was flat and had no intellectual gravitas. Rich and I disagreed, but we couldn't change their minds. These had been very supportive colleagues and we didn't want to alienate them'.[29]

In early 1995, the Provost's Ad Hoc Committee completed its work and recommended the establishment of a separate administrative locale bearing the compromise name, Global & International Studies. Located directly under the provost's office rather than the divisional dean's, it was to serve as the institutional umbrella for a variety of undergraduate programs and additional planning committees, including a Global, Peace and Security undergraduate minor; an Islamic and Near Eastern Studies major; a Jewish Studies minor; a South Asia Studies committee; and the planning committees for a new major in Global and International Studies and a Global Policy graduate program. Impressed with the work of the committee, the provost approved its recommendations and appointed Mark Juergensmeyer as the first director of the program to guide the necessary campus review and approval process for the new unit. The growing global studies team managed to secure its approval within a year, when it was formally approved as a separate campus unit. The 'Global, Peace, and Security program' was renamed the 'Global & International Studies program' (G&IS), and then, in the 1996–7 academic year, it was elevated from a 'little-p' program located within a department to a 'big-P' program with independent status and its own budget and faculty positions. Supported by a single staff position, Juergensmeyer continued on as director and governed the program together with an executive committee comprised of the chairs of all programs and planning committees associated with G&IS. In addition, an advisory committee of the major was formed, which consisted of ten faculty members appointed by the Executive Committee of the College of Letters and Sciences.

By this time, Giles Gunn, who had been a participant in many of these negotiations, joined Juergensmeyer and Appelbaum in taking the considerable professional risk of also switching half of his academic appointment to the new G&IS Program. Former Chair of the English department, Gunn had long nurtured and pursued the vision of multidisciplinary program dedicated to the study of global issues. A noted scholar of cultural and literary criticism as well as American pragmatism, Gunn was guided by his philosophical commitment to an inclusive 'cosmopolitan pragmatism' suitable for a globalizing world.[30] In fact, it was Gunn who had convinced Mattison Mines, Chair of the Academic Senate Committee in charge of the ongoing 'global issues discussion', to agree that any further planning for a global studies curriculum of whatever kind had to reserve a large place for the humanities in its construction. As it turned out, Gunn's vision of designing a global studies curriculum around the interlinked study of culture and of society and politics was to become the distinguishing cornerstone and chief feature of doing global studies at UCSB. And Gunn's vision was to be reinforced by a conviction shared by Appelbaum, and particularly by Juergensmeyer, that global studies should be at once historical as well as contemporary. Hence, it is no coincidence that once the program had been established, its first outside appointment was to be of a global historian named Dominic Sachsenmaier, now a professor at the University of Heidelberg, Germany.

No sooner had Juergensmeyer, Gunn, and Appelbaum had secured much-needed office and meeting spaces than they were joined by Sucheng Chan, a tenured Asian studies expert who also requested the permanent transfer of half of her positions to G&IS. One of the leaders in the process that culminated in a full-fledged, stand-alone major in Global and International Studies, Chan had started her academic career as a political scientist trained at UC Berkeley, where she met her future partner Mark Juergensmeyer. She quickly became one of the founders of the emerging field of Asian American Studies, authoring both basic textbooks and some of the most influential research publications in the field.[31] In the last years before her early retirement, Chan took the courageous step of joining the young global studies program, and her expertise proved to be invaluable in developing the global studies curriculum at UCSB.

Over the next decade of the 2000s, Gunn continued his mission to integrate a strong humanities perspective into a program dominated by social scientists. A scholar of unusual intellectual breadth as well as a seasoned academic administrator, Gunn was also willing to step into central administrative positions and eventually served as the Chair of the G&IS program, guiding it through a decade of phenomenal growth. Within the first year of the establishment of the G&IS Program, more than a dozen UCSB tenured faculty applied for affiliate studies and committed themselves to cross-listing some of their courses with the new program. In a genuine team effort, G&IS faculty embarked on creating new courses for the major. 'Global Conflict' and 'Global Ideology' were followed by the creative action of splitting the quarter-long introductory course in global studies into a two-semester sequence: 'Global 1: History, Culture, and Ideology', and 'Global 2: Socioeconomic and Political Processes'. Aided by a 1997 system-wide call to internationalize the University of California as well as developing new interdisciplinary programs, the global studies BA program at UCSB was approved in Spring 1998, thus allowing the first undergraduate students to be admitted into it.

There were ten tracks within the major: five area studies tracks (the Americas, Europe, Africa and the Middle East, South and Southeast Asia, East Asia and the Pacific), and five global issues tracks (global economy, environment, politics and world order, culture and society, and global science and technology). Students were expected to choose one or two of these ten tracks as their focus within the major. For example, student A could focus on East Asia and the Pacific and on global science and technology. All students were required to take the introductory G&IS course as a prerequisite and also complete two years of a foreign language. An 'outside concentration' requirement for majors ensured that students were taking at least four courses in a disciplinary field (such as history or political science) and thus would graduate with a good knowledge of at least one liberal arts discipline in addition to the interdisciplinary knowledge fostered through the G&IS major. Double-majoring was encouraged as well. Only a year later, Sajeed Titu Asghar became the first student to graduate with a BA from G&IS and later decided to pursue a graduate degree in International Service at American University. Within three years, student enrollment in global studies skyrocketed to 800 majors, making it the most popular undergraduate major on campus. Like Asghar, many of these students were keen to pursue graduate work on the subject. Consequently, the growing global studies faculty embarked on the lengthy process of establishing two new graduate programs in global studies: (1) a transdisciplinary PhD 'Emphasis in Global Studies' that ultimately included twelve departments across campus: political science, sociology, geography, communication, history, English, comparative literature, feminist studies, film and media studies, religious studies, anthropology, and education (2003); and, (2) a terminal MA program focusing on global civil society and designed to prepare students to work for international non-governmental organizations (NGOs) (2005).

This process was greatly aided by the generosity of philanthropist, Kinko's founder, and serial entrepreneur Paul Orfalea who began teaching an immensely popular seminar in global business and leadership at UCSB in Spring 2002. Sharing the global vision of Juergensmeyer and Appelbaum, the investing guru and the Orfalea Family Foundation provided a ten million dollar endowment at UCSB that permitted not only the successful inauguration of the proposed terminal MA program under Director Appelbaum, but also the establishment of the Orfalea Center for Global and International Studies (2005). Providing the intellectual and programmatic focus for UCSB's activities in global studies, international studies, and area studies, the Orfalea Center under the directorship of Mark Juergensmeyer began to work closely with G&IS and other international units on campus. It also pursued projects with academic collaborators around the world, thus engaging in research and policy questions of global scope, implications, and relevance.

In 2015, precisely a decade after the inauguration of the Orfalea Center, the G&IS Program dropped 'international' from its name and became the Department of Global Studies. In the same year, it launched the first doctoral program in global studies at a Tier-1 research university in the United States. But it is worth remembering that this auspicious moment was preceded by eight years of hard collective labor of designing the PhD program and shepherding it through various faculty committees and administrative levels. Gunn had pushed for it from the moment he took over as chair in 2005, and then worked with his colleagues to triple the faculty's size at the same time as the University of California system was dealing with a one billion dollar deficit. Gunn conceived and wrote the proposal for the doctoral program, and then, with the new Chair Eve Darian-Smith's assistance at the end of the long process, worked for its acceptance by the university in the face of considerable institutional skepticism and opposition. Moreover, the PhD proposal would never have come into being, much less received approval, without the unwavering support and creative assistance the global studies team received from Dean Melvin Oliver. Reflecting areas of centrality in the field of global studies at large, UCSB's doctoral curriculum was configured around three areas of specialization: (1) global political economy, sustainable development, and the environment; (2) global culture, ideology, and religion; and (3) global governance, human rights, and civil society. In designing and developing this landmark program, the successive chairs Giles Gunn and legal scholar Eve Darian-Smith drew on the skills, expertise, and contributions of their growing core of junior and senior faculty members Jan Nederveen Pieterse, Alison Brysk, Paul Amar, Aashish Mehta, Esther Lezra, Nadège Clitandre, Javiera Barandiarán, Marguerite Bouraad-Nash, Raymond Clémençon, and Philip McCarty. Along the way, the department benefited in numerous ways from the contributions of the prominent political scientist Richard Falk and the legal expert Hilal Elver, two scholars who held adjunct positions on the faculty for nearly a decade. To be sure, the many processes that led to the establishment and development of global studies at UCSB were not always smooth and uncontroversial. The troubling flipside of relative departmental autonomy in American higher education is the all too frequent dominance of a 'silo mentality' that breeds resistance to the development of new programs perceived as threatening the disciplinary terrain of existing departments. As we shall discuss in more detail in Chapter 3, it is one thing to pay lip service to inter- and multidisciplinarity as a noble *ideal*, but it is quite another to turn the concept into institutional reality. As Richard Appelbaum remembers, one UCSB social science department, in particular, put up a hard and protracted fight to prevent the approval of the one-year introductory course sequence in global studies, claiming that many themes and issues taught in these classes trespassed into areas of knowledge that properly 'belonged' to its area of expertise.[32]

Other obstacles in the evolution of global studies at UCSB included procuring the necessary faculty lines for the very quickly growing program; motivating core global studies faculty to put countless unpaid overtime hours into serving on planning committees, developing new gateway courses, and teaching sometimes unremunerated course overloads to keep up with the exploding enrollments; engaging in long discussions with faculty senators from other colleges suspicious of the value of 'global studies' while wielding the power to delay or block time-sensitive curricular or administrative proposals; and getting bogged down in seemingly endless negotiations with deans and other high-level administrators reluctant to allocate scarce resources to untested ideas and initiatives. In the end, however, the UCSB global studies faculty succeeded in taking a giant step toward the realization of a dream that Appelbaum, Juergensmeyer, and Gunn had shared since the beginning of their auspicious collaboration in 1990s: the ultimate establishment of a Global Studies School at UCSB that would be at the vanguard of twenty-first century 'global affairs' to the same extent that Princeton University's Woodrow Wilson School of Public and International Affairs and Columbia University's School of International and Public Affairs had spearheaded the study of 'international affairs' in the twentieth century.

The Globalism Institute (now Centre for Global Research) at RMIT University

In the late 1990s, roughly around the same time Appelbaum, Gunn, and Juergensmeyer were putting the finishing touches on their pioneering BA program in global and international studies, another process commenced thousands of miles away in Melbourne, Australia. It would ultimately result in the establishment of a trailblazing global studies program at RMIT University. Serving as the Deputy Head of the Politics Program in the School of Social Inquiry at Monash University, the political and social theorist Paul James was working with a small team of mostly early-career scholars who were exasperated with the traditional nation-state focus of IR, which seemed to ignore the increasingly prominent role played by globalization dynamics in world politics. In particular, James had been engaging in close research collaborations with his senior colleague Tom Nairn, a prominent Scottish nationalism scholar who had recently turned his attention to the multiplying intersections between national and global politics in the aftermath of the Cold War. Pondering the reasons for the seemingly anachronistic resurgence of violent nationalisms in Yugoslavia and other parts of the old continent, Nairn focused on what he called 'the European enigma' as reflected in his central research question, 'Why has globalization engendered nationalism, rather than transcending it?' James shared his colleague's fascination with the apparent globalization of nationalisms, but approached Nairn's enigma of the strange return of nationality politics in a globalizing world from a decidedly socio-theoretical angle. While James's reflections drew inspiration from the contributions of both classical and contemporary social thinkers like Karl Marx, Émile Durkheim, Ernest Gellner, and Anthony Giddens, he also recognized the importance of bridging the divide between social theory and political practice by anchoring his theoretical investigations in political crises of global impact such as the Bosnian war and the 1994 Rwandan genocide. In the course of these critical engagements, James produced a sophisticated 'theory of nation formation', which analyzed the entangled dynamics of globalization processes and 'postmodern capitalism' in reconstituting the communal framework and institutional functions of conventional nation-states.[33]

In 1999, James, Nairn, and their small group of like-minded colleagues enthusiastically responded to a university-wide call for proposals to establish new internally funded research units at Monash organized around cutting-edge research themes. But their formal proposal to establish a transdisciplinary 'global politics' unit dedicated to probing the productive tension between the national and the global went nowhere. Deeming that the research team consisted of too many 'junior scholars' to be successful in the national hunt for external research grants, Monash University turned its back on what James and Nairn had begun to call 'globalism research'. Within a year, most of the group's junior members proved the academic value of their collective research vision by obtaining academic posts at other prestigious universities in Australia and the United Kingdom. James and Nairn, too, decided to leave Monash University and accepted RMIT University's offer to take up senior positions as 'Professor of Globalization and Cultural Diversity' (James) and 'Professor of Nationalism and Cultural Diversity' (Nairn). James thus became the first professor of globalization in Australia, They were joined by two full-time research fellow appointments, Christopher Ziguras, a former PhD student of Paul James, and Peter Phipps, working on global indigeneity. In one bold stroke, RMIT had acquired four talented globalization scholars who would put their new university at the forefront of what would soon be known as 'global studies'.

On the surface, Monash University and RMIT University could not have been any more different. The former was a leading national university with an international reputation in the arts and sciences, whereas the latter originally constituted a vocationally oriented 'Institute of Technology' that had merged with similar institutions to expand into a large and comprehensive university of technology specializing in engineering, architecture, design, business, education, and select social science disciplines such as urban and environmental planning, criminal justice administration, sociology, and international studies. Surprisingly, James and Nairn had been recruited by an education expert, Mary Kalantzis. The entrepreneurial Dean of the Faculty of Education, Language, and Community Services had just received significant federal funding for the establishment of new teaching programs and research centers in the area of 'Global and International Learning'. James and Nairn jumped on her offer to create a new research center located in her Faculty that would coordinate university-wide research on globalization and cultural diversity. James assumed the leading role in the design and faculty recruitment of the new unit, which was inaugurated in early 2002 as RMIT's 'Globalism Institute' (GI). Charged with undertaking engaged research into globalism, transnationalism, nationalism, and cultural diversity, the new research center attracted promising early-career scholars such as environmental planner Martin Mulligan, educational anthropologist Yaso Nadarajah, and security studies expert Damian Grenfell whose work examined and critically evaluated new directions of global-local change, with an emphasis on the cultural implications of global political and economic transformations. These three newcomers also provided valuable leadership in the creation and development of *Local-Global*, a peer-reviewed, collaborative international journal addressing critical issues concerning the relationship between the local and the global such as community resilience, border control, and climate change.

In the first annual Globalism Institute report published in early 2003, founding Director Paul James emphasized the tight connection between 'globalism' and 'globalization'—the twin key concepts of the conceptual framework that defined the new center.

> A working definition of the cluster of terms around 'globalism' begins through relating the various intersecting modes of practice to their extension across world space. Globalisation is thus most simply the name given to the matrix of those practices as they extend across world-space. The associated concept of 'globalism' is defined as the dominant ideology and subjectivity associated with different historical formations of global extension. . . . The definition thus is sensitive to Roland Robertson's argument that globalism is a deep historical and variable process.[34]

At the same time, however, James made abundantly clear that research undertaken by core members of the new unit would focus on both the tensions and complementarities between the global and the national and local. Indeed, the GI's 'manifesto' promised to contribute to the process of 'rethinking the relationship between the global and the local' that included such varied dynamics as the remaking of institutions of global governance and global civil society through the reconstitution of the nation-state and the reformations of local regions and communities.

Another goal highlighted in the GI's manifesto was the importance of building transnational links with other world centers of excellence committed to the study of globalization. To that purpose, James embarked, in December 2002, on a trip to the University of Hawai'i- Mānoa where a large Globalization Research Center (GRC) had been inaugurated two years earlier. Deane Neubauer, its founding director, had been successful in securing a large federal grant which had established the Globalization Network, a consortium of four affiliated globalization research centers located at George Washington University, the University of California Los Angeles, the University of South Florida, and the University of Hawai'i-Mānoa. A noted expert on global health and higher education policy, Neubauer had just accepted an appointment as the university's interim chancellor and thus recognized the need to attract additional globalization scholars to maintain the center's ambitious research agenda. He persuaded his colleague and former graduate student Manfred Steger (co-author of this book) to serve in a consulting role as the GRC's Director of Publications. In addition to launching a successful book series 'Globalization' with Rowman & Littlefield—co-sponsored by the center—Steger was given the task to organize and chair a small international conference in Honolulu on the theme, 'The Ideological Dimensions of Globalization'. A number of prominent globalization scholars attended, including Leslie Sklair, James Mittelman, Mohammed Bamyeh, Mark Rupert, and Mary Hawkesworth. Having just welcomed Paul James to the GRC, James White, its deputy director, managed to convince the reluctant conference chair on the evening before the opening of the three-day event to include the Australian visitor in the program as a full participant. James' brilliantly delivered *ad hoc* presentation on the changing relevance of nationalism in a globalizing world convinced Steger that he had made the right decision.

A Rutgers University-trained historian of political thought who had penned political biographies of both the Marxist revisionist Eduard Bernstein and Mahatma Gandhi, the Indian 'Father of the Nation', Steger had recently turned his research interests in political ideologies toward the subjective dimensions of globalization. In fact, his conceptual analysis of the core concepts and neoliberal claims of what he called the dominant ideology of 'market globalism' had resulted in an award-winning book that served as the thematic framework for the GRC-sponsored conference papers, which were published in an academic anthology a year later.[35] Sharing a strong research interest in social theory and nationalism studies, both Steger and James had seized upon the term 'globalism' to explore various aspects of globalization. During the conference, the two theorists found time to deepen their intellectual affinity in intense one-on-one conversations. Having taught comparative political theory at Illinois State University for a number of years, Steger confided in his new friend that he was ready for a relocation to a university that showed greater commitment to transdisciplinary globalization research—or what he had recently begun to call 'globalization studies'.

Two years later, James convinced Steger to apply for Head of the newly constituted School of International and Community Studies at RMIT University. This position had been created as a result of the reorganization of Kalantzis's Faculty into three separate schools. Steger was offered the job and assumed his headship in August 2005. Beset by administrative problems resulting from overlapping disciplinary programs in RMIT's two separate social science and humanities schools—International and Community Studies, and Social Science and Planning—Steger assembled a transdisciplinary team of reform-minded faculty willing to support his vision to merge the two schools into a large 'global studies' unit. As was the case at UCSB, it required a dedicated team effort to turn the merger into reality—but not without suggesting some compromise measures to assuage more narrow disciplinary interests. These were reflected in the name of the newly merged unit: School of Global Studies, Social Science, and Planning. Officially inaugurated on January 1, 2006, the new school became the first large academic unit in the English-speaking world to adopt 'global studies' in its appellation.

Their location under the new institutional umbrella made it possible for research-only faculty in the GI and instructional faculty serving the two international studies programs—a BA track in international studies and the terminal MA program in international development—to meet and interact closely. Thus began their long and often difficult, but ultimately successful, journey to coordinate their respective research and teaching activities in the newly created transdisciplinary Global Studies Program. Under the leadership of Paul Battersby, the Convener of the Program, the predominantly IR curriculum of the BA track in international studies was significantly altered and reconfigured around a new globalization focus reflected in the creation of new courses such as 'From Nationalism to Globalism', 'Globalizing Societies', 'Global Processes', 'Gender Development and Globalization', 'Digital Technology and Globalization', 'Global Mobility and Ethnic Relations', and 'Global Governance and International Law'. The restructured curriculum also included a language requirement and integrated modules of international fieldwork, internships, study abroad, and international professional practice opportunities. But perhaps the most innovative feature of the Global Studies Program was a built-in schedule of guest lectures delivered by research faculty from the Globalism Institute who introduced students to various methodological toolboxes for conducting research in global studies. The restructured curriculum proved to be enormously successful as applications soared and selectivity criteria were tightened. By the late 2000s, RMIT's BA in International Studies had become the leading undergraduate program of its kind in Australia as measured by the stellar entry scores of its first-year students.

In the meantime, the Globalism Institute had expanded rapidly as a result of successful external research grant applications that provided substantial funding for new doctoral students, postdoctoral research fellows, and junior researchers—some of whom eventually obtained permanent faculty positions in the Global Studies Program. When Steger assumed the Directorship of the Globalism Institute in 2007—renamed in the same year as 'Globalism Research Centre'—he joined an extraordinary team of academics eager to push global studies research into new directions. As the following three examples show, the innovative character of their work was reflected in the themes and scope of their funded research projects.

The international development and security studies expert Damian Grenfell had assembled a transdisciplinary group of scholars engaged in what they called the 'Timor-Leste Research Program'. Focusing on East

Timor's postcolonial process of nation-formation, research moved across the disciplines of political science, sociology, and anthropology as the group explored the impact of globalization on social change and different patterns of social integration, from the customary to the modern. In particular, the group tackled aspects of globalization where change has been felt acutely, such as culture, community and polity, and across the domains of security, development, gender, justice, and governance.

In similar transdisciplinary fashion, postdoctoral fellow Anne McNevin led a collaborative research project probing the relationship between Australia's increasing role in security and development in Pacific states and irregular labor migration flowing from these ties. In particular, her work explored the exacerbation of tensions in Australia around multiculturalism and national identity that had surfaced in violent public disturbances and in debates on border protection, migration, and guest worker schemes. Thus, McNevin's project drew on regional and Australian experiences of irregular migration to inform policy and political questions on the prominent issues of citizenship, migration and globalization.

Finally, the cultural anthropologist Peter Phipps spearheaded a successful collaborative grant proposal that provided funding for a small research group investigating evolving forms of 'globalizing indigeneity'. Investigating the role of cultural festivals in supporting community wellbeing in selected indigenous communities in the Asia–Pacific region, the project was grounded in fieldwork-based case studies of each festival. Ultimately, Phipps's team found that despite the very different penetration and impacts of globalization in these places, these festivals could be understood through a common framework, which both deployed and exceeded human rights-based discourses as a local assertion of indigenous global presence.

In 2008, UCSB's Global and International Studies Program and RMIT's Globalism Research Center established enduring interactions and exchanges through the Global Studies Consortium (GSC). Founded by Mark Juergensmeyer in 2007 with the support of the Orfalea Center and its Program Director, Victor Faessel, the GSC promoted and facilitated both research and graduate teaching programs in global studies. This professional umbrella organization organized annual global studies conferences and offered membership to any academic program in the world interested in the development of transdisciplinary graduate programs related to global studies. Indeed, the establishment of the GSC not only reflected the increasing acceptance and popularity of the 'global studies' label, but also marked the beginning of a new, more mature phase in the development of the new field.

Concluding Remarks

Tracing the origins and evolution of global studies this chapter emphasized the interconnected trajectory of globalization and the emerging transdisciplinary field. We noted that, far from being invented during the neoliberal Roaring Nineties as shorthand for the liberalization and worldwide integration of markets, 'globalization' had been used for decades in academic fields as varied as education and psychology, society and culture, politics and international relations, and economics and business. At the same time, the powerful ideological and political dynamics of the 1990s served as crucial catalysts for the cross-fertilization of public and academic discourses on the subject. These raging globalization debates stimulated growing interest in the academic study of globalization as a multidimensional phenomenon. Emerging from these debates, the heading 'global studies' competed with a number of other pertinent terms such as 'globalization studies', 'critical globalization studies', 'transnational studies', and 'globalism research'. It was not until the early 2000s that global studies established its status as the most frequently used designation for the new field and imaginary. To a large extent, the reasons for its popularity were pragmatic—its brevity and generality as well as the success of some pioneering teaching programs and research centers that consciously embraced the heading. As we saw in the case of UCSB and RMIT, innovative teams of scholars collaborated to create independent degree-granting global studies units consisting of global studies programs and centers with their own courses and their own instructional and research faculty. Such trailblazing units usually evolved from rather modest teaching programs granting a BA degree to full-fledged departments or schools offering both undergraduate and graduate degrees in global studies.

Throughout the 2000s, a growing number of universities and colleges in the US and around the world followed suit by creating their own 'global studies' units on campus. However, as Jan Nederveen Pieterse pointed out, in many cases these activities did not involve the generation of brand new programs *ex nihilo*, but the upgrading and reconfiguring of existing offerings in IR, comparative studies, regional studies programs, or development studies.[36] Other universities, like the University of Hawai'i-Mānoa, chose the route of interdisciplinary undergraduate major and minor programs in global studies. These tend to be supported by faculty in traditional departments who volunteer their time or are assigned to teach global studies on a released-time basis. In some cases, such interdisciplinary global studies programs offered few if any courses of their own as the curriculum consisted entirely of courses in existing departments that are designated as appropriate for a global studies major. Still other universities, like the University of Illinois, Urbana-Champaign or the London School of Economics opted for integrating global studies as a subfield within conventional departments that increased their program menus by offering global studies degrees.

Perhaps the most 'global' novelty in the ongoing evolution of global studies as an academic field involved the creation of interuniversity consortia that offered degrees in global studies. In such cases, a group of universities entered into binding collaboration agreements for the purpose of sponsoring a common course of study. The global studies degree is given by the consortium itself and the course of study is taught by professors from the sponsoring universities. Perhaps the best known such consortium is the European Union's *Erasmus Mundus* program, which sponsors a global studies MA program supported by faculty from Leipzig University (Germany), the University of Vienna (Austria), Wroclaw University (Poland), and the London School of Economics (UK). Students ordinarily spend one year at one university, and another year at any of the other three universities. In 2010, two Danish universities, Aarhus and Roskilde, joined the EU consortium, which is also supported by Stellenbosch (South Africa), Macquarie (Australia), Dalhousie (Canada), and UCSB (United States) and, since 2009, Jawaharlal Nehru University (India) and Fudan University (China).

Finally, in recent years we have noticed the rising popularity of joint degree programs in global studies at the undergraduate or graduate levels that are offered by two or more universities in partnership. Students rotate from one campus to another and may receive a degree solely from the partnership, or from two or more universities in the joint degree arrangement. Among the largest joint degree programs in global studies is the Global Studies Programme, which offers both MA and PhD degrees in global studies, and which is sponsored by the Albert Ludwigs Universität (Freiburg, Germany), the University of Cape Town (South Africa), FLACSO (Buenos Aires, Argentina), Chulalongkorn University (Bangkok, Thailand), and Jawaharlal Nehru University (New Delhi, India). The MA degree in global studies is a two-year program that requires students to begin with a four-month course at Freiburg, then four months at either Cape Town or Buenos Aires, then another four months at either New Delhi or Bangkok, concluding with an internship period, and a final four months at Freiburg. In addition, the program sponsors joint degree programs between Freiburg and Buenos Aires, and between Freiburg and Cape Town.[37] This increasing variety of programs and research centers, together with the rapidly growing number of global studies graduates at both the undergraduate and graduate levels serves as the most convincing evidence for the rising popularity of global studies.

Having provided the necessary background on the origins and evolution of the field, we are now in a position to make our case for the gradual coalescence of an academic space of tension into a reasonably coherent field that employs shared analytical frameworks in order to explore the integrating world of the twenty-first century and its problems. To this purpose, the next four chapters explore in some detail what we consider the four major pillars of the field: globalization, transdisciplinarity, space and time, and critical thinking.

NOTES

1 See also Habibul Haque Khondker, 'Globalization, Glocalization, or Global Studies? What's in a Name?' *Globalizations* 10.4 (2013), p. 530; and Nayan Chanda, *Bound Together: How Traders, Preachers, Adventurers, and Warriors Shaped Globalization* (New Haven: Yale University Press, 2007), pp. xxi.

2 This segment of the chapter draws on materials presented in the full genealogical account of 'globalization' in Paul James and Manfred B. Steger, 'A Genealogy of "Globalization" : The Career of a Concept', *Globalizations* 11.4 (2014), pp. 417–34.

3 In both the academic and public discourse, this generic meaning of globalization is usually imbued with economic-technical signifiers. Cultural meanings play a secondary role.

4 James and Steger, 'Globalization: The Career of a Concept'.

5 William Boyd, *The History of Western Education,* 3rd ed. (London: A. & C. Black, 1932).

6 William Boyd and M. M. MacKenzie, eds., *Towards a New Education* (New York: A. Knopf, 1930), p. 350.

7 Ovide Decroly, *La Fonction de Globalisation et l'Enseignement* (Brussels: Lamertin, 1929).

8 Richard C. Snyder, *Thinking, Teaching, Politicking about the Globalization of the World: Toward a Synthesis and Possible Future Strategy* (Washington, DC: ERIC Clearinghouse, 1990). http://catalogue.nla.gov.au/record/5538423. Accessed on 1 January 2016.

9 See, for example, Jaishree Kak Odin and Peter T. Manicas, eds., *Globalization and Higher Education* (Honolulu: University of Hawai'i Press, 2004); Benjamin Wildavsky, *The Great Brain Race: How Global Universities Are Reshaping the World* (Princeton, NJ: Princeton University Press, 2010); and Deane E. Neubauer, ed., *The Emergent Knowledge Society and the Future of Higher Education: Asian Perspectives* (London and New York: Routledge, 2013).

10 Lucius C. Harper, 'He is Rich in the Spirit of Spreading Hatred', *Chicago Defender,* (15 January 1944), p.4.

11 David Runciman, 'Destiny vs. Democracy', *London Review of Books,* 35.8 (25 April 2013), pp. 13–16.

12 Paul Meadows, 'Culture and Industrial Analysis', *Annals of the American Academy of Political and Social Science* 274 (1951), p. 11.

13 Ibid.

14 Roland Robertson, *Globalization: Social Theory and Global Culture.* (London: SAGE, 1992); Mike Featherstone, ed., *Global Culture: Nationalism, Globalization, and Modernity* (London: SAGE, 1990); Anthony Giddens, *The Consequences of*

Modernity (Stanford: Stanford University Press, 1990); John Tomlinson, *Globalization and Culture* (Chicago: University of Chicago Press, 1999); and Arjun Appadurai, *Modernity at Large: The Cultural Dimensions of Globalization* (Minneapolis, MN: University of Minnesota Press, 1996).

15 Inis L. Claude, 'Implications and Questions for the Future', *International Organization* 19.3 (1965), p.837.

16 George Modelski, 'Communism and the Globalization of Politics', *International Studies Quarterly* 12.4 (1968), p. 389.

17 See, for example, Kenichi Ohmae, *The End of the Nation State: The Rise of Regional Economies* (New York: Free Press, 1995).

18 Anonymous, 'European Communities', *International Organization*, 13.1 (1959), pp. 174–8.

19 François Perroux and Therese Jaeger, 'The Conquest of Space and National Sovereignty', *Diogenes* 10.1 (1962), pp. 1–16; and Stéphane Dufoix, 'Between Scylla and Charybdis: French Social Science Faces Globalization', unpublished manuscript, p.2. It should be noted that some meanings of *mondialisation* are quite different from the one that is now usually translated as 'globalization'.

20 Thomas Friedman, *The World Is Flat 3.0: A Brief History of the Twenty-First Century* (New York: Picador, 2007).

21 Theodore Levitt, 'The Globalization of Markets', *Harvard Business Review* 61.3 (May-June 1983), pp. 92–102.

22 For a detailed discussion of the major claims of market globalism, see Chapter 2.

23 See the 'Interviews' section in the special issue of *Globalizations* 11.4 (2014), pp. 435–572 (edited by Manfred B. Steger and Paul James).

24 James Mittelman, ed., *Globalization: Critical Reflections* (Boulder: Lynne Rienner, 1996); and David Held, Anthony McGrew, David Goldblatt, and Jonathan Perraton, *Global Transformations: Politics, Economics, and Culture* (Stanford: Stanford University Press, 1999).

25 Paul James, 'Globalization, Approaches To', in Helmut K. Anheier and Mark Juergensmeyer, eds. *Encyclopedia of Global Studies*, vol. 2 (London and Thousand Oaks: SAGE, 2012), p. 753.

26 Interview with Richard Appelbaum, Santa Barbara, CA, 13 February 2015.

27 Benjamin R. Barber, *Jihad vs. McWorld* (New York: Crown, 1995).

28 Mark Juergensmeyer, *The New Cold War? Religious Nationalism Confronts the Secular State* (Berkeley, CA: University of California Press, 1993).

29 Mark Juergensmeyer, 'Interview Mark Juergensmeyer', *Globalizations* 11.4 (2014), p. 541.

30 See, for example, Giles Gunn, *The Culture of Criticism and the Criticism of Culture* (Oxford: Oxford University Press, 1988); *Beyond Solidarity: Pragmatism and Difference in a Globalizing World* (Chicago: University of Chicago Press, 2001); and *Ideas to Die For: The Cosmopolitan Challenge* (London and New York: Routledge, 2013).

31 See, for example, Sucheng Chan, *Asian Americans: An Interpretive History* (Farmington Hills, MI: Twayne Publishers, 1991).

32 Interview with Richard Appelbaum, Santa Barbara, CA, 13 February 2015.

33 Tom Nairn, *Faces of Nationalism: Janus Revisited* (London and New York: Verso, 1997), p. 63; and Paul James, *Nation Formation: Towards a Theory of Abstract Community* (London and Thousand Oaks: SAGE, 1996), p. xv.

34 Paul James, 'What Is Globalism', *Globalism Institute RMIT Annual Report* (January 2002–January 2003), pp. 8–9.

35 Manfred B. Steger, *Globalism: The New Market Ideology* (Lanham, MD: Rowman & Littlefield, 2002); and Manfred B. Steger, ed., *Rethinking Globalism* (Lanham, MD: Rowman & Littlefield, 2004).

36 Jan Nederveen Pieterse, 'What Is Global Studies?', *Globalizations* 10.4 (2013), p. 499.

37 Our thanks go to Giles Gunn and his colleagues at the Department of Global Studies at UCSB for making this important information available to us.

2

THE FIRST PILLAR OF GLOBAL STUDIES

Globalization

Defining Globalization

Globalization is the principal subject of the emerging field of global studies. At the same time, the global also serves as the conceptual framework through which global studies scholars investigate the contemporary and historical dynamics of thickening interdependence. As we noted in the Introduction, most academic inquiries into globalization focus on its objective dynamics involving global financial transactions, the impact of new digital technologies, enhanced global mobility in terms of the movements of goods and people, and global cultural flows. Indeed, attempts to develop objective, quantifiable assessments of the causes, contents, and consequences of globalization have become a key issue for contemporary social science research and social policy. Since 2000, researchers have sought to develop empirical measures of globalization based on various indicators. These efforts led to the rapid proliferation of major globalization indices such as the KOF Index of Globalization.[1]

While these material aspects of intensifying social relations are certainly important, we also ought to bear in mind that globalization additionally involves equally significant subjective processes, particularly the heightening of people's awareness of the world as an interlinked whole. The forging of new objective connectivities produces a growing consciousness of interconnectivity just as much as people's increasing awareness of those interdependencies goes hand-in-hand with the proliferation of interconnections in the external world. Today, readers interested in globalization

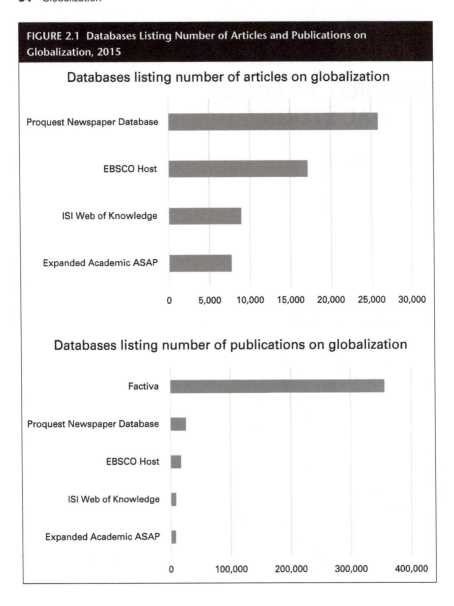

FIGURE 2.1 Databases Listing Number of Articles and Publications on Globalization, 2015

can select among thousands and thousands of pertinent books, articles, and encyclopedia entries. In our digital age, these writings can be tracked down with unprecedented speed and precision through new technologies such as the search engine *Ngram*, Google's mammoth database collated from more than five million digitized books available free to the public for online searches. Their systematic attempts to develop workable definitions reflect their desire to arrive at shared understandings in the transdisciplinary field of global studies.

One major obstacle in the way of producing useful definitions of 'globalization' is that the term has been variously used in both academic literature and the popular press to describe a process, a condition, a system, a force, and an age.[2] Given that these concepts have very different meanings, their indiscriminate usage is often obscure and invites confusion. For example, a sloppy conflation of process and condition encourages circular definitions that explain little. The familiar truism that globalization [the process] leads to more globalization [the condition] does not allow us to draw meaningful analytical distinctions between causes and effects. Hence, we suggest the adoption of the term *globality* to signify a *social condition* characterized by extremely tight global economic, political, cultural, and environmental interconnections across national borders and civilizational boundaries. Yet, we should neither assume that globality is already upon us nor that it refers to a determinate endpoint that precludes any further development. Rather, it signifies a future social condition beyond the currently existing nation-state system. Moreover, we could easily imagine different social manifestations of globality: one might be based primarily on values of individualism, competition, and laissez-faire capitalism, while another might draw on more communal and cooperative norms. These possible alternatives point to the fundamentally indeterminate character of globality.

The term 'globalization' applies not to a condition but a multidimensional *set of social processes*. By 'process' we mean an observable sequence of social change that gradually transforms the social condition of nationality into one of globality. As we noted in the Introduction, however, this does not mean that the national or the local are becoming extinct or irrelevant. In fact, the national and local remain important arenas but are changing their appearance, functions, and character as a result of increasing global connectivity. At its core, then, globalization is about shifting forms of human contact that imply three assumptions: first, that we are slowly leaving behind the condition of modern nationality that gradually unfolded from the eighteenth-century onwards; second, that we are moving toward the new condition of 'late modern' or 'postmodern' globality; and, third, that we have not yet reached it. Indeed, like 'modernization' and other verbal nouns that end in the suffix '-ization', the term 'globalization' suggests a sort of dynamism best captured by the notion of 'development' or 'unfolding' along discernible patterns. Such unfolding may occur quickly or slowly, but it always corresponds to the idea of change, and, therefore, denotes transformation.

Hence, global studies scholars exploring the dynamics of globalization are particularly keen on pursuing research questions related to the theme of change that connects the human and natural sciences. How does globalization proceed? What is driving it? Is it one cause or a combination of factors? Is globalization a continuation of modernity or is it a radical break? Does it create new forms of inequality and hierarchy or is it lifting millions of people out of poverty? Is it producing cultural homogeneity or diversity? What is the role of new technologies in accelerating and intensifying global processes? Note that the conceptualization of globalization as a dynamic process rather than as a static condition highlights the ever-increasing significance of *social change* in the Global Age. Forcing global studies researchers to pay close attention to multiple aspects of the phenomenon, it also foregrounds the fact that globalization is an uneven process: people living in various parts of the world are affected very differently by this 'glocal' transformation of social structures and cultural zones.

To argue that globalization constitutes a set of social processes enveloped by the rising global imaginary that propel us towards the condition of globality may eliminate the danger of circular definitions, but it gives us only one defining characteristic of the process: movement towards more intense forms of global connectivity, integration, and also new fissures and ruptures. But such a general outlook on globalization tells us little about its remaining qualities. In order to overcome this deficiency, it behooves us to identify a number of additional qualities that make globalization different from other sets of social processes.

First, it involves both the *creation* of new social networks and the *multiplication* of existing connections that cut across traditional political, economic, cultural, and geographical boundaries. For example, today's global media combines conventional TV coverage with multiple feeds into digital devices and networks that transcend nationally-based services.

The second quality of globalization is reflected in the *expansion* and the *stretching* of social relations, activities, and connections. Today's financial markets reach around the globe, and electronic trading occurs around the clock. Gigantic and virtually identical shopping malls have emerged on all continents, catering to those consumers who can afford commodities from all regions of the world—including products whose various components were manufactured in different countries. Indeed, we have moved to a truly transnational capitalism that integrates people around the world in global production chains and gigantic financial flows. Its gravitational pull cannot be resisted by a single nation, no matter how powerful or insignificant. As William Robinson puts it, 'We have gone from a *world economy*, in which countries and regions were linked to each other via trade and financial flows in an integrated international market, to a *global economy*, in which nations are linked to each other more organically through the transnationalization of the production process, of finance, and of the circuits of capital accumulation'.[3]

Third, globalization involves the *intensification* and *acceleration* of social exchanges and activities. As Manuel Castells has pointed out, the creation of a global 'network society' is fueled by 'communication power' that required a technological revolution—one that has been powered chiefly by the rapid development of new information and communication technologies.[4] Proceeding at breakneck speed, these innovations are reshaping the social landscape of human life. The World Wide Web relays distant information in real time, and satellites provide consumers with instant pictures of remote events. Sophisticated forms of social networking by means of Facebook, Twitter, Instagram, or YouTube have become routine activities for more than a billion people around the globe. The intensification of worldwide social relations means that local happenings are shaped by events occurring far away, and vice versa. To make the point again, the seemingly opposing processes of globalization and localization actually involve each other in the global-local nexus of 'glocalization'.

Fourth, as we emphasized in our discussion of the global imaginary, globalization impacts both the macrostructures of a 'global community' and the microstructures of 'global personhood'. It extends deep into the core of the self and its dispositions, facilitating the creation of multiple individual and collective identities nurtured by the intensifying relations between the personal and the global.

Compressing all of these core qualities of globalization into a single sentence, we arrive at the following definition of globalization: *Globalization refers to the multidimensional expansion and intensification of social relations and consciousness across world-time and world-space.*

Globalization Pioneers in the 1990s: Four Profiles

As we noted in the previous chapter, 'globalization' exploded in the 1990s and quickly achieved the illustrious status of what Raymond Williams called 'keywords'. What the British cultural theorist had in mind were words that were critical to understanding the modern world. He called them 'keywords' in two connected senses: 'They are significant, binding words in certain activities and their interpretation; they are significant, indicative words in certain forms of thought'.[5] There has been a dramatic increase of publications containing references to the keyword during the 1990s, as measured by JSTOR, a digital library established in 1995 that offers full text searches for almost 2,000 academic periodicals across a broad swath of academic disciplines.

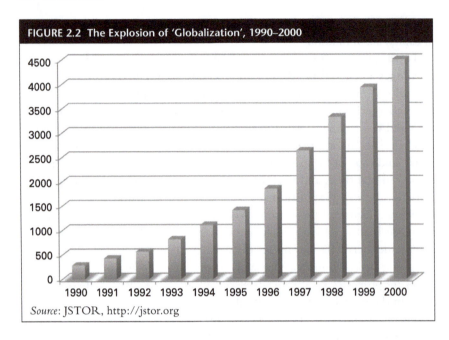

FIGURE 2.2 The Explosion of 'Globalization', 1990–2000

Source: JSTOR, http://jstor.org

The development of global studies in the 1990s was greatly enhanced by the contributions of groundbreaking thinkers who made the study of globalization the centerpiece of their academic endeavors. From the long list of these globalization pioneers, let us select four scholars whose work turned out to be especially influential in setting the theoretical agenda of the emerging field.

It is perhaps most fitting to start these four short profiles with the British sociologist of religion Roland Robertson—not only because he began to use the term regularly in his academic articles as early as the 1980s, but also because he believed that he had actually coined the term in 1979 when he had been in the process of rethinking the sociological key concept 'modernization': 'Consciously, I first heard it [globalization] from my own mouth . . . I said to myself, "Modernization is not just about a particular society—it's the modernization of the world." So if it is clumsy to call it "modernization of the whole world", so what should I call it? So I called it "globalization," and that's how it all began'.[6] His conviction that he had invented a brand new concept reflects not only his unawareness of its long genealogical evolution but also its extremely low profile in the academic community before the 1990s. Still, for many of us working in global studies today, Roland Robertson is a tremendously influential thinker who deserves the recognition of having put 'globalization' on the agenda of the social sciences for good. His pioneering insights into the relationship between globalization and modernity preceded and most likely influenced Anthony Giddens, Mike Featherstone, Scott Lash, and other significant early writers on the subject. His early articles on the subject in the 1980s resurrected the socio-cultural branch of 'globalization' that had withered after Paul Meadows's initial musings in the 1950s.[7]

Robertson's pioneering early contributions came in three parts. First, he criticized the economistic meaning of globalization as a material process of marketization that dominated the public discourse. Emphasizing the equal importance of the cultural and subjective aspect of the phenomenon, his definition of globalization contained two dimensions: increasing transnational social connectivity on the one hand and growing reflexive global consciousness on the other. As he emphasized in his magisterial and immensely influential study, *Globalization: Social Theory and Global Culture* (1992): 'Globalization as a concept refers both to the compression of the world and intensification of consciousness of the world as a whole'.[8] Robertson's definition—particularly his insight that the intensification of global consciousness played a crucial role in the contemporary phase of globalization—made a huge impression on other scholars steeped in cultural theory yet relatively new to the subject. It also drew greater attention to the fact that globalization was a multidimensional phenomenon. In the first short introductory survey on the subject published in 1995, the Australian sociologist Malcolm Waters emphasized Robertson's status as 'the key figure in the formalization and specification of the concept of globalization. . . . His [Robertson's] own biography might itself be seen as an instance of a link between what might be called transnationalization and global consciousness'.[9]

Robertson's second major contribution came in the form of an influential periodization of five successive phases of globalization processes. Focusing on developments in Europe from the early fifteenth to mid-eighteenth centuries, Phase I—'The Germinal Phase'—was characterized by the accentuation of ideas about humanity as a whole, and the development of scientific theories of the world as a planet. Again set mostly in Europe in the early to mid-nineteenth century, Phase II—'The Incipient Phase'—encompassed the formalization of conceptions of international relations and of standardized citizenry. Ranging from the 1870s to the 1920s, Phase III—'The Take-Off Phase'—described a worldwide dynamic favoring more integrated forms of globalization and relatively unified conceptions of humankind. Phase IV—'The Struggle-for Hegemony Phase'—concentrated on conflict and worldwide war while still extending the globalization process through the 1960s. The current Phase V—'The Uncertainty Phase'—is characterized by an unprecedented intensification of global consciousness as well as a sharp acceleration in means of global communications coupled with a greater fluidity of the international system.[10] Robertson's mapping of distinct historical phases of globalization constituted a major intellectual achievement. As Paul James noted, it challenged a dominant tendency in both the scholarly literature and in popular representations to treat globalization as if it had only just begun during the last few years or decades.[11] On the downside, Robertson's outline largely remained a prisoner of conventional stage models of history that overemphasize the role of Europe as the originating source of world-encompassing dynamics.

Robertson's third seminal contribution to the study of globalization relates to his argument that globalization was inseparable from localization. Popularizing the hybrid term 'glocalization', the social thinker insisted that in the 'real world' of lived social relations, the macroscopic level of the global always intersected with microscopic aspects of the local. Thus, globalization did not occur on an isolated spatial scale hovering above the national and local, but only became concrete and empirically observable in the local. Robertson derived his notion of glocalization from the Japanese _dochakuka_ ('global localization'), which had achieved special salience in the 1980s in Japanese marketing circles concerned with their country's success in the global economy.[12] Liberating the concept from such business understandings, the British scholar extended the meaning of the term into the cultural sphere by investing the interdependence of local and global process in the formation of identities and symbolic interactions. Moreover, he used this term to combat influential views that cultural globalization inevitably led to homogenization such as 'Americanization' or 'McDonaldization'.[13] Rather, Robertson argued that homogenization tendencies coexisted with equally strong social dynamics favoring expressions of cultural diversification and hybridization.

If Roland Robertson should be credited with initiating a 'cultural turn' in the study of globalization, then David Harvey, the second featured profile on our list of globalization pioneers, deserves recognition for inspiring a 'spatial turn'. In the early 1990s, the British political geographer emerged as perhaps the most insightful and innovative Marxist intellectual committed to analyzing the latest tendencies of capital on a global scale. In his groundbreaking study, _The Condition of Postmodernity_ (1989), he coined the famous phrase 'time-space compression'—the forerunner to Robertson's 'compression of the world', thus capturing the crucial role of spatial and temporal dynamics in the creation of what neoliberals celebrated as 'the globalization of free markets'. In particular, Harvey had drawn attention to capitalism's growing ability to provide a 'spatial fix' to its 1970s crisis of expansion. The speeding up of production, circulation, and exchange of commodities by harnessing new information and communication technologies had to be accompanied by new spatial strategies to overcome national barriers. Appropriately subtitled *An Enquiry into the Origins of Cultural Change*, Harvey's book had also pointed to a link between globalizing capitalism and the growing intellectual and aesthetic appeal of postmodern sensibilities during the 1980s—particularly their appreciation of discontinuity, plurality, and difference. However, rather than ceding autonomy to the cultural sphere, Harvey had explained the popularity of postmodernist theories largely as a cultural response to the decentering time-space compression inherent in the latest globalizing phase of capitalism.[14]

By the mid-1990s, Harvey linked his insights into the time-space compression of the global economy to the collective efforts of intellectuals on the political Left to respond more effectively to the powerful neoliberal charge that Marxism was drifting into historical irrelevance. Thus focusing on the new post-Cold War context of 'capitalism-gone-global', he channeled the main thrust of his arguments against the dominant neoliberal meaning construction of globalization. In a seminal essay published in 1995, Harvey discussed the theoretical and political implications and consequences of 'important changes in western discourses' for the socialist movement in general and the Marxist tradition in particular. From the start, he flagged the central position of globalization in the postcommunist political vocabulary, noting that it had 'become a key word for organizing our thoughts as to how the world works'.[15] For Harvey, conventional Marxist preoccupations with imperialism and colonialism were secondary to 'globalization' in organizing novel theoretical frameworks and charting new political possibilities. At the same time, he recognized that the dominance of neoliberal meanings associated with the concept operated as a powerful deterrent by shrinking the room for political maneuver and amplifying a sense of powerlessness on the part of national, regional, and local working-class movements. Pointing to the severe political price exacted by globalization and its associated neoliberal meanings, he advised progressives to neither reject nor abandon the term but to accept its centrality and explore how new meanings might be incorporated and used in productive ways by alternative globalization movements around the world.

As we noted, Harvey's central contribution to the early study of globalization involved a spatial turn that both influenced and interacted with the writings of other space-centered globalization pioneers like Saskia Sassen, Manuel Castells, Neil Brenner, Jan Aart Scholte, John Agnew, and Mike Douglass.[16] As we discuss in more detail in Chapter 4, Harvey started with the suggestion that globalization should be understood as an ongoing *spatial process* rather than a *political-economic condition* that had only come into being recently—as asserted by neoliberals like Theodore Levitt and Thomas Friedman. Reminding his readers that globalization processes had always been integral to capitalist development because the accumulation of capital had always involved profoundly geographical and spatial dynamics, Harvey called for a good dose of 'spatial thinking' to analyze the contemporary phase of global capitalism. Presenting the famous authors of the *Communist Manifesto* as early theorists of globalization, the British thinker proposed a spatial redefinition of globalization as an ongoing 'process of production of uneven temporal and geographical development'. This discursive alternative rooted in early Marxist insights allowed him to charge the radical Left with its most pressing political task: the reorganization of its material struggles—both locally and globally—in step with a revised Marxist discourse centered on a spatialized understanding of globalization. A unified promotion of such critical and alternative globalization narratives would, according to Harvey, serve to expose the 'violence and creative destruction of uneven geographic development . . . just as widely felt in the traditional heartlands of capitalism as elsewhere . . .'[17] In other words, his redefinition of 'globalization' made it much easier to demonstrate that the contemporary time-space compression of global capitalism came not just with unprecedented gains for the wealthy few, but with all its accompanying evils, such as people's enhanced vulnerability to violence; increasing unemployment and inequality; collapse of services; and degradation in living standards and in environmental qualities.

Harvey's theoretical interventions inspired scores of progressive intellectuals to articulate the rising global imaginary in geographically sensitive ways that challenged hegemonic neoliberal definitions and understandings of globalization as the liberalization and global integration of markets. Most of these publications shared the same elements of Harvey's essay: close attention to the centrality of globalization in current political discourse; an emphasis on the relevance of Marxist insights for our global age; the introduction of critical-alternative meanings of globalization; an enhanced role for geography and spatial thinking; and expressions of sympathy for a more decentralized, locally embedded, and diverse global network of anticapitalist actors. Although the majority of these critical voices hailed from the global North, the late 1990s and early 2000s began to see a remarkable upsurge of pertinent contributions from the global South.[18] Finally, Harvey's spatialized approach to the study of globalization also flowed into the self-understanding of the fledgling global justice movement at the beginning of the new century. It contributed to the rise of a new optimism on the political Left, perhaps best reflected in the popular slogan of the newly minted World Social Forum: 'Another World Is Possible!'

The chapter's third featured globalization pioneer, Arjun Appadurai, was born and raised in Mumbai, India, and completed his graduate education in the United States. Possessing the rare qualities of a genuine multidisci- plinary and multilingual scholar, Appadurai was anchored in socio-cultural anthropology but pursued a number of research interests in other fields, such as political economy, media studies, and urban studies. In a series of related scholarly articles that culminated in the publication of *Modernity at Large* (1996), he linked contemporary globalization dynamics to the larger framework of a 'global cultural economy'. In what would become one of the most influential early books exploring the cultural dimensions of global- ization, Appadurai rejected the then dominant opposing views that global- ization gave rise to either cultural sameness ('Americanization' or 'McDonaldization') or greater differentiation (proliferation and/or frag- mentation of cultures). He employed concrete examples from South Asia and other parts of the global South to argue that increasing global interde- pendence had simultaneously produced both of these extremes. The outcome was an 'infinitely varied mutual contest of sameness and differ- ence' characterized by radical 'disjunctures' between different sorts of global flows, which were intimately connected to forms of global consciousness he called 'constructed landscapes of collective aspirations'. Thus, he fore- grounded the role of imagination in contemporary social practices that shape new global subjectivities.

Appadurai's pioneering intellectual contribution to the study of global- ization lay in his introduction of a five-dimensional conceptual model by which to analyze these complex disjunctures between economic, cultural, and political flows. He argued that the conditions under which current global flows occur could be classified in terms of five 'landscapes'— 'ethnoscapes', 'mediascapes', 'technoscapes', 'finanscapes', and 'ideoscapes'. These combined into concrete perspectives or 'imaginaries' that allowed individuals and groups to make sense of the shrinking world.[19] Noting that human history had always been characterized by disjunctures in the flows of people, machinery, money, images, and ideas, he nonetheless emphasized that the sheer speed, scale, and volume of each of these flows had become so great in the late twentieth century that the contemporary disjunctures had become central to the politics of global culture. These disjunctures in the global flows of goods, services, information, and ideas encouraged the formation of 'multiple worlds' constituted by the historically and politi- cally situated interactions of persons and groups spread around the globe: transnational corporations, nation-states, diasporic communities, non- governmental organizations (NGOs), as well as subnational groupings and movements.

Like Robertson, Appadurai favored a balanced approach that gave equal attention to objective and subjective dimensions of globalization. Most importantly, he demonstrated how globalization—reflected in transnational capital as well as international clothing styles—provided innovative resources for new identities and subjectivities that were no longer exclusively anchored in the modern nation or the traditional tribe. Appadurai's reflections generated tremendous interest in global cultural dynamics and stimulated established cultural theorists to add their significant insights to the study of globalization.[20]

The final globalization pioneer of the 1990s covered in this section is the social and urban theorist Saskia Sassen who chairs the Committee on Global Thought at Columbia University. Born in the Netherlands, she grew up in Argentina and Italy but has pursued her academic career primarily in the United States. Focusing primarily on transnational migration, gender, and labor issues, her early work in the 1980s suggested that foreign investment in less-developed countries can actually raise the likelihood of emigration if that investment goes to labor-intensive sectors and devastates the traditional economy. Her thesis went against established notions that such investment would retain potential emigrants.[21]

But Sassen's key contribution to global studies consists of her development of a 'global city model' that offered new ways of analyzing the strategic roles of global cities like New York, London, Tokyo, Shanghai, Seoul, and Paris. Although most of these global cities had long served as international economic and cultural centers, Sassen argued that globalization processes had produced 'massive and parallel changes in their economic base, spatial organization and social structure'.[22] Thus, global cities had assumed great significance as pivotal places of spatial dispersal and global integration located at the intersection of multiple global circuits and flows involving migrants, ideas, commodities, and money. In other words, the global economy needs very specific territorial insertions, and this need is sharpest in the case of highly globalized and digitized sectors such as finance.

As a result of globalization, Sassen insisted, global cities should no longer be conceptualized as bounded units but as complex structures capable of coordinating a variety of cross-boundary processes and reconstituting them as urban activities. Functioning as highly specific places encased in national territory and a transnational network linked to hinterlands and other urban centers, global cities owed their growing stature to processes of deterritorialization while at the same time serving as crucial catalysts for the formation of new transboundary spatialities epitomized in the global economic system.

Countering established notions at the time that the global economy transcended territory and its associated regulatory umbrellas, Sassen's work on global cities emphasized the partial embeddedness of the global in the subglobal. Indeed, she developed this line of inquiry throughout the 1990s and early 2000s by showing that contemporary social transformations—from economic to cultural and subjective—are taking place largely inside thick national settings and institutions.[23] As we discuss in more detail in Chapter 4, she conceptualized these transformations as denationalizing dynamics that operate alongside the more familiar globalizing dynamics. For Sassen, the denationalizing of what was historically constructed as national is more significant than much of the self-evidently global.

Academic Globalization Debates: Four Intellectual Camps

The globalization pioneers of the 1990s inspired the development of an intellectual framework of global studies that involved inquiries into the main dimensions of globalization: economic, political, cultural, ideological, and ecological. As we argue in Chapter 3, researching these principal domains involves *transdisciplinary* explorations of definitions, impacts, networks, flows, hybridities, and new research orientations. These contemporary globalization debates have taken place over the last two decades in two separate but related arenas. As we discussed in the previous chapter, the evolution of the dominant economistic meaning branch of 'globalization' underwent what we might call a 'double movement'. Decisively shaped by Theodore Levitt in a business school academic context, the term escaped into the public discourse while also remaining in its scholarly terrain. Moreover, the public globalization debates heating up in the immediate aftermath of the Cold War stimulated new academic studies of the phenomenon in its many dimensions, not just its economic-technological aspects, but also its socio-cultural and political aspects.

Hence, one discussion—introduced in this section—has proceeded mostly within the narrow walls of academia. The other—covered in the next section—has unfolded in the more visible arena of public discourse. Although there are some common themes and overlapping observations, the academic debate differs from the more general discussion in that a good number of participants tend to emphasize the various analytical aspects of globalization rather than its ideological dimensions. Many of the principal contributors to this academic discourse reside and teach in the wealthy countries of the Northern Hemisphere, particularly the United States, Canada, the European Union, and Australia. Their disproportionate intellectual influence reflects not only existing power relations in the world, but also the global dominance of Anglo-American ideas. The principal voices in the academic globalization debates can be divided into four distinct intellectual 'camps': globalizers, rejectionists, skeptics, and modifiers.[24] Let us examine these influential perspectives in more detail.

Globalizers

Most global studies scholars fall into the category of 'globalizers' who argue that globalization is a profoundly transformative set of social processes that is moving human societies toward unprecedented levels of interconnectivity.[25] Emphasizing that globalization is not a single monolithic process but a complex and often contradictory and uneven dynamic of simultaneous social integration and fragmentation, they insist that empirical research clearly points to the intensification of significant worldwide flows that can be appropriately subsumed under the general term 'globalization'. While committed to a big picture approach, globalizers nonetheless tend to focus their research efforts on one of the principal dimensions of globalization: economics, politics, culture, or ecology.

For example, globalizers researching economic aspects suggest that a quantum change in human affairs has taken place in the last decades as the flow of large quantities of trade, investment, and technologies across national borders has expanded from a trickle to a flood. In addition to these issues, perhaps the two most important aspects of economic globalization relate to the changing nature of the production process and the increasing power of transnational organizations. Globalizers interested in political aspects of globalization approach their subject often from the perspective of global governance. Representatives of this group analyze the role of various national and multilateral responses to the fragmentation of economic and political systems and the transnational flows permeating through national borders. Some of these researchers argue that political globalization might facilitate the emergence of democratic transnational social forces emerging from a thriving sphere of 'global civil society'.[26] This topic is often connected to discussions focused on the impact of globalization on human rights and vice versa.[27] For example, Martin Shaw emphasizes the role of global political struggles in creating a 'global revolution' that would give rise to an internationalized, rights-based state conglomerate symbolically linked to global institutions. Thus, he raises the fascinating prospect of 'state formation beyond the national level'.[28] Finally, the thematic landscape traversed by scholars of cultural globalization is vast. Perhaps the two most central questions raised by these researchers are, first, does globalization increase cultural homogeneity, or does it lead to greater diversity or hybridity? And second, how does the dominant culture of consumerism impact the natural environment?

To be sure, some of the global studies scholars located on the extreme end of the spectrum could be labeled 'hyperglobalizers' for they see globalization as the main driver of nearly all of social change today and often adopt quite deterministic perspectives situated within economistic frameworks.[29] More moderate globalizers, however, caution against such sweeping generalizations and overarching narratives of globalization, opting instead for less ambitious approaches designed to provide specific explanations of particular domains of the phenomenon. Still, both of these two globalizer wings are united in their conviction that the contemporary phase in the expansion and intensification of social relations is highly significant and truly global in its reach and impact. Today, globalizers constitute the bulk of global studies scholars.

Rejectionists

By contrast, 'rejectionists' contend that most of the accounts offered by globalizers are incorrect, imprecise, or exaggerated. They note that just about everything that can be linked to some transnational process is cited as evidence for globalization and its growing influence. Considering 'globalization' a prime example of a 'big idea resting on slim foundations', they claim that the term is so broad and hazy that it could be associated with 'anything from the Internet to a hamburger'.[30] Arguing that such generalizations often amount to little more than 'globaloney', rejectionists dismiss the utility of 'globalization' for scientific academic discourse.[31] They also charge that the term obscures more than it illuminates and, therefore, suggest breaking the concept of globalization into smaller, more manageable parts that could be linked more easily to processes of interconnections in the 'real world'. However, as empirical studies in the last decade have provided more evidence for the existence of significant globalization dynamics, the number of rejectionists has dramatically dwindled in recent years.

Skeptics

The third camp in the contemporary globalization debates consists of 'skeptics' who acknowledge some forms and manifestations of globalization while also emphasizing its limited nature. This perspective is perhaps best reflected in the writings of Robert Wade, Paul Hirst, and Grahame Thompson.[32] In their detailed historical analysis of economic globalization, Hirst and Thompson claim that the world economy is not a truly global phenomenon, but one centered on Europe, East Asia, Australia, and North

America. The authors emphasize that the majority of economic activity around the world still remains primarily national in origin and scope. Presenting relevant data on trade, foreign direct investment, and financial flows, the authors warn against drawing premature conclusions from increased levels of economic interaction in advanced industrial countries. Ultimately, their argument against the existence of economic globalization is linked to their criticism of the general misuse of the concept. Without a truly global economic system, they insist, there can be no such thing as globalization: '[A]s we proceeded [with our economic research] our skepticism deepened until we became convinced that globalization, as conceived by the more extreme globalizers, is largely a myth'.[33] Buried under an avalanche of quantitative data, one can detect a critical-normative message in the Hirst–Thompson thesis: exaggerated accounts of an 'iron logic of economic globalization' tend to produce disempowering political effects. For example, the authors convincingly demonstrate that certain political forces have used the thesis of an inexorable economic globalization to propose national economic deregulation and the reduction of welfare programs. Obviously, the implementation of such policies stands to benefit neoliberal interests.

But there also remain a number of problems with the Hirst–Thompson thesis. As several critics have pointed out, the authors set overly high standards for the economy in order to be considered 'fully globalized'. Second, their construction of an abstract model of a perfectly globalized economy unnecessarily polarizes the topic by pressuring the reader to either completely embrace or entirely reject the concept of globalization. Third, as critics like William Robinson have pointed out, Hirst and Thompson collect and make sense of their data from within their nation-state-centric framework of analysis that prevents them 'from interpreting facts in a new way that provide greater explanatory power with regard to novel developments in the late twentieth- and early twenty-first century world'.[34] Perhaps the most serious problem with the Hirst–Thompson thesis lies in its attempt to counteract neoliberal economic determinism with a good dose of economic determinism. Their argument implicitly assumes that globalization is primarily an economic phenomenon. As a result, they portray all other dimensions of globalization—culture, politics, and ideology—as reflections of deeper economic processes. While paying lip service to the multidimensional character of globalization, their own analysis ignores the logical implications of this assertion. After all, if globalization is truly a complex, multilevel phenomenon, then economic relations constitute only one among many globalizing tendencies. It would therefore be entirely possible to argue for the significance of globalization even if it can be shown that increased transnational economic activity appears to be limited to advanced industrial countries.

Modifiers

The fourth camp in the contemporary globalization debates consists of 'modifiers' who acknowledge the power of globalization but dispute its novelty and thus the innovative character of globalization theory. Thus, they seek to modify and assimilate globalization theory with tried and tested approaches in IR, IS, or other related fields, claiming that a new conceptual paradigm is unwarranted.[35] Implying that the term has been used in a historically imprecise manner, they suggest current globalization theories that would highlight the longevity of the phenomenon. Robert Gilpin, for example, cites relevant data collected by the prominent American economist Paul Krugman to note that the world economy in the late 1990s appeared to be even less integrated in a number of important respects than it was prior to the outbreak of World War I. Even if one were to accept the most optimistic assessment of the actual volume of transnational economic activity, the most that could be said is that the postwar international economy has simply restored globalization to approximately the same level that existed in 1913. Gilpin also points to two additional factors that seem to support his position: the globalization of labor was actually much greater prior to World War I, and international migration declined considerably after 1918. Warning his readers against accepting the arguments of 'hyper-globalizers', the political economist insists that such ahistorical short-term thinking requires serious modifications.[36]

Similar calls for adapting globalization theory to previous perspectives come from the proponents of 'world-systems analysis'—a generic label for various explanations of long-term, large-scale social change favoring the emergence of a single world-system rooted in structural components of the world economy. Pioneered in the 1970s by neo-Marxist scholars like Immanuel Wallerstein, Andre Gunder Frank, Giovanni Arrighi, and Christopher Chase-Dunn, world-systems theorists argue that globalization theory should be adapted to fit their own framework, which suggests that the modern capitalist economy in which we live today has been global since its inception five centuries ago.[37] They contend that, driven by the exploitative logic of capital accumulation, the capitalist world system has created global inequalities based on the domination of modernizing Western 'core' countries over non-Western 'peripheral' areas. States are crucial subentities within the capitalist world-system with the capacity to coordinate and reproduce the core-periphery hierarchy. These structural forms of exploitation were inscribed in nineteenth-century systems of colonialism and imperialism and have persisted in the twentieth and twenty-first centuries in different forms. World-systems analysts reject, therefore, the use of the term 'globalization' as referring exclusively to the relatively recent phenomenon of the last few decades. Instead, they emphasize that globalizing tendencies have been proceeding along the continuum of modernization for a long time. As Wallerstein puts it, 'The proponents of world-systems analysis . . . have been talking about "globalization" since long before the word was invented—not, however, as something new but as something that has been basic to the modern world-system ever since it began in the sixteenth century'.[38]

Still, world-systems analysis shares a number of features with global studies. First, the proponents of the former are as interested as the latter in capturing the 'big picture'. They emphasize that all forms of 'systemic knowledge' necessarily involve the construction of overarching narratives capable of explaining interconnected social relations. Second, world-systems analysts, too, embrace transdisciplinary approaches that abolish the lines between economic, political, and sociocultural modes of analysis. Seeking to analyze materials within a single analytical framework, Wallerstein has characterized his method as a 'unidisciplinary approach' that does not recognize the intellectual legitimacy of disciplinary divisions. Finally, like global studies scholars, world-systems analysts emphasize the significance of space and time. In their view, serious discussions of globalization pay attention to cross-regional transfers of resources, technology, and culture. Extending their historical sensitivity beyond the temporal spectrum of most globalizers, world-systems thinkers have drawn on the insights of world historian Fernand Braudel to suggest that the origins of globalizing tendencies ought to be traced back to the political and cultural interactions that sustained the ancient empires of Persia, China, and Rome. Thus, the study of globalization should involve a single-frame analysis of total social systems over long periods of time (*longue durée*).[39]

At the same time, however, there are also clear differences between the world-systems and global studies outlook. While both approaches dismiss the utility of accepting the nation-state as the basic unit of analysis, world-systems analysts focus their research efforts on 'world-systems' rather than globally circulating flows and worldwide interconnectivities. In fact, as Wallerstein points out, their use of the term 'world-system' should not be equated with the idea of a 'global system':

> Note the hyphen in "world-systems" and its two subcategories, "world-economies" and "world-empires." Putting in the hyphen was

intended to underline that we are talking not about systems, economies, empires *of the* (whole) world, but about systems, economies,
empires *that are* a world (but quite possibly, and indeed usually, not
encompassing the entire globe).[40]

Second, Wallerstein and other major world-systems theorists leave little
doubt that they consider world-integration to be a process driven largely by
economic forces whose essence can be captured by economistic analytical
models. Accordingly, they assign to culture and ideology merely a subordinate role as 'idea systems' dependent on the 'real' movements of the capitalist world economy.[41] Although some global studies researchers analyzing
the economic dimensions of globalization subscribe to similar forms of
reductionism, this does not hold true for the field in general.

To be fair, however, we should point out that more recent studies
produced by world-systems scholars like Barry K. Gills acknowledge the
interaction between dominant-class interests and cultural transnational
practices. In so doing, they have begun to raise important normative
questions, suggesting that the elements of the 'ideological superstructure'—
politics, ideas, values, and beliefs—may, at times, neutralize or supersede
economic forces. Leslie Sklair, for example, highlights the importance of
what he calls 'the culture-ideology of global consumerism'. Other world-
systems thinkers like Ash Amin concede that the pace of globalization has
significantly quickened in the last few decades of the twentieth century.
This unprecedented compression of space and time since the 1970s suggests
that much of the criticism of globalization as a new phenomenon has been
based on quantitative analyses of trade and output that neglect these recent
qualitative shifts in social and political relations. These spectacular changes
in the globalizing process, Amin argues, may indeed warrant a new label as
they produced new configurations in the capitalist world-system such as
complex networks of transnational corporations, financial flows, and
cultural homogenization.[42]

Overall, then, skeptics and modifiers have made important contributions
to the contemporary academic debate on globalization. Their insistence on
a more careful and precise usage of the term forced globalizers to hone their
analytical skills and pay attention to larger temporal frames. Moreover, their
critical intervention serves as an important reminder that some aspects of
globalization may neither constitute brand new developments nor reach to
all corners of the earth. However, by focusing too narrowly on abstract
issues of terminology, the critics of the globalizer camp tend to downplay
the significance and extent of today's intensifying connectivities. Finally,
skeptics and modifiers are inclined to conceptualize globalization mostly

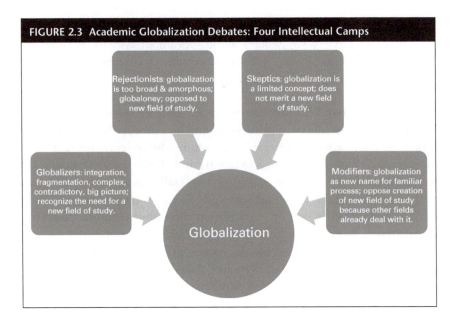

FIGURE 2.3 Academic Globalization Debates: Four Intellectual Camps

along economic lines, thereby often losing sight of its multidimensional character. As we demonstrate in the next chapter, it is precisely the willingness to tackle globalization as a complex phenomenon involving multiple aspects and logics that sets most global studies perspectives apart from unidisciplinary approaches.

Public Globalization Debates: Three Ideological Perspectives

The public debate over globalization has occurred largely outside the walls of academia. Attesting to the discursive power of 'globalization' as a value-laden keyword, this dominant public discourse represents an important aspect of the phenomenon itself. Indeed, the discursive explosion of 'globalization' in the 1990s was not an ideologically neutral affair. As we noted in the previous chapters, it occurred within the dominant Anglo-American framework that imbued the general concept with neoliberal meanings linked to particular power interests. Consider, for example, this ideological definition taken from Thomas Friedman's 1999 runaway bestseller *The Lexus and the Olive Tree: Understanding Globalization*:

> The driving idea behind globalization is free-market capitalism—the more you let market forces rule and the more you open your economy to trade and competition, the more efficient and flourishing your

economy will be. Globalization means the spread of free-market capitalism to virtually every country in the world. Therefore, globalization has its own set of economic rules—rules that revolve around opening, deregulating, and privatizing your economy, in order to make it more competitive and attractive to foreign investment. . . . Globalization has its own defining technologies: computerization, miniaturization, digitization, satellite communications, fiber optics, and the Internet, which reinforce its defining perspective on integration.[43]

Explaining the phenomenon to a global mass audience, Friedman's globalization blockbuster both reflected and helped sustain the dominant public discourse of the 1990s that shackled 'globalization' (the concept describing a process) to the political belief system of 'globalism' (a neoliberal market ideology).

Ideologies are shared mental maps that help people navigate their complex social and political environment. Ideas and norms articulated on this explicitly political level are connected to the deeper levels of social imaginaries and ontologies. The late twentieth century saw the reconfiguration of conventional ideologies around an increasingly globalized political landscape. People's increasing sensitivity to ideological novelty is reflected in the prefix 'neo' that became attached to most traditional political belief systems such as liberalism, conservatism, and Marxism. As we noted in the Introduction, powerful social elites in the 1980s and 1990s reconfigured their neoliberal ideas around the buzzword 'globalization', thereby articulating the rising global imaginary in concrete 'neoliberal' political agendas and programs.

Enamored with free-market economics, these mostly Anglo-American framers of 'market globalism' consisted mostly of corporate managers, executives of large transnational corporations, corporate lobbyists, prominent journalists and public relations specialists, cultural elites and entertainment celebrities, academics writing for large audiences, high-level state bureaucrats, and political leaders. Many members of this neoliberal corporate elite have been exchanging ideas at the annual meeting of the World Economic Forum in Davos, Switzerland.

The members of this transnational phalanx spoke softly and persuasively as they sought to attract people worldwide to their vision of globalization as a leaderless, inevitable juggernaut that would ultimately engulf the entire world. They marshaled their considerable material and ideal resources to sell to the public the alleged benefits of the liberalization of trade and the global integration of markets: rising living standards, reduction of global poverty, economic efficiency, individual freedom and democracy, and

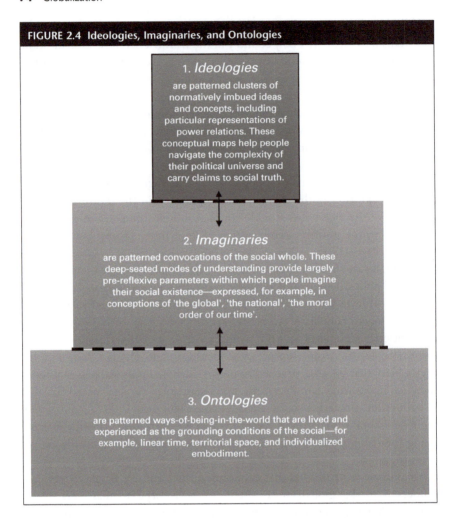

FIGURE 2.4 Ideologies, Imaginaries, and Ontologies

1. *Ideologies*

are patterned clusters of normatively imbued ideas and concepts, including particular representations of power relations. These conceptual maps help people navigate the complexity of their political universe and carry claims to social truth.

2. *Imaginaries*

are patterned convocations of the social whole. These deep-seated modes of understanding provide largely pre-reflexive parameters within which people imagine their social existence—expressed, for example, in conceptions of 'the global', 'the national', 'the moral order of our time'.

3. *Ontologies*

are patterned ways-of-being-in-the-world that are lived and experienced as the grounding conditions of the social—for example, linear time, territorial space, and individualized embodiment.

unprecedented technological progress. State initiated public-policy initiatives should be confined to those measures that liberate the economy from social constraints: privatization of public enterprises, deregulation instead of state control, liberalization of trade and industry, massive tax cuts, strict control of organized labor, and the reduction of public expenditures.

The discursive preeminence of the 'market' of course, harkened back to the heyday of liberalism in mid-Victorian England. And yet, contemporary market globalists tie this concept no longer exclusively to the old paradigm of self-contained national economies but refer primarily to a model of global exchanges among national actors, subnational agencies, supranational bodies, networks of NGOs, and transnational corporations. As we noted in

IMAGE 2.1 World Economic Forum Meeting in Davos, Switzerland, 2016
Source: Keystone/Associated Press, AP Photo ID 308388914157

the Introduction, market globalism emerged in the 1990s as a comprehensive ideology extolling, among other things, the virtues of globally integrating markets. Ideationally much richer than the more familiar term 'neoliberalism' suggests, market globalism discarded, absorbed, and rearranged large chunks of the grand ideologies while at the same time incorporating genuinely new ideas. Seeking to enshrine their neoliberal paradigm as the self-evident and universal order of our global era, transnational power elites articulated the rising global imaginary along the lines of five major ideological claims: (1) globalization is about the liberalization and global integration of markets, (2) globalization is inevitable and irreversible, (3) nobody is in charge of globalization, (4) globalization benefits everyone, and (5) globalization furthers the spread of democracy in the world.[44]

Even after two severe social crises in our new century—global terrorism and the global financial upheavals of 2008–10—market globalism has remained the dominant ideology of our global age. Although the influential proponents of such 'globalization from above' share a common belief in the shrinking of government and the power of free markets to create a better world, their neoliberal doctrine comes in different hues and multiple variations. Moreover, political elites in the global South (often educated at the elite universities of the North) have learned to fit the dictates of the market-oriented 'Washington Consensus' to their local contexts and political objectives. Thus, market globalism has adapted to specific environments, problems, and opportunities across the world.

As we discuss in some detail in Chapter 5, the so-called 'anti-globalization' forces of the political Left have challenged market globalism since the massive anti-WTO demonstration in Seattle in 1999. But their democratic vision of 'globalization from below' did not represent a rejection of globalization per se, but an alternative translation of the global imaginary critical of corporate 'globalization from above'. These transnational voices of the 'global justice movement' (GJM) provided an alternative translation of the rising global imaginary. At the core of this 'justice globalism' lies the ideological claim that the liberalization and global integration of markets leads, in fact, to greater social inequalities, environmental destruction, the escalation of global conflicts and violence, the weakening of participatory forms of democracy, the proliferation of self-interest and consumerism, and the further marginalization of the powerless around the world.

The justice-globalist vision is neither about reviving a moribund Marxism nor a return to the 'good old days' of 1968. Although justice globalism contains elements of Gandhian Third-World liberationism and traditional European social democracy, it goes beyond these Cold War ideational clusters in several respects—most importantly in its ability to bring together a large number of New Left concerns around a more pronounced orientation toward the globe as a single, interconnected arena for political action. One example of the GJM's strong global focus is its publicity campaign to highlight the negative consequences of deregulated global capitalism on the planet's environmental health. Indeed, in the first two decades of the new century, the issue of global climate change has advanced to the forefront of public discourse around the world, second only to the specter of global terrorism and warfare.

The policy vision of justice globalism lays out in some detail by now rather familiar proposals. The programmatic core of these demands is a 'global Marshall Plan'—now a fashionable buzzword that has entered the mainstream discourse as a result of the lingering 2008–9 Great Recession—that would create more political space for people around the world to determine what kind of social arrangements they want. Members of the global justice movement argue that the possibility of 'another world' has to begin with a new, worldwide Keynesian-type program of taxation and redistribution, exactly as it took off at the national level in the now-rich countries a century or so ago. The necessary funds for this global regulatory framework should come from the profits of transnational corporations and financial markets—hence their worldwide campaign for the introduction of the global 'Tobin Tax' on short-term, speculative transactions. Other proposals include: the cancellation of poor countries' debts, the closing of offshore financial centers offering tax havens for wealthy individuals and corporations, the ratification and implementation of stringent global environmental agreements, the implementation of a more equitable global development agenda, the establishment of a new world development institution financed largely by the global North and administered largely by the global South, establishment of international labor protection standards, greater transparency and accountability provided to citizens by national governments and global economic institutions, making all governance of globalization explicitly gender sensitive, the transformation of 'free trade' into 'fair trade', and a binding commitment to non-violent direct action as the sole vehicle of social and political change.[45]

But market globalism has also been challenged from the political Right by various 'religious globalisms'. Indeed, globalization has impacted all traditional religious belief systems. It led to noticeable weakening, if not a reversal, of the powerful secularization dynamic that had served as a midwife to Western modernity for two centuries. It is unlikely that secularism in the West will disappear any time soon, but the growing power of religious discourses has forced secular governments into previously unimagined forms of accommodation and compromise. And it is likely that the rising global imaginary will continue to create fertile conditions for 'religious politics' or 'political religions'. Consequently, we ought to treat religious ideas and beliefs as an increasingly integral part of certain global ideologies.

While religious globalisms are not tied to one specific religion, the radical form of 'Islamist globalism' embraced by ISIS or al-Qaeda represents one of the most potent religious globalisms of our time. As can be gleaned from the vast literature on 'Islamism', this term has been used in many different ways by both Muslims and non-Muslims to refer to various movements and ideologies dedicated to the revival of Islam and its political realization. Related terms currently in circulation include 'political Islam', 'Islamic fundamentalism', 'Islamist purism', and the pejorative 'Islamo-fascism'.[46] Although different in causes, responses, strategies, and collective identities, various forms of Islamism share the common proclivity to synthesize certain religious elements of their traditional political discourses with certain elements of modern ideologies. Indeed, Islamisms are about the politicization of religion just as much as they represent the sacralization of modern politics.

The extremist version articulated by the leaders of ISIS or al-Qaeda has been the most prominent example of Islamist globalism. Its tremendous influence around the world points to the rise of new political ideologies resulting from the ongoing deterritorialization of Islam. Islamist globalism constitutes the most successful ideological attempt yet to articulate the rising global imaginary around its core concepts of *umma* (Islamic community of believers in the one and only God), *jihad* (armed or unarmed 'struggle' against unbelief purely for the sake of God and his *umma*), and *tawhid* (the absolute unity of God). As Bruce Lawrence notes, the bulk of Osama bin Laden's writings and public addresses emerged in the global context of a 'virtual world' moving from print to the Internet and from wired to wireless communication. Largely scriptural in mode, the al-Qaeda leader's 'messages to the world' were deliberately designed for the new global media.[47]

Decontesting their core concepts of *umma*, *jihad*, and *tawhid* in potent ideological claims, ISIS and al-Qaeda developed a potent narrative predicated upon globalization's destabilization of the national imaginary. Seeing themselves as members of a global *umma*, their leaders consciously addressed a global audience of believers and non-believers. Their desired Islamization of modernity has taken place in global space emancipated from the confining national or regional territoriality of 'Egypt' or the 'Middle East' that used to constitute the political framework of religious nationalists fighting modern secular regimes in the twentieth century. As Olivier Roy observes, 'The Muslim *umma* no longer has anything to do with a territorial entity. It has to be thought of in abstract and imaginary terms'.[48] Similarly, Faisal Devji argues that extremist Islamism projects no national ambitions, for it is as global as the West itself, both being intertwined and even internal to each other: 'This is why Osama bin Laden's calls for the United States to leave the Muslim world do not entail the return to a cold-war geopolitics of détente, but are conceived rather in terms of a global reciprocity on equal terms'.[49] Hence, the leaders of ISIS and al-Qaeda have urged their followers to make the war against Islam's enemies global. Al-Qaeda's simple ideological imperative—rebuild a unified global *umma* through global *jihad* against global *kufr* ('unbelief')—resonates with the dynamics of a globalizing world.[50]

Although some political commentators have suggested that virulent forms of national-populism embodied by the likes of Marine Le Pen in France or Donald Trump in the United States constitute the most powerful right-wing challenge to market globalism, we contend that this designation belongs to extremist 'religious globalisms'. Far from being a regionally contained 'last gasp' of a backward-looking, militant offshoot of political Islam, the religious globalism of the ISIS and al-Qaeda variety still represents a potent globalism of worldwide appeal. These organizations desire for

IMAGE 2.2 Anti-ISIS Demonstration in India, 2015
Source: Manish Swarup/Associated Press, AP Photo ID 346378426713

their version of a global religious community to be all encompassing and to be given primacy and superiority over state- and secular-based political structures. And they are prepared to use violent means to achieve this goal. But we must not forget that religious globalisms come in the plural. Other religiously inspired visions of global political community include Pentecostalism and other fundamentalist Christian branches, Jewish organizations such as Chabad, the eclectic pan-Chinese Falun Gong movement, and the Soka Gakkai International Buddhist global network originating in Japan. This substantial list suggests that not *all* religiously inspired visions of global community embrace political violence to realize their vision.

In summary, then, we note that 'globalization', in the dominant public discourse, is associated with three types of contesting global ideologies: market globalism, justice globalism, and religious globalisms. If global studies researchers want to understand the material and ideal stakes raised in public globalization debates, then these multiple ideological frames of reference regarding the meanings and likely consequences of globalization represent an important subject of study. Thus, as we emphasize in Chapter 5, most global studies scholars enter the value-laden arena of ideology and engage in critical assessments of the language about globalization that is constitutive of the phenomenon itself.[51] Rather than being rejected as a confusing cacophony of subjective assertions, the normative preferences and rhetorical maneuvers

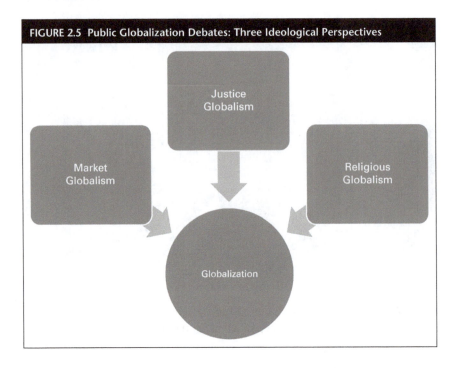

FIGURE 2.5 Public Globalization Debates: Three Ideological Perspectives

performed by the main participants in globalization debates have become a legitimate research focus. In a world of ongoing political contestations, a general discussion about 'globalization'—the material process—makes little sense without a proper recognition that the former is inextricably intertwined with the various 'globalisms'—the ideological package.

Concluding Remarks

As we have emphasized in this chapter, globalization is the subject of global studies and thus constitutes its first and most central pillar. Bursting into the public discourse toward the end of the Cold War era, the keyword proved to be an equally powerful catalyst for new academic initiatives. The globalization pioneers of the 1990s prepared the ground for what quickly became an avalanche of scholarly inquiries into the dimensions and dynamics of the phenomenon. The unfolding academic globalization debates placed participants into four distinct camps that engage in fruitful exchanges of ideas.

As we noted in the Introduction, even after two decades of intense scholarly scrutiny, 'globalization' has remained a hotly contested and surprisingly slippery concept. In spite of the remarkable proliferation of research programs for the study of globalization, academics have remained divided on the utility of various methodological approaches, the value of available empirical evidence for gauging the extent, impact, and direction of globalization, and, of course, its normative implications. But the failure to arrive at a broad scholarly consensus on the subject attests not only to the contentious nature of academic inquiry in general, but also reflects the uneven, contradictory, and ambiguous nature of the phenomenon itself. In recent years, it has become increasingly evident that neither 'hyper-globalizers' nor 'rejectionists' have offered convincing arguments for their respective views. While objections to the overuse of the term has forced the participants in the globalization debates to hone their analytic skills, the wholesale rejection of globalization as a 'vacuous concept' has often served as a convenient excuse to avoid dealing with the actual phenomenon itself. Rather than constructing overarching 'grand narratives' of globalization, many researchers have instead wisely opted for modest methodological middle-range approaches designed to provide specific explanations of particular manifestations of globalization.

The persistence of academic divisions on some theoretical issues notwithstanding, it should be pointed out that an increasing number of global studies scholars seem to have settled on similar understandings of 'globalization'. Most influential definitions of globalization highlight certain characteristics that are said to constitute the core of the phenomenon. These common elements are expressed in the following three assertions. First, globalization is not a single monolithic process but a *complex set* of often *conflicting* and *contradictory* social processes. Second, globalization involves the *creation* of new networks of social interconnections as well as the uneven *multiplication, expansion, intensification,* and *acceleration* of existing social exchanges and activities. Third, the resulting 'compression of time and space' is not merely an objective phenomenon, but also manifests itself on the subjective level of individual and collective consciousness.

Thus, it would be intellectually dishonest not to acknowledge a noticeable convergence of scholarly views on the subject that has taken place in global studies over the last decade or so. While covering a broad intellectual landscape, the existence of clearly articulated areas of intellectual agreement nonetheless allows us to make a strong case for the significance of common features in global studies. The next chapters of this study are devoted to the discussion of the three remaining 'pillars' of the new field: transdisciplinarity, space and time, and critical thinking.

NOTES

1 For a recent discussion of 'objective' measurements of globalization with a view toward advancing the construction of new globalization indices, see Pim Martens, Marco Caselli, Philippe de Lombaerde, Lukas Figge, and Jan Aart

Scholte, 'New Directions in Globalization Indices', *Globalizations* 12.2 (2015), pp. 217–228.

2 See Steger, *Globalization*, Chapter 1.

3 William I. Robinson, *Global Capitalism and the Crisis of Humanity* (Cambridge, UK: Cambridge University Press, 2014), p. 2.

4 Manuel Castells, *Communication Power*, 2nd ed. (Oxford: Oxford University Press, 2013).

5 Raymond Williams, *Keywords: A Vocabulary of Culture and Society* (Oxford: Oxford University Press, 2014 [1983]), p. xxvii.

6 Roland Robertson Interview in *Globalizations* 11.4 (2014), p. 447.

7 Anthony Giddens, *The Consequences of Modernity* (Stanford: Stanford University Press, 1990); and Mike Featherstone, ed., *Global Culture: Nationalism, Globalization, and Modernity* (London and Thousand Oaks: SAGE, 1990); and Mike Featherstone, Scott Lash, and Roland Robertson, *Global Modernities* (London and Thousand Oaks, CA: SAGE, 1995).

8 Roland Robertson, *Globalization: Social Theory and Global Culture* (London and Thousand Oaks: SAGE, 1992), p. 8.

9 Malcolm Waters, *Globalization*, 2nd ed. (London and New York: Routledge, 2001 [1st ed. 1995]), p. 3.

10 Robertson, *Globalization*, pp. 58–9.

11 Paul James, 'Globalization, Phenomenon of', *Encyclopedia of Global Studies*, vol. 2 (London and Thousand Oaks: SAGE, 2012), p. 763.

12 Robertson, *Globalization*, pp. 173–4. See also Roland Robertson, 'Globalisation or Glocalization?', *The Journal of International Communication* 1.1 (1994), pp. 33–52.

13 See George Ritzer, *The McDonaldization of Society* (London and Thousand Oaks: SAGE, 1992).

14 David Harvey, *The Condition of Postmodernity: An Enquiry into the Origins of Cultural Change* (Oxford: Blackwell, 1989).

15 David Harvey, 'Globalization in Question', *Rethinking Marxism*, 8.4 (Winter 1995), p. 1.

16 See Saskia Sassen, *The Global City: New York, London, Tokyo* (Princeton, NJ: Princeton University Press, 1991); and Manuel Castells, *The Information Age: Economy, Society, Culture* 3 vols. (Chichester, UK: Wiley-Blackwell, 1996–8); Neil Brenner, 'Beyond State-Centrism? Space, Territoriality, and Geographical Scale in Globalization Studies', *Theory and Society* 28.1 (1999), pp. 38–79; Jan Aart Scholte, *Globalization: A Critical Introduction* (Houndmills, UK: Palgrave Macmillan, 2000); Mike Douglass and John Friedmann, eds., *Cities for Citizens: Planning and the Rise of Civil Society in a Global Age* (New York: John Wiley, 1998); and John Agnew, *Globalization and Sovereignty* (Lanham, MD: Rowman & Littlefield, 2009).

17 Harvey, 'Globalization in Question', p. 12.

18 See, for example, Mohammed A. Bamyeh, *The Ends of Globalization* (Minneapolis, MN: University of Minnesota Press, 2000); Tom Mertes, Walden Bello, Bernard Cassen, Jose Bove, *A Movement of Movements: Is Another World Possible?* (London and New York: Verso, 2004); Paul Tiyambe Zeleza, *Rethinking Africa's Globalization* (Trenton, NJ: Africa World Press, 2003); Sankaran Krishna, *Globalization and Postcolonialism: Hegemony and Resistance in the Twenty-First Century* (Lanham, MD: Rowman & Littlefield, 2009); and Supriya Singh, *Globalization and Money: A Global South Perspective* (Lanham, MD: Rowman & Littlefield, 2013).

19 Arjun Appadurai, *Modernity at Large: Cultural Dimensions of Globalization* (Minneapolis, MN: University of Minnesota Press, 1996), p. 33.

20 See, for example, Mike Featherstone, ed., *Global Culture* (London: SAGE, 1990); Ulf Hannerz, *Transnational Connection: Culture, People, Places* (London and New York: Routledge, 1996); Fredric Jameson and Masao Miyoshi, eds., *The Cultures of Globalization* (Durham and London: Duke University Press, 1998); John Tomlinson, *Globalization and Culture* (Chicago: The University of Chicago Press, 1999); Walter Mignolo, *Local Histories/Global Designs: Coloniality, Subaltern Knowledges, and Border Thinking* (Princeton, NJ: Princeton University Press, 2000); Ulrich Beck, *What is Globalization?* (Cambridge, UK: Polity Press, 2000); Peter L. Berger and Samuel P. Huntington, eds., *Many Globalizations: Cultural Diversity in the Contemporary World* (Oxford: Oxford University Press, 2002); George Yúdice, *The Expediency of Culture: Uses of Culture in the Global Era* (Durham and London: Duke University Press, 2003); Jan Nederveen Pieterse, *Globalization and Culture: Global Mélange*, 3rd ed. (Lanham, MD: Rowman & Littlefield, 2015).

21 Saskia Sassen, *The Mobility of Labor and Capital* (Cambridge, UK: Cambridge University Press, 1988).

22 Saskia Sassen, *The Global City: New York, London, Tokyo*, 2nd ed. (Princeton, NJ: Princeton University Press, 2001), pp. 3–4.

23 Saskia Sassen, *Territory, Authority, Rights: From Medieval to Global Assemblages* (Princeton, NJ: Princeton University Press, 2006).

24 For related attempts to distinguish between various camps in the globalization debates, see David Held and Anthony McGrew, David Goldblatt and Jonathan Perraton, *Global Transformations: Politics, Economics, and Culture* (Stanford: Stanford University Press, 1999); and James H. Mittelman, 'Globalization: An Ascendant Paradigm?', *International Studies Perspectives* 3.1 (February 2002), pp. 1–14.

25 See, for example, David Held and Anthony McGrew, *Globalization/Anti-Globalization* (Cambridge, UK: Polity Press, 2002); James H. Mittelman, *The Globalization Syndrome: Transformation and Resistance* (Princeton, NJ: Princeton University Press, 2000); and Jan Aart Scholte, *Globalization: A Critical Introduction*, 2nd ed. (Houndmills, UK: Palgrave Mamillan, 2005).

26 See, for example, John Keane, *Global Civil Society?* (Cambridge, UK: Cambridge University Press, 2003); and Mary Kaldor, Henrietta L. Moore, and Sabine Selchow, eds., *Global Civil Society 2012: Ten Years of Critical Reflection* (Houndmills, UK: Palgrave Macmillan, 2012).

27 See, for example, Alison Brysk, ed., *Globalization and Human Rights* (Berkeley, CA: University of California Press, 2002).

28 Martin Shaw, *Theory of the Global State: Globality as an Unfinished Revolution* (Cambridge, UK: Cambridge University Press, 2000), p. 16.

29 See, for example, Kenichi Ohmae, *The End of the Nation State: The Rise of Regional Economies* (New York: Free Press, 1995); and Martin Albrow, *The Global Age* (Stanford: Stanford University Press, 1996).

30 Susan Strange, *The Retreat of the State: The Diffusion of Power in the World Economy* (Cambridge, UK: Cambridge University Press, 1996), pp. xii–xiii; and Linda Weiss, *The Myth of the Powerless State: Governing the Economy in a Global Era* (Ithaca, NY: Cornell University Press, 1998), p. 212.

31 For an illuminating discussion on the notion of 'globaloney', see Michael Veseth, *Globaloney 2.0: The Crash of 2008 and the Future of Globalization* (Lanham, MD: Rowman & Littlefield, 2010).

32 Robert Wade, 'Globalization and Its Limits: Reports on the Death of the National Economy Are Greatly Exaggerated', in Suzanne Berger and Ronald Dore, eds., *National Diversity and Global Capitalism* (Ithaca, NY: Cornell University Press, 1996), pp. 60–88; and Paul Hirst and Grahame Thompson, *Globalization in Question: The International Economy and the Possibilities of Governance*, 2nd ed. (Cambridge, UK: Polity Press, 1999). See also Alan Rugman, *The End of Globalization* (New York: Random House, 2001).

33 Hirst and Thompson, *Globalization in Question*, p. 2.

34 Robinson, *Global Capitalism and the Crisis of Humanity*, p. 2.

35 See Mittelman, 'Globalization: An Ascendant Paradigm?', p. 5.

36 Robert Gilpin, *The Challenge of Global Capitalism: The World Economy in the 21st Century* (Princeton, NJ: Princeton University Press, 2000), pp. 294–95. For a similar assessment, see Dani Rodrik, *Has Globalization Gone Too Far?* (Washington, DC: Institute for International Economics, 1997), pp. 7–8; and Gary T. Burtless, Robert Z. Lawrence, Robert E. Litan, and Robert J. Shapiro, *Globaphobia: Confronting Fears about Open Trade* (Washington, DC: Brookings Institution Press, 1998), pp. 6–7.

37 Immanuel Wallerstein, *The Capitalist World-Economy* (Cambridge, UK: Cambridge University Press, 1979), and *The Politics of the World-Economy: The States, the Movements, and the Civilizations* (Cambridge, UK: Cambridge University Press, 1984); and Andre Gunder Frank, *ReORIENT: Global Economy in the Asian Age* (Berkeley, CA: University of California Press, 1998); Giovanni Arrighi, *The Long Twentieth Century: Money, Power, and the Origins of Our Times* (London and New York: Verso, 1994); and Christopher K. Chase-Dunn, *Global Formation: Structures of the World-Economy* (Lanham, MD: Rowman & Littlefield, 1998).

38 Immanuel Wallerstein, *World-Systems Analysis: An Introduction* (Durham and London: Duke University Press, 2004), p. x.

39 Ibid., p. 19; and Fernand Braudel, Sarah Matthews, trans. *On History* (Chicago: University of Chicago Press, 1982).

40 Wallerstein, *World-Systems Analysis*, pp. 16–17.

41 Immanuel Wallerstein, 'Culture as the Ideological Battleground of the Modern World System', in Mike Featherstone, ed., *Global Culture: Nationalism, Globalization, and Modernity* (London and Thousand Oaks: SAGE, 1990), p. 38.

42 Ash Amin, 'Placing Globalization', *Theory, Culture & Society* 14.2 (1997), pp. 123–38; Barry K. Gills, ed., *Globalization and the Politics of Resistance* (Houndmills, UK: Palgrave Macmillan, 2002); and Leslie Sklair, *Globalization: Capitalism and Its Alternatives*, 3d ed. (Oxford: Oxford University Press, 2002). See also William I. Robinson, *A Theory of Global Capitalism: Production, Class, and the State in a Transnational World* (Baltimore, MD: Johns Hopkins University Press, 2004).

43 Thomas Friedman, *The Lexus and the Olive Tree: Understanding Globalization* (New York: Anchor Books, 1999), p. 9.

44 For a broader discussion of these claims, see Manfred B. Steger, *Globalisms: The Great Ideological Struggle of the Twenty-First Century*, 3rd ed. (Lanham, MD: Rowman & Littlefield, 2009).

45 See the online supplemented resources for an instructive example of a global studies research project exploring the conceptual composition of justice globalism.

46 See, for example, Olivier Roy, *Globalizing Islam: The Search for a New Ummah* (New York: Columbia University Press, 2004).

47 Bruce B. Lawrence, 'Introduction', in *Messages to the World: The Statements of Osama Bin Laden,* edited by Bruce B. Lawrence and translated by James Howarth

(London and New York: Verso, 2005). For the most recent collection of writings by al-Qaeda leaders, see Gilles Kepel and Jean-Pierre Milelli, eds., *Al Qaeda in Its Own Words* (Cambridge, MA: The Belknap Press of Harvard University Press, 2008).

48 Roy, *Globalizing Islam*, p. 19.

49 Faisal Devji, 'Osama Bin Laden's Message to the World', *OpenDemocracy* (December 2005), p. 2. www.opendemocracy.net/conflict-terrorism/osama_ 3140.jsp. Accessed 1 June 2016. See also Faisal Devji, *Landscapes of the Jihad: Militancy, Morality, Modernity* (Ithaca, NY: Cornell University Press, 2005), p. 144.

50 Osama Bin Laden, 'A Muslim Bomb', in *Messages to the World*, p. 91. See also Fawaz A. Gerges, *The Far Enemy: Why Jihad Went Global*, 2nd ed. (Cambridge, UK: Cambridge University Press, 2009).

51 See, for example, Manfred B. Steger, ed., *Rethinking Globalism* (Lanham, MD: Rowman & Littlefield, 2004); Angus Cameron and Ronen Palan, *The Imagined Economies of Globalization* (London and Thousand Oaks: SAGE, 2004); James H. Mittelman, *Whither Globalization: The Vortex of Knowledge and Ideology* (London and New York: Routledge, 2004); and Norman Fairclough, *Language and Globalization* (London and New York: Routledge, 2007).

3

THE SECOND PILLAR OF GLOBAL STUDIES

Transdisciplinarity

Examining the second pillar of global studies, this chapter introduces some common themes and concrete illustrations of the many ways in which transdisciplinarity animates global studies. We proceed from the premise that understanding the profound changes affecting social life in the Global Age increasingly requires an examination of the growing forms of complexity. This means that global problems and dynamics of interconnectivity can no longer be approached from a single academic discipline or area of knowledge. Multidimensional processes of globalization and their associated global challenges such as climate change, pandemics, terrorism, digital technologies, marketization, migration, urbanization, and human rights represent examples of transnational issues that both cut across and reach beyond conventional disciplinary boundaries. However, the disciplinary organization of knowledge—institutionalized for the first time in nineteenth-century European universities—still shapes contemporary academic settings. Even though university administrators in the US and elsewhere have warmed up to ideas of 'interdisciplinarity', most instructional activities in today's institutions of higher education still occur within an overarching framework of the disciplinary divisions. The same holds true for academic research in the social sciences and humanities where scholars continue to produce specialized problems to which solutions can be found primarily within their own disciplinary orientations.[1]

Contemporary globalization debates, however, have raised a plethora of empirical, normative, and epistemic concerns that cannot be sorted out by specialists operating within the narrow and often rather arbitrary confines of single disciplines and their associated idioms. Critical of this tendency to compartmentalize the complexity of social existence into discreet spheres of activity, global studies has evolved as a self-consciously transdisciplinary field committed to the engagement and integration of multiple knowledge systems and research methodologies. In the United States, global studies is part of a small but growing interdisciplinary trend in the academy that started in the 1970s as a response to the methodological rigidity of dominant behavioral approaches. At the time, some scholars championed interdisciplinarity to address 'real-world' issues and develop broader and problem-centered perspectives. In the 1980s and 1990s, these academics turned to interdisciplinary modes of teaching and research primarily for intellectual and political reasons. They soon discovered that the increasingly neoliberal environment of higher education began to favor interdisciplinarity for financial, rather than intellectual, reasons. Budget-conscious administrators often saw interdisciplinary programs as a way of circumventing self-governance at the department level and reduce labor costs. Public and private funding agencies external to the university appreciated its enhanced focus on policy-relevant issues. As Isaac Kamola has noted, interdisciplinarity in the twenty-first century constitutes a mixed blessing. While it challenges epistemologically conservative regimes of disciplinary knowledge production, it also complements the defunding of established departments and programs.[2]

Typically hailing from traditional disciplinary backgrounds, faculty members are often attracted to global studies because they are deeply critical of the entrenched conventions of disciplinary specialization inherent in the Eurocentric academic framework. Each discipline is said to cover a particular field and then an analytical cartography is superimposed on the world. Thus, Western modes of producing and disseminating knowledge have profoundly shaped higher education in the non-Western world.[3] Appreciative of a more flexible intellectual environment that allows for the bundling of otherwise disparate conceptual fields and geographical areas into a single object of study, global studies scholars seek to overcome such Western forms of disciplinary 'silo thinking'. Unsurprisingly, they often draw skeptical, and sometimes even hostile, responses from more conventional colleagues trained to analyze various phenomena through discipline-specific lenses. Thus, 'unorthodox' interdisciplinarians who embrace synthesis and integration face considerable professional risks in the dominant academic environment of taken-for-granted disciplinary divides.

The Evolution of Disciplines

Let us start with pertinent etymological clarifications involving the concept 'discipline'. Its Latin roots are the verb *discere* ('to learn') and the nouns *disciplina* and *discipulus*, which translate into 'education' and 'student', respectively. However, the meanings associated with these nouns are far broader. *Disciplina*, for example, took her place in the ancient Roman pantheon as a minor deity, worshipped fervently by soldiers for her martial virtues of strict training, self-control, and determination rather than her equally strong affinities for education and knowledge. These potentially violent and confining aspects of *disciplina* were brilliantly deconstructed in Michel Foucault's postmodern interpretation of 'discipline' as involving modern micropractices of power capable of producing and normalizing new 'scientific' institutional arrangements responsible for the creation of docile bodies and minds.[4] The French philosopher also pointed to the formation of academic disciplines as part and parcel of this all-pervasive 'power-knowledge' matrix—a crucial insight worth remembering for those exploring the role of *trans*disciplinarity in global studies.

To be sure, conventional academic usage embraces the concept's etymological strand linked to 'study' and 'education'. In this case, 'discipline' refers to a defined body or branch of knowledge that can be learned—and taught—and involves special skills, techniques, training, and modes of communication. Securely ensconced in contemporary English language dictionaries, this definition of 'discipline' is usually traced back to the earliest appearance of academic branches of inquiry in the classical world. For example, Aristotle introduced in the fourth century BCE his influential three-fold division of 'theoretical', 'practical', and 'productive' forms of knowledge, which he further subdivided into seven specialized disciplines that included biology, ethics, rhetoric, and mathematics. Martianus Capella's important fifth-century CE work, *De septem disciplines*, provides clear evidence for the continued relevance of Aristotelian classification schemes in the ancient Roman context. Further refined in European medieval universities, the discipline-oriented ordering of knowledge for the purposes of academic instruction and research did not receive its full expression until the nineteenth century when external demands for specialization resulting from processes of industrialization and advances in information and communication technology served as catalysts for the creation of the European system of higher education in which single disciplines functioned as the basic units of 'scientific knowledge'.[5]

The ensuing institutional addition of new disciplines (especially the menu of the 'social sciences') and the gradual refinement of disciplinary specialisms are often seen as crucial steps in the evolution of 'modernity'. These disciplinary dynamics were complemented by the creation and rapid diffusion of the associated educational roles of individual scholars who worked within these relatively narrow fields of scientific activity. The resulting discipline-based academic order fueled a distinctive academic *esprit de corps* that valorized sharply delineated 'scientific communities' that made intellectual claims to particular subjects, raised discreet research questions, and employed distinct methodologies. The ensuing practices of epistemic gatekeeping assigned to academic insiders the privileged task of drawing and defending the boundaries of 'their' disciplinary territory. Such increasingly specialized communities of shared ideal and material interests also standardized curricular activities and scientific production processes by establishing new discipline-focused publications ('academic journals') and elaborate professional codes and requirements governing disciplinary careers.[6]

The further fortification of these disciplinary bulwarks in the mid-twentieth century encouraged the formation and differentiation of even more strictly bounded disciplinary clusters attached to particular intellectual lineages and distinct professional idioms. Disciplinary differentiation and knowledge specialization acted as the twin midwives for the birth of the modern academic order. As Armin Krishnan observes, in the second half the twentieth century, academic disciplines could be categorized according to six criteria or characteristics: (1) a particular object of research, (2) a body of accumulated specialist knowledge, (3) theories and concepts that could organize such knowledge effectively, (4) specific terminologies and technical languages, (5) specific research methods, and (6) concrete institutional manifestations in the form of subjects taught in separate departments at universities or colleges.[7] New fields of inquiry that were perceived as falling short of one or more of these six characteristics usually emerged with the lesser status of 'studies'—a marker indicating a supposed lack of theoretical sophistication or methodological thinness. To a significant extent, then, the contemporary disciplinary order emerged as the result of an artificial differentiation of fields and the production of specialized and fractured knowledge that served dominant interests.

However, as intensifying globalization dynamics added extra layers of complexity to social life, 'real-world' problems seemed to conform less and less to the conventional disciplinary organization of knowledge. As philosopher Thomas Kuhn famously pointed out more than fifty years ago, the proliferation of knowledge requires periodic 'scientific revolutions' driven by provocative ideas and theories that are capable of interrupting the workings of 'normal science', that is, the confirmation of the type of knowledge already established and legitimized by the paradigm in which it arises.[8] In other words, the challenges to dominant forms of knowledge arise to a significant degree as a result of unorthodox insights generated by interactions on the fringes and across existing disciplines. This means that intellectual innovation capable of creating new epistemic paradigms depends on transdisciplinary initiatives that counteract the compartmentalization of knowledge while at the same time stimulating new forms of sub- and multidisciplinary differentiation. At their best, such transdisciplinary practices are capable of producing novel intellectual insights, shifting knowledge boundaries, and reconfiguring existing constellations of academic inquiry.

Interdisciplinarity, Multidisciplinarity, or Transdisciplinarity?

Most of us are quite familiar with the notion of 'interdisciplinarity'. But what about the term 'transdisciplinarity' that seems to have become a trendy expression in the academy? Does it carry the same meanings as the more established concept of 'interdisciplinarity'? Some experts on the subject warn against using these terms synonymously in order to avoid conceptual confusion. Others propose conceptualizing them on a spectrum that runs from 'multidisciplinarity' through 'interdisciplinarity' to 'transdisciplinarity'. Most global studies programs have approached these concepts in rather pragmatic ways that allow for their interchangeable usage. Although it may not be possible—and, indeed may be undesirable—to establish rigid distinctions among these three major terms in applied settings like university teaching or research, it does makes sense to separate them for analytic reasons.[9]

Derived from the Latin word *multus* ('many'), the concept of 'multidisciplinarity' refers to activities drawing on knowledge from different disciplines that involve tight coordination among disciplines but fall short of deep integration. In most cases, members from different disciplines come together around a particular project that would benefit from a variety of methodological approaches. Still, multidisciplinarians work independently on different aspects of their common project—often in a parallel or sequential manner. Proceeding in a self-contained fashion, they stay largely within their own disciplinary boundaries and require only few opportunities for intercommunication. Allen Repko compares multidisciplinarity to 'a bowl of fruit containing a variety of fruits, each fruit representing a discipline and being in close proximity to the others'.[10] Their lack of interest in integration, however, does not mean that multidisciplinary scholars fail to make valuable contributions to their collaborative projects. By adding, contrasting, and juxtaposing their distinct insights, multidisciplinarians extend and enhance existing knowledge. Rather than learning *from* each other, they learn *about* each other's separate modes of approaching a joint question or problem. The ultimate outcome of multidisciplinary efforts is cumulative, that is, the sum of the individual parts. Examples include a team-taught course on climate change mitigation in which faculty from different disciplines provide serial or parallel lectures, or the study of a Michelangelo sculpture from the distinct perspectives of art, history, religion, and philosophy.[11]

Continuing with our second concept, let us recall that the Latin prefix *inter* means 'among'—as in the word 'international' ('among nations'). However, as in 'interchange', it can also signify 'together', 'mutually', or 'reciprocally'. Interdisciplinarity refers to any form of dialogue or interaction among two or more disciplines that might in some cases lead to an enduring reciprocal relationship between them. Still, as David Alvargonzález notes, just as international relationships between different countries do not imply denying the sovereignty of each, interdisciplinarity does not eliminate the independence of each discipline.[12] Indeed, many scholars associate 'interdisciplinarity' with circumscribed or overlapping spaces of interaction involving no more than two or three disciplines that leave each field largely unaltered. Although some of these interactions might at times necessitate a departure from some disciplinary aspects, scholars usually do not give up their area-specific base. Thus, members from different disciplines come together as interdisciplinary teams to collaborate on teaching or research projects that are seen as benefiting their own areas of expertise. Team members learn from each other, thus expanding their own disciplinary horizons. In some cases, such established routines of mixing or sharing disciplinary-specific knowledge lead to moderate forms of integration that can give rise to new 'hyphenated' fields and subdisciplines such as political economy, mathematical physics, environmental planning, or biochemistry. Biologists, for example, encourage some interdisciplinary integration when they grant a defined purpose to issues or contents traditionally represented by chemists (and vice versa).

Hence, it is important to distinguish between weak and strong forms of interdisciplinarity. The former involve generalists engaged in modes of dialogue or interaction between disciplines that consciously minimize or reject integration, while the latter group is comprised of academics Allen Repko calls 'integrationist interdisciplianarians'.[13] Though hailing from separate disciplines, they are dedicated to creating enduring common ground in their efforts to solve a particular problem. Integrationist interdisciplianarians believe that many contemporary issues are far too complex and wide-ranging to be dealt with adequately by a single field. Consequently, their interdisciplinary activities aim at constructing more comprehensive and holistic understandings.

Finally, the concept of 'transdisciplinarity' is configured around the Latin prefix *trans* ('across' or 'beyond'). It signifies the systemic and holistic integration of diverse forms of knowledge by cutting *across* and through existing disciplinary boundaries and paradigms in ways that reach *beyond* each individual discipline. If interdisciplinarity can be characterized by the mixing of disciplinary perspectives involving little or moderate integration, then transdisciplinarity should be thought of as a deep fusion of disciplinary knowledge that produces new understandings capable of transforming or restructuring existing disciplinary paradigms. But the transdisciplinary imperative to challenge, go beyond, transgress, and unify separate orientations does not ignore the importance of attracting scholars with specific disciplinary backgrounds. Rather, as Bernard Choi and Anita Pak have pointed out, 'Transdisciplinary teams work using a shared conceptual framework, drawing together discipline-specific theories, concepts and approaches to address a common problem'.[14] In other words, transdisciplinarians put complex 'real-world problems' at the heart of their intellectual efforts. These include such life-world issues as poverty, inequality, violence, or environmental degradation. The formulation of possible resolutions of these problems requires the deep integration of a broad range of perspectives from multiple disciplinary backgrounds. As we discuss below, transdisciplinarians approach the complexity of the problem from various angles and link abstract theory to case-specific knowledge in order to develop knowledge and social practices that promote what is perceived to be the common good.[15]

By favoring issue-driven projects based on shared concerns, transdisciplinary scholars typically adopt a critical stance vis-à-vis the requirements of 'normal science' and existing organizational arrangements. Ideally, their criticism is constructive in the sense of supporting common definitions and holistic frameworks that might stake out new knowledge territories with an explicit focus on solving complex problems. It is not surprising that transdisciplinarians routinely encourage the research participation of non-academic experts from public and private sectors whose relevant applied skills can add much value to their academic efforts. It is not enough for the transdisciplinary scholars to simply acknowledge the relativity of their perspective and look at things from different angles, but they must also acquire the skills to differentiate, compare, contrast, relate, clarify, reconcile, and synthesize multiple perspectives.[16] Rather than just mixing together various insights drawn from different disciplinary backgrounds, they aim at a deep integration—even fusion—of disciplinary knowledge that invites contributions from non-academic experts.

Far from merely constituting the latest fad in our rapidly globalizing higher education environment, transdisciplinarity and its corresponding methodological toolkits steeped in pluralism and eclecticism have become indispensable modes of unifying knowledge about the world and expanding the research capabilities of academic institutions. In recent years, transdisciplinary activities have become especially closely associated with the emergence of global studies and other integrative fields such as 'sustainability studies' or 'future studies'. After all, new modes of knowledge production associated with globalization processes require diverse, problem-based, and collaborative forms of research capable of transcending both methodological nationalism and disciplinary boundaries in the integration and synthesis of multiple contents, theories, and methodologies.[17]

At the same time, let us remember that full transdisciplinarity—understood as activities that transcend, recombine, and integrate separate disciplinary paradigms—remains an elusive goal for most academics. This includes global studies scholars associated with currently existing academic programs in the field. Some, like the Global Studies Department at UCSB have achieved a high degree of transdisciplinary integration, whereas others, like the Global Studies Initiative at Whitman College (Walla Walla, WA), rely more on multi- and interdisciplinary activities that benefit students and faculty alike. Although there exists no transdisciplinary litmus test in global studies, it is nonetheless important to point out that all programs are oriented towards interdependent practices of teaching and research that challenge the existing disciplinary order in higher education. In some cases, these challenges become more effective when they assume less transformative forms to navigate a number of existing institutional obstacles. These include the dominance of discipline-based assessment schemes for teaching programs and research projects seeking internal or external funding; difficulty in attracting faculty or students prepared to risk moving outside the conventional disciplinary matrix; or the unwillingness of academic administrators to distribute funds and resources to new and relatively untested programs that do not operate within the familiar disciplinary framework. Hence, as related to global studies, we suggest a more flexible use of the term 'transdisciplinarity' containing both a strict indication of a very high level of disciplinary integration and a more pragmatic reference to a broad range of practices and dynamics that occur between disciplines, across disciplines, and beyond any single discipline, thus encompassing multidisciplinarity and interdisciplinarity practices as well.[18]

Transdisciplinary approaches can only be effective if there is a significant shift in disciplinary thinking and practice. Although most contemporary universities and colleges tend to pay lip service to the virtues of transdisciplinarity, many institutions still marginalize such programs in separate 'interdisciplinary' units that suffer from chronic underfunding and thus are forced to rely in large part on the voluntary efforts of engaged faculty who

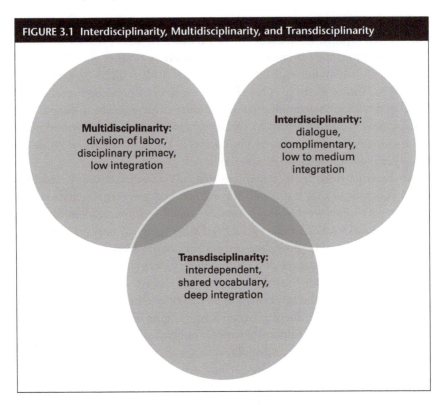

FIGURE 3.1 Interdisciplinarity, Multidisciplinarity, and Transdisciplinarity

Multidisciplinarity:
division of labor,
disciplinary primacy,
low integration

Interdisciplinarity:
dialogue,
complimentary,
low to medium
integration

Transdisciplinarity:
interdependent,
shared vocabulary,
deep integration

remain tied to their home departments and centers. Powerful as they may be, these structural constraints must not condemn transdisciplinary activists to assume a paralyzing wait-and-see posture or to settle for other forms of passivity. Strengthening transdisciplinarity requires enduring engagement with new phenomena and shifting social contexts. The academic story of global studies, in particular, shows that the mere rhetorical enthusiasm for transdisciplinarity on the part of some university administrators can indeed be transformed into the successful institutionalization of global studies programs around the world.

Transdisciplinarity and Global Complexity

As we have noted previously, global studies scholars frequently disagree with each other on various pertinent issues related to globalization. But one can also point to a growing number of agreements that allow us to sketch the contours of the emerging field. One claim, above all, seems to enjoy virtual consensus in the global studies community: the study of globalization requires close encounters with multiple forms of complexity and differentiation. One of the earliest definitions of globalization offered by the political scientist George Modelski in 1968 revolves around the recognition of the significance of growing complexity in an incipient global society: 'A condition for the emergence of a multiple-autonomy form of world politics arguably is the development of a global layer of interaction substantial enough to support continuous and diversified institutionaliza-tion. We may define this process as globalization; it is the result of the increasing size, complexity and sophistication of world society'.[19] Similarly, John Tomlinson argues in his influential study on cultural globalization that 'complex connectivity' captures in a 'simple and relatively uncontentious way' the basic understanding of globalization as a 'rapidly developing and ever-densening network of interconnections and interdependencies that characterize modern social life'.[20]

We argued earlier in this chapter that the prevailing compartmentaliza-tion of scientific and professional knowledge reflected in the modern disci-plinary order fails to capture the increasingly diverse and multilayered social contexts of the twenty-first century. By recognizing the importance of increasing complexity for their systematic inquiries, global studies experts consciously embrace transdisciplinarity in their efforts to understand the shifting dynamics of interconnectedness. Thus, their exploration of complex forms of interdependence not only combats knowledge fragmentation and scientific reductionism, but also facilitates an understanding of the 'big picture', which is indispensable for stimulating the political commitment needed to tackle the pressing global problems of our time such as large-scale human migration, advanced digital technologies, and novel pandemics. For this reason, transdisciplinarity expert Christian Pohl emphasizes the imper-ative to grasp the complexity of socially relevant issues as the overriding rationale for engaging in transdisciplinarity research.[21]

Since global complexity appears in many forms and pervades different social arenas, it makes sense to approach it from different angles and through multiple levels of analysis. The goal, in particular, is to illuminate the inten-sifying complexities involved in the interconnectivity of microscopic, 'local' phenomena and macroscopic dynamics involved in the creation of globality. As we shall see in the next chapter on space and time, grasping these 'glocalized' forms of interdependence requires researchers to experiment with innovative methodological approaches that reject the local/global binary. Calling for the conscious application of a 'methodo-logical glocalism', Robert Holton suggests a non-reductionist account of interactions across multiple, often overlapping, spatial scales and dimensions at which social action takes place in our globalizing world.[22] To illustrate such new modes of transdisciplinary thinking as they apply to global studies, let us consider the treatment of six concrete manifestations of global complexity in the writings of some notable globalization scholars: domains, dimensions, networks, flows, fluids, and hybrids.

Domains and Dimensions

Approaching globalization as a complex set of social processes—enveloped by the rising global imaginary and propelling us toward the condition of globality—implies an affirmation of the multidimensional character of the phenomenon. From its beginnings two decades ago, the ability of global studies to engage transdisciplinary perspectives to capture these complex forms of multidimensionality was considered the Holy Grail of critical globalization scholarship. As Barrie Axford puts it, the challenge was to present 'a systematic account of the analytically separate but interconnected and perhaps mutually constitutive dynamics of economics, politics, and culture, delivered through a robust *interdisciplinarity* or *transdisciplinarity* . . .'[23]

Embarking on their intellectual journeys in the 1990s, the pioneers of global studies recognized the difficulty of developing a comprehensive theoretical framework of globalization as a *differentiated* process that could not be reduced to a single phenomenon yet remained cognizant of the numerous dimensions of social life. In most cases, their first step in maneuvering around this obstacle consisted of initiating a globalization dialogue across the disciplines that would lead to the identification of the central 'domains' or 'dimensions' of the phenomenon. Moreover, such bundling of disciplinary perspectives made it easier for global studies researchers to cope with the enormous range and complexity of globalization processes as well as tackling the new problems they generated. At the dawn of the new century, the most frequently studied dimensions of globalization included the following:

- *Economic* globalization refers to the intensification and stretching of economic connections across the globe. Gigantic flows of capital mediated by digital technology have stimulated trade in goods and services. Extending their reach around the world, markets have migrated to cyberspace and created new linkages among national and regional economies. Huge transnational corporations, powerful international economic institutions, and gigantic regional trading networks like Asia-Pacific Economic Cooperation (APEC) or the European Union (EU) have emerged as the major building blocks of the twenty-first century's global economic order.
- *Political* globalization refers to the intensification and expansion of political interrelations across the globe. These processes raise an

important set of political issues pertaining to the principle of state sovereignty, the growing impact of intergovernmental organizations, and the future prospects for regional and global governance. Obviously, these themes respond to the evolution of political arrangements beyond the framework of the nation-state, thus breaking new conceptual and institutional ground.

- *Cultural* globalization refers to the intensification and expansion of cultural flows across the globe. The exploding network of cultural interconnections and interdependencies in the last decades has led some commentators to suggest that cultural practices lie at the very heart of contemporary globalization. The thematic landscape traversed by scholars of cultural globalization is vast and the numerous issues raised include the tension between sameness and difference in the emerging global culture, the crucial role of transnational media corporations in disseminating popular culture, and the globalization of languages.

- *Environmental* globalization refers to the increasing biological inter-dependencies that emerge from the compression of social and natural environments. Centered on the question of global sustainability, global studies scholars dealing with this domain who explore global environ-mental issues such as global climate change and transboundary pollu-tion have received enormous attention from research institutes, the media, politicians, and economists. Indeed, the ecological effects of globalization are increasingly recognized as the most significant and potentially life-threatening for the world as we have inherited it from our ancestors. The worldwide impact of natural and man-made disas-ters such as the horrifying nuclear plant accidents at Chernobyl, Ukraine (1986), and Fukushima, Japan (2011), clearly shows that the formidable ecological problems of our time can only be tackled by a global alliance of states and civil society actors.

- *Ideological* globalization refers to the expansion of political belief systems across world-space and world-time. Most importantly, this process includes the transformation of the conventional ideological landscape consisting of traditional 'isms' such as liberalism, conservatism, socialism, and so on. As we noted in the Introduction, ideological globalization has led to the emergence of new political thought-systems—'globalisms'—that articulate the rising global imaginary in concrete political agendas and programs capable of transcending the limited framework of the nation-state.

To be sure, one could add more dimensions to this list, and most of them would be equally deserving of scholarly scrutiny. For example, the

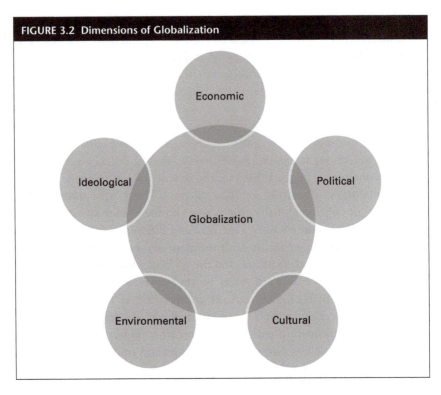

FIGURE 3.2 Dimensions of Globalization

influential social thinker Anthony Giddens includes the globalizing of military power ('world military order') in his four-fold classification scheme.[24] Although major aspects of globalization are often examined separately, it is important to remember that each dimension interacts with all the other domains.

One of the most impressive early projects to wrestle with global complexity by assigning various globalization dynamics to analytically distinct social 'domains' was the 500–page tome, *Global Transformations: Politics, Economics, and Culture.* First published in 1999, this transdisciplinary study offers readers the impressive results of collective academic globalization research stretching over nearly a decade.[25] Aiming at nothing less than developing a general theory of globalization, the book brought together four British academics dedicated to extending their individual research efforts on the subject across disciplinary boundaries. The team leader was David Held, a political theorist who had previously analyzed the changing nature and form of liberal democratic nation-states in the context of intensifying global relations. He was joined by Anthony McGrew, an IR specialist who approached domestic politics as a product of more powerful interstate forces; David Goldblatt, a social theorist with a strong background in environmental policy; and Jonathan Perraton, an economist and international finance expert.

Putting the analysis of global complexity squarely at the core of their project, the authors promise to 'develop a more comprehensive explanation of globalization which highlights the complex intersection between a multiplicity of driving forces, embracing economic, technological, cultural and political change'.[26] But the success of their attempts to unravel global complexity depends to a significant degree on overturning the conventional wisdom of the 1990s, which had reduced the topic of globalization largely to contemporary economic issues like the liberalization of trade and business matters such as the deregulation of national stock and commodity exchanges. According to such influential interpreters, 'globalization' could be boiled down to the workings of a techno-economic force responsible for the 'spread of free-market capitalism to virtually every country in the world.'[27] Conversely, Held and his collaborators envision globalization as an extremely complex and differentiated set of processes that could only be grasped in its totality through an innovative model of multidimensionality. Thus, their first and perhaps most difficult task was to make a convincing case for the complexity of globalization that countered, in effective ways, the simplistic arguments of these economistic 'hyperglobalists'. Although various proponents of this perspective disagreed with each other on the normative implications of the liberalization and global integration of markets, they found common ground in their understanding of globalization as a singular dynamic: a wholly economic phenomenon reflected in the creation of new transnational networks of commodity production, trade, and finance.

In their attempt to refute both these hyperglobalizers and the equally economistic camp of globalization skeptics who argued that worldwide levels of economic integration were falling far short of truly 'global' proportions, Held and his colleagues ultimately articulated a new 'transformationalist' perspective that affirms the growing importance of globalization while at the same time conceding that it was an uneven and contingent historical process replete with contradictions:

> In comparison with the skeptical and hyperglobalist accounts, the transformationalists make no claims about the future trajectory of globalization; nor do they evaluate the present in relation to some single, fixed ideal-type 'globalized world', whether a global market or a global civilization. Rather, transformationalist accounts emphasize globalization as a long-term historical process which is inscribed with contradictions and which is significantly shaped by conjunctural factors.[28]

According to the authors, one of those crucial 'conjunctural factors' relates to complex political dynamics resulting in the 'unbundling of the relationship between sovereignty, territoriality, and state power'. The deregulation and global integration of markets should not been seen as the single driver of globalization, but as a dynamic tightly linked to the reconfigured power of national governments in response to the growing complexity of a globalizing world. Thus reasserting the significance of the political domain, they emphasized that globalization must not be understood in terms of a singular economic logic, but as 'a highly differentiated process involving social domains of activity and interaction as diverse as the political, military, economic, cultural, migratory, and environmental'. For the authors, each of these domains of social life contained different patterns of relations and activities. Though connected to all the other dimensions, these dynamics operated at times largely autonomously according to impulses and forces that were internally created and applied. The social domains of globalization also served as pivotal sites of power understood as 'interaction contexts and organizational milieus in and through which power operates to shape action capacities of peoples and communities'.[29]

The authors' efforts culminated in their attempt to develop a generalized theory and typology of globalization capable of shedding light on the growing social complexity of our changing world. The linchpin of this comprehensive theoretical framework was the postulation of analytically distinct but empirically connected social domains that corresponded to the central arenas of human interaction. Their detailed examinations of deeply embedded processes of change taking place within six different social domains (political, military, economic, cultural, migratory, and environmental)—and in different historical periods—met the requirements of 'methodological glocalism' by linking a holistic conceptualization of globalization (as complex patterns of growing global complexity) to profoundly contingent, indeterminate, uncertain, uneven, multicausal, and multifaceted interactions in specific local settings.

However, their central concern with the delineation of major social domains privileged social processes over spatial dynamics. In other words, a differentiation of globalization into various sites and sources of social power did little to address what David Harvey and other spatial thinkers considered the core of globalization: the transformation in the spatial organization of social relations and transactions. Recognizing this problem, Held and his colleagues expanded their general framework of globalization by adding the four 'spatio-temporal dimensions' to their six social domains: the extensity of global networks; the intensity of global interconnectedness; the velocity of global flows; and the impact of global interconnectedness.

Since we'll discuss matters of space and time in more detail in the next chapter, let us direct our attention at this stage to the 'network' terminology that frames their four spatial dimensions. Adopted primarily from the work of globalization theorist Manuel Castells (discussed in the next section), the phrase 'global flows' referred to in *Global Transformations* characterizes the 'movements of physical artifacts, people, symbols, tokens and information across space and time'. The term 'global networks' signified 'regularized or patterned interactions between independent agents, nodes of activity, or sites of power'.[30]

Some commentators have pointed to a problem with the latter definition. Held and his team had previously linked the notion of 'sites of power' to social domains. Connecting it to 'networks' (a spatio-temporal category) blurred the distinction between 'social domains' and 'spatio-temporal dimensions' thus inviting conceptual confusion. To make matters worse, the authors added yet another set of four 'organizational dimensions' necessary for sketching the broad shape of globalization: infrastructures, institutionalization, stratification, and modes of interaction. In short, their laudable attempts to capture global complexity in its myriad forms and manifestations led them to introduce three sets of overlapping 'domains' and 'dimensions'. In addition, proper explanations of their internal workings required degrees of abstraction that rendered their grand theory quite abstract and sterile. As Andrew Jones argues, such high degrees of abstraction and generality made their multidimensional model of globalization quite vulnerable to criticism concerning the capacity of *any* 'grand' theoretical framework to universally and adequately capture every possible aspect of global interconnectedness.[31] In other words, their preoccupation with the macro-level—domains and dimensions—detracted from a necessary attention to the micro-level where globalization actually becomes concrete. Although the authors attempted to make up some of this 'local' ground in chapters that are organized around a more detailed examination of the contours and character of different domains of globalization, their discussion had a tendency to lapse into generalizations.

Despite these limitations, *Global Transformations* came closer than any previous attempt to providing researchers in the field with the outline of a general theory of globalization. Moreover, Held, McGrew, Goldblatt, and Perraton succeeded in making a convincing case for the suitability of transdisciplinary approaches in tackling the complexity and multidimensionality of globalization processes. Their study constitutes an impressive scholarly achievement that deservedly ranks near the top of the list of key texts in global studies. Indeed, it comes remarkably close to the possibility of developing a generalized globalization theory that cuts across a variety of disciplinary perspectives.

Networks, Flows, Fluids, and Hybrids

As we noted above, Held and his co-authors drew heavily on the relatively new terminology of 'networks' and 'flows' that had intensified in the early 1990s in the context of novel computer-based technologies that were at the center of what came to be known as the Information and Communication Technology (ICT) Revolution. In this foundational decade for global studies, nobody did more to integrate the technological discourse centered on 'electronically processed information networks' with the emerging globalization debate configured around 'social interdependencies' than the Spanish social scientist Manuel Castells. Examining complex globalization processes operating in economic, social, and cultural domains, his path-breaking three-volume study of *The Information Age* (1996–8) constitutes an encompassing theoretical treatise constructed from a series of specific 'network analyses' of these interlinked spheres of globalization. Somewhat more context-specific than Held's endeavor, Castells's project offers an empirically grounded, coherent account of globalization capable of explaining changing social and organizational arrangements of what he called the 'network society'. To that end, the author introduced new concepts into a comprehensive theoretical perspective that stopped just short of proposing the sort of general, unitary theory of society that Held and his collaborators hoped to assemble.[32]

Castells's most basic concept is that of a 'network', which he defines as a set of 'nodes' interconnected by 'ties' that are capable of directing all sort of 'flows'. Conceding that networks have existed in various forms throughout human history, Castells emphasized that their current manifestations were infinitely more complex and expansive. Their unprecedented combination of flexibility and task-implementation allowed for a superior coordination and management of growing social complexity. Emerging as the indispensable medium for the absorption, organization, and dissemination of microelectronics-based communication and information, networks appeared in the contemporary context in myriad forms and dynamics, most importantly as the capitalist world economy greased by transnational financial flows that are directed by 24/7 stock exchange markets; globally connected webs of civil society and their proliferating nodes of information-sharing NGOs; mobile digital devices generating, transmitting, and receiving signals in interlinking global media systems; expanding crime cartels and drug traffic routes cutting across national and regional geographies; and so on. Presenting these new communication/information networks as open structures capable of infinite expansion and integration of a large number of new nodes and ties, Castells argued that their global expansion at the turn of the century made them animating forces of *all* dimensions of contemporary social life. Indeed, Castells claimed that the new 'technological paradigm' constituted around digital networks represented a new period in human history. The global 'Information Age'— configured around the rising 'network society' and embedded in interconnected networks of production, power, and experience—was replacing the Industrial Age and its centrally organized, vertical chains of command and control geared toward the production and distribution of energy.[33]

Although Castells emphasized the crucial impact of economic and technological developments—especially the significance of digital 'systems of horizontal communication networks' in the liberalization and global integration of markets—he was careful to point out that the impact of the Internet and wireless communication technologies had to be analyzed in explicit transdisciplinary modes that eschewed determinist and reductionist explanations of globalization as 'technology plus markets'. For example, while the evolution of digital technology in the Information Age went hand-in-hand with the formation of 'informational capitalism', it also sparked a series of fundamental cultural and political transformations that make 'virtuality' an essential aspect of people's sense of the social whole.[34] After all, Castells insisted, communication is a process of sharing meaning through the exchange of information. The ongoing transformation of communication technology in the digital age—and the environment in which such communication occurs—directly affects the forms of meaning construction, and therefore the production of culture.

But Castells's theory of the network society raised as many questions as it answered. For example, how did these sophisticated digital technologies of networked information and communication mediate a vast array of social, political, and economic practices? How, precisely, did networks operating primarily in one domain interact with networks unfolding in other dimensions? And how did multiple expanding interdependencies form a coherent whole that could be conceptualized as the 'rise of the network society' in the Information Age? Like Held, Castells insisted that the key to understanding the evolving network society—and the diffusion of its logic of interconnectivity across all social domains—lay in an in-depth analysis of the globalizing forms of social *complexity* in the contemporary context. As he explained:

> [D]igital networking technologies, characteristic of the Information Age, powered social and organizational networks in ways that allowed their endless expansion and reconfiguration, overcoming the

traditional limitations of networking forms of organization to *manage complexity* beyond a certain size of the network. Because networks do not stop at the border of the nation-state, the network society constitutes itself as a global system, ushering in the new form of globalization characteristic of our time.[35]

In particular, Castells sought to unlock the complexities of the global network society by concentrating on the 'flows'—purposeful and repetitive sequences of exchange and interaction involving such things as language, data, money, or drugs—that pass through nodes along the ties of the network. However, under conditions of increasing complexity, flows can assume many different forms, characteristics, and qualities. As Darin Barney suggests, they can be constant or intermittent, one-way or reciprocal, uni- or multidirectional, balanced or imbalanced, strong or weak.[36] Castells recognized this difficulty and acknowledged that his empirical analysis of specific flows in the network society could not proceed without a prior consideration of larger space-time transformations in the human experience resulting from the new patterns of connection and mobility.

Hence, as we will discuss in more detail in the next chapter, the emergence of new modes and dimensions of space and time mediated by information technologies assumed a place of great significance in Castells's investigation of global networks. As for now, let us limit our discussion of spatial matters in his theory to our concern with transdisciplinary attempts to understand complexity in the Global Age. Introducing his influential notion of 'space of flows', Castells argued that microelectronics-based digital communication, advanced telecommunication networks, and computerized information systems had transformed conventional forms of social space by 'introducing simultaneity, or any chosen time frame, in social practices, regardless of the location of the actors engaged in the communication process'. Unlike a 'space of places'—conventionally bounded space linked to specific locations such as delineated suburbs, villages, towns, and the nation-state—Castells's 'space of flows' referred to a new interrelationship of knowledge, power, and communication that 'involves the production, transmission, and processing of flows of information'. To be sure, the space of flows on the Internet still relied on the production of localities as nodes of expanding communication networks, but the primary function of such 'places' consisted of providing 'material support of simultaneous social practices communicated at a distance'.[37]

In other words, Castells argued that the network society reorganizes and manages globalizing forms of social complexity through the space of flows. Localized constraints of place and time no longer limit expanding and proliferating manifestations of human activity mediated by global communication networks. Castells's approach to global complexity emphasized the materiality inherent in the space of flows. He pointed to the rise of a flexible 'new economy' organized in countless circuits of electronic exchanges that directed billions of financial transactions around the world. The production of significant nodes and hubs such as 'global cities' like New York and Shanghai not only facilitated the global division of labor or the global distribution centers for countless products and services, but also served as crucial social meeting places for global elites. As Barney sums it up, 'The network society is "always on" and the placement of its members in territorial space is less important than their existence as "space of flows" where crucial economic and other activity occurs'.[38]

Thus, Castells consciously broadened his transdisciplinary approach to complexity beyond the conventional focus on the dynamics of global capitalism to include flows of organizational templates, technical knowledge, images, sounds, symbols, and so on. But his pioneering analysis of the network society in terms of 'space of flows' allowed Castells not only to explain how networking forms of organization managed complexity but also showed how global networks included some people and territories while excluding others, 'so inducing a geography of social, economic, and technological inequality'. Indeed, Castells's exploration of various forms and processes of power in the network society moved to the center of his research efforts in the 2000s and 2010s.[39] In particular, he focused on the exercise of hegemonic power by programming and switching political, military, and financial networks, and the enactment of counterpower by dominated groups willing to disrupt prevailing networks and reprogram them around alternative interests and values. This significant expansion of his theory into the world of social movements and identity politics brought the author of The Information Age trilogy closer to his transdisciplinary goal of examining the different dimensions of the global network society so that together they provided a more holistic understanding of 'the trends that characterize the structure and dynamics of our societies in the world of the twenty-first century'.[40]

Building on Castells's theory of the global network society and Zygmunt Bauman's notion of 'liquid modernity', John Urry emerged in the 2000s as one of the most influential academic voices urging the reconfiguration of sociological and social-scientific research around the 'liquid' nature of 'complexity'.[41] Citing the transformative impact of globalization—reflected especially in the increasing mobility of people, commodities, technologies, and ideas—the British social scientist embarked on the transdisciplinary quest to connect social inquiries into the nature of the global with the 'complexity sciences' and 'chaos theory' in order to capture these new transnational dynamics. In particular, he argued that new concepts and methods borrowed from physics and biology had the capacity to expand our understanding of the global as a complex system or series of interdependent systems. Appreciative of Castells's innovative examination of intersecting global networks as the new framework for studying globalization, Urry nonetheless criticized his colleague for lacking a sufficiently broad range of theoretical terms necessary to illuminate the intensification of global complexity. As he saw it, Castells's notion of 'network' was 'too undifferentiated a term' to capture the dynamic properties of global processes and worldwide connections. Hence, the basic premise of Urry's path-breaking book, *Global Complexity* (2003), was to overcome the 'limitations of many globalization analyses that deal insufficiently with the *complex* character of emergent global relations'.[42] In this constructive spirit, the author proceeded to advance his innovative transdisciplinary project by introducing three key concepts to the study of globalization.

As his starting point, Urry proposed that emergent global systems should be conceptualized as interdependent and self-organizing 'global hybrids'. Combining both physical and social relations in curious and unexpected ways, these formations were capable of evolving toward both disorganization and order. Teetering 'on the edge of chaos,' global hybrids often moved away from points of equilibrium and stability, thus exhibiting the qualities of unpredictability, contingency, nonlinearity, irreversibility, and indeterminacy that have long been described and analyzed in natural sciences devoted to the study of complexity such as quantum physics, thermodynamics, cybernetics, ecology, and biology.[43] Citing informational systems, automobility, global media, world money, the Internet, climate change, health hazards, and worldwide protests as examples of such global hybrids, Urry argued that all of these manifestations could be classified as either 'globally integrated networks' or 'global fluids'.

For Urry, globally integrated networks (GINs) consisted of complex and enduring 'networked connections between peoples, objects and technologies stretching across multiple and distant spaces and times'. The purpose of GINs was to manage global complexity by introducing regularity and predictability into the chaotic multiplicity of emergent globality. For example, global enterprises like McDonald's, American Express, or Sony were organized through GINs that interweave technologies, skills, texts, and brands to ensure that the same service or product was delivered more or less the same way across the entire network. This made outcomes predictable, calculable, routinized, and standardized. However, as Urry notes, GINs also showed important weaknesses under conditions of advanced globalization. For example, the power of a global brand based within a GIN could evaporate almost overnight as a consequence of relatively minor occurrences. Local protests against global sweatshop practices or locally organized resistances to global corporations such as Starbucks could produce powerful effects that were difficult to analyze within a 'network' framework. Urry also noted that large transnational corporations organized through GINs (like Microsoft) had failed to react quickly to such social challenges or rapidly changing consumer preferences. They exhibited insufficient flexibility and fluidity to implement appropriate modes of organizational learning.[44] Urry's main point here was to argue that, under conditions of intensifying globalization, analytic frameworks centered on 'network' metaphors no longer sufficed as explanatory models of growing social complexity.

Thus, Urry introduced his third and perhaps most significant key concept to the study of globalization: global fluids (GFs). While these highly evolved manifestations of global hybridity undoubtedly involved 'networks', this term did not do justice to the 'uneven, emergent and unpredictable shapes' that 'fluids' might take. Structured by the various dimensions and domains of global order, GFs travelled along network ties from node to node, but their movements were much less stable and predictable than Castells suggested when he introduced the notion 'space of flows' within 'global networks'. Urry argued that GFs 'may escape, rather like white blood corpuscles, through the "wall" into surrounding matter and effect unpredictable consequences upon the matter'. Seizing upon the quantum physics metaphor of matter exhibiting qualities of both particles and waves, he suggested that GFs were constituted by 'particles' of 'people, information, objects, money, images, risk and networks' that moved 'within and across diverse regions forming heterogeneous, uneven, unpredictable and often unplanned waves'. For example, powerful 'fluids' of travelling people or health hazards such as global pandemics travelled across national borders at changing speeds and 'at different levels of viscosity with no necessary end state or purpose'. Unlike the 'network' metaphor, the notion of GFs (of different viscosity) was quite capable of explaining how the 'messy power of complexity processes' was organized in the Global Age. As Urry emphasized, GFs managed complexity by creating over time 'their own context for action rather than being seen as "caused" by such a context'.[45]

For the author of *Global Complexity*, the advantage of substituting the new 'global fluids' metaphor for the more conventional notion of 'network flows' lay in the superior representational powers of the former. It allowed researchers to better grasp the intersecting dynamics of globalization while at the same time acknowledging their complex and ultimately unpredictable forms. While Urry has been criticized for providing a rather abstract set of metaphors and concepts—and also for his tendency to indulge in patterns of assertion without much elaboration or specification—he deserves much praise for his intellectual modesty. Troubled by the ambitious attempts of researchers like Castells or Held to produce a unified and generalizable theory of globalization, Urry suggested that globalization was neither unified nor could it be presented as a linear and orderly set of processes unfolding in different domains. But his willingness to accept limits to his analysis of the global set by the growing complexity of globalization itself did not mean abandoning the academic task of inquiring into the wide array of rapidly evolving GINs and GFs. Rather, Urry encouraged fellow scholars to engage in a 'thoroughgoing post-disciplinarity' capable of transcending the physical science/social science divide. In short, such new post-disciplinary initiatives constitute the heart of global studies and thus should inspire the analysis of contemporary global relations.[46]

Concluding Reflections: Globalizing the Research Imagination

In a book presenting a series of interviews with some of the world's leading global studies scholars, Jane Kenway and Johannah Fahey conclude that globalization has deeply challenged many prevailing ideas and practices in the social sciences and humanities. The resulting imperative to 'globalize the research imagination' has put pressure on conventional academic land-scapes and architectures shaped by Western disciplinary logics developed in the previous two centuries. As Kenway and Fahey put it, mobilizing this global imagination 'becomes a form of "disciplinary urging" encouraging those in the field to move beyond its impasses and absences, even beyond inherited ways of thinking'.[47] But their suggested intellectual enterprise of globalizing our 'inherited ways of thinking' stands in stark contrast to established forms of academic tribalism that discourage relationships and exchanges between different disciplines.

As we have emphasized in this chapter, transgressing disciplinary space means establishing relationships to knowledge that are more open to the perpetual intellectual demands for change and self-alteration. As one among many manifestations of this transdisciplinary spirit, global studies encourages intellectual travel of the sort that produces wider academic horizons. But such a journey cannot be made without accepting the intellectual and institutional risks that come from challenging deeply engrained disciplinary modes of theory and practice. As we have seen, global studies research must stretch far beyond the confines of conventional bounded concepts like 'society' or 'nation' that have long dominated academic thinking. Exploring global complexity means revising the existing intellectual vocabulary without sacrificing the holism that does justice to the expanding parameters of social science research. In short, one of the most formidable challenges facing global studies today is transdisciplinarity: finding new *and* applicable ways of globalizing the research imagination.

We have noted that full transdisciplinarity involves at least four major dynamics: the systematic integration of knowledge in the never-ending search for knowledge unification; the transgression of disciplinary boundaries; transcendence of the scope of disciplinary views by articulating them in a holistic framework; and an issue-driven focus on problem-solving in the life-world that elevates concrete research questions and practices over disciplinary concerns.[48] As various transdisciplinary initiatives have gathered strength in the last two decades, some of these new fields have turned into trendy academic programs that often contain the denotation 'studies'— such as environmental studies, urban studies, cultural studies, ethnic studies, black studies, poverty studies, development studies, internet studies, and, of course, global studies. As Allen Repko observes, such 'studies' programs in general not only represent fundamental challenges to the dominant academic superstructure, but their growing popularity also indicates widespread dissatisfaction with the prevailing order of knowledge embodied in the traditional forms of disciplinary organization.[49] And yet, mainstream disciplinary discourses often assign such 'studies' an inferior role, implying that they lack the coherence, structure, evenness, depth, and sophistication of 'real' disciplines like sociology or political science.

While it may be true that 'studies' often lack a traditional 'canon' or established methodologies that are celebrated within disciplinary boundaries, a more generous, and perhaps accurate, perspective would replace such derision with the recognition of the *novelty* and *innovation* that one finds at the heart of many of these unorthodox newcomers. As Jan Nederveen Pieterse notes, the real distinction between disciplines and studies is one of seniority: 'The earlycomers claim to be foundational while the latecomers claim new objects of study. . . Hence "studies" are often introduced first at younger or newcomer universities, which cannot compete with the established universities in the disciplines, but can try to establish themselves and attract faculty and students in new terrains'.[50] The most convincing intellectual rationale for the legitimacy of 'studies' is, therefore, that established disciplines are too defensive in their self-assigned roles of knowledge gatekeepers to allow for the necessary process of innovation in a given field of study. As a result, knowledge innovators often choose a transdisciplinary approach as the best strategy to pursue their research path with a minimum of disciplinary interference.

While newly emerging transdisciplinary initiatives might surpass the conventional disciplines in performing the necessary task of realigning changing forms of knowledge to the global challenges of the twenty-first century, the success of such 'studies' programs might actually weaken the transgressive impulse at the heart of transdisciplinarity. How so? In order to be effective within the still dominant academic order of largely self-contained disciplines, global studies—and other 'studies' fields—face considerable pressures (and incentives) to join the existing single-discipline club as—yes—yet another separate-discipline member. In other words, the more popular global studies becomes, the greater the danger of contracting the disciplinary disease of drawing conceptual boundaries between 'us' and 'them', which is institutionally fortified by the erection of protective departmental walls and the separate allocation of resources.

The task, then, is for the new transdisciplinary field to attract talented scholars willing to assume the burden of intellectual leadership. They must develop a clear agenda for transdisciplinarity in global studies that can inspire followers among students and faculty. Global studies needs to expand its foothold in the dominant academic landscape while at the same time continue its work against the prevailing order. To satisfy these seemingly contradictory imperatives, global studies must retain its perilous ambition to project 'globalization' across the conventional disciplinary matrix yet accept with equal determination the pragmatic task of finding some accommodation within the very disciplinary structure it seeks to transform. Such necessary attempts to reconcile these diverging impulses forces scholars to play at least one, and preferably more, of three distinct roles—depending on the concrete institutional opportunities and constraints they encounter in their academic home environment.

First, global studies sympathizers might have to assume the role of *intrepid mavericks* willing to establish global studies as a separate discipline—as a first but necessary step toward the more holistic goal of comprehensive integration. The collective efforts of scholars located in the UCSB global studies department or RMIT University's Globalism Research Center (now Centre for Global Research) represent an impressive model of how such difficult maverick activities can lead to remarkably successful outcomes. However, as Armin Krishnan has pointed out, leaving one's discipline behind does not mean the wholesale abandonment of one's original disciplinary interests: '[P]ractically every new discipline starts off necessarily as an interdisciplinary project that combines elements from some parent discipline(s) with original new elements and insights'.[51] To be sure, mavericks must possess a certain spirit of adventure that makes it easier for them to leave their original disciplinary setting behind to cover new ground.

And being a maverick always carries the considerable risk that they and their new field will possibly fail.

Second, global studies scholars must be prepared—if their academic context demands it—to embrace the role of *radical insurgents* seeking to globalize established disciplines from *within*. This means working toward the goal of carving out a 'global studies' dimension or status for specific disciplines such as political science or sociology. A specific example for such 'insurgence' activity would be Peter Dicken's 2004 fierce critique of his own discipline—geography—for failing to engage properly with intellectually and economically significant globalization debates. He challenged his colleagues to take up what he considers the 'central task for geographers'—to pay more attention to contemporary global issues and concerns such as the spatial outcomes of globalization that set the framework for crucial social dynamics in the twenty-first century.[52] Dicken's plea did not fall on deaf ears for one can find today many human geographers at the cutting-edge frontiers of global studies research.

Finally, students of global studies must slip into the role of *tireless nomads* travelling perpetually across and beyond disciplines in order to reconfigure existing and new knowledge around concrete globalization research questions and projects. The nomadic role, in particular, demands that global studies scholars familiarize themselves with vast literatures on pertinent subjects that are usually studied in isolation from each other.

Indeed, one of the most formidable intellectual challenges facing global studies today lies in its enduring commitment to making transdisciplinarity work in concrete university settings. This task requires the integration and synthesis of multiple strands of knowledge in a way that does justice to the ever-growing complexity, fluidity, and connectivity of our globalizing world.

NOTES

1 In this chapter, we employ a very broad definition of 'science' that extends to the humanities. The discussion of what does and what does not constitute science is certainly germane with respect to our topic of transdisciplinarity, but extends well beyond the scope of this chapter.
2 Kamola, *Producing the Global Imaginary*, Chapter 4: 'The U.S. Academy and the Production of the Global Imaginary'.
3 Lie, 'Asian Studies/Global Studies: Transcending Area Studies in the Social Sciences', p. 4.
4 See, for example, Michel Foucault, *Discipline and Punish: The Birth of Prison* (New York: Vintage, 1995).
5 David Alvargonzález, 'Multidisciplinarity, Interdisciplinarity, Transdisciplinarity, and the Sciences', *International Studies in the Philosophy of Science* 25.4 (2011), p. 387;

Rudolf Stichweh, 'Differentiation of Scientific Disciplines: Causes and Consequences', *Encyclopedia of Life Support Systems* (Paris: UNESCO, 2003), p. 2; Julie Thompson Klein, *Interdisciplinarity: History, Theory, and Practice* (Detroit: Wayne State University Press, 1990), pp. 20–25; and Joe Moran, *Interdisciplinarity* (London and New York: Routledge, 2002), p. 13.

6　Stichweh, 'Differentiation of Scientific Disciplines: Causes and Consequences', p. 5.

7　Armin Krishnan, 'What are Academic Disciplines? Some Observations on the Disciplinarity vs. Interdisciplinarity Debate', ESRC National Centre for Research Methods NCRM Working Paper Series (January 2009), pp. 9–10.

8　Thomas Kuhn, *The Structure of Scientific Revolutions* (Chicago: The University of Chicago Press, 1962).

9　See, for example, Alvargonzález, 'Multidisciplinarity, Interdisciplinarity, Transdisciplinarity, and the Sciences', pp. 387–8; Alice W. Russell, 'No Academic Borders? Transdisciplinarity in University Teaching and Research', *Australian Universities' Review* 48.1 (2005), pp. 35–41; Manfred A. Max-Neef, 'Foundations of Transdisciplinarity', *Ecological Economics* 53.1 (2005), pp. 35–41; Bernard C. K. Choi and Anita W. P. Pak, 'Multidisciplinarity, Interdisciplinarity, and Transdisciplinarity in Health Research, Services, Education and Policy: Definitions, Objectives, and Evidence of Effectiveness', *Clinical & Investigative Medicine* 29.6 (2006), pp. 351–364; and Allen F. Repko, *Interdisciplinary Research: Process and Theory*, 2nd ed. (London and Thousand Oaks: SAGE, 2011).

10　Repko, *Interdisciplinary Research: Process and Theory*, p. 17.

11　Choi and Pak, 'Multidisciplinarity, Interdisciplinarity, and Transdisciplinarity', pp. 355–6.

12　Alvargonzález, 'Multidisciplinarity, Interdisciplinarity, Transdisciplinarity, and the Sciences', p. 388.

13　Repko, *Interdisciplinary Research: Process and Theory*, pp. 4, 16.

14　Choi and Pak, 'Multidisciplinarity, Interdisciplinarity, and Transdisciplinarity', p. 355.

15　Christian Pohl and Gertrude Hirsch Hadorn, 'Methodological Challenges of Transdisciplinary Research', *Natures Sciences Sociétés* 16.2 (2008), p. 112; and Christian Pohl, 'From Transdisciplinarity to Transdisciplinary Research', *Transdisciplinary Journal of Engineering & Science* 1.1 (December 2010), p. 69.

16　See Klein, *Interdisciplinarity*.

17　Russell, 'No Academic Borders? Transdisciplinarity in University Teaching and Research', pp. 35–41.

18　Roderick J. Lawrence and Carole Després, Editors' Introduction, 'Futures of Transdisciplinarity', *Futures* 36 (2004), p. 400.

19　George Modelski, 'Communism and the Globalization of Politics', *International Studies Quarterly* 12.4 (1968), p. 389.

20　John Tomlinson, *Globalization and Culture* (Chicago: University of Chicago Press, 1999), pp. 1–2. See also Ulf Hannerz, *Cultural Complexity: Studies in the Social Organization of Meaning* (New York: Columbia University Press, 1992), pp. 6–8.

21　Pohl, 'From Transdisciplinarity to Transdisciplinary Research', p. 68.

22　Robert Holton, *Global Networks* (Houndmills, UK: Palgrave Macmillan, 2008), pp. 199–200.

23　Axford, *Theories of Globalization*, p. 8.

24　Giddens, *The Consequences of Modernity*, pp. 74–5.

25 David Held and Anthony McGrew, David Goldblatt and Jonathan Perraton, *Global Transformations: Politics, Economics, and Culture* (Stanford: Stanford University Press, 1999).

26 Held et. al, *Global Transformations*, p. 12.

27 Thomas Friedman, *The Lexus and the Olive Tree: Understanding Globalization* (New York: Anchor Books, 1999), p. 9.

28 Held et. al, *Global Transformations*, p. 7.

29 Ibid., pp. 8, 12, 23.

30 Ibid., p. 16.

31 Andrew Jones, *Globalization: Key Thinkers* (Cambridge, UK: Polity Press, 2010), p. 88.

32 Manuel Castells, *The Information Age: Economy, Society, and Culture*, 3 vols., 2nd ed. (Chichester, UK: Wiley-Blackwell, 2010). For excellent discussions of Castells's theory of the global network society, see Darin Barney, *The Network Society* (Cambridge, UK: Polity Press, 2004), Holton, *Global Networks*, and Jones, *Globalization*.

33 Castells, *The Information Age, Volume I: The Rise of the Network Society*; and Manuel Castells, 'Materials for an Exploratory Theory of the Network Society', *British Journal of Sociology* 51.1 (2000), pp. 5–24.

34 Ibid., p. xviii, 6.

35 Ibid., our emphasis.

36 Barney, *The Network Society*, p. 26.

37 Castells, *The Information Age Volume I: The Rise of the Network Society*, p. xxxii.

38 Barney, *The Network Society*, p. 29.

39 See Manuel Castells, *Communication Power* (Oxford: Oxford University Press, 2009); and Manuel Castells, *Networks of Outrage and Hope: Social Movements in the Internet Age* (Cambridge, UK: Polity Press, 2012). For a different theory of network power that explores the possibility of global social coordination via the production of new global standards, see David Grewal Singh, *Network Power: The Social Dynamics of Globalization* (New Haven: Yale University Press, 2008).

40 Castells, *The Information Age Volume I: The Rise of the Network Society*, p. xix.

41 See Zygmunt Bauman, *Liquid Modernity* (Cambridge, UK: Polity Press, 2000).

42 John Urry, *Global Complexity* (Cambridge, UK: Polity Press, 2003), p. 39; p. 15.

43 Ibid., p. 14. We discuss cultural forms of 'hybridity' and their significance for global studies in Chapter 5.

44 Ibid., pp. 56–9.

45 Ibid., pp. 60–1.

46 Ibid., p. 124.

47 Jane Kenway and Johannah Fahey, eds., *Globalizing the Research Imagination* (London and New York: Routledge, 2009), p. 4.

48 Alvargonzález, 'Multidisciplinarity, Interdisciplinarity, Transdisciplinarity, and the Sciences', pp. 394–5.

49 Repko, *Interdisciplinary Research: Process and Theory*, p. 9.

50 Pieterse, 'What is Global Studies?', pp. 503–4.

51 Krishnan, 'What are Academic Disciplines? Some Observations on the Disciplinarity vs. Interdisciplinarity Debate', p. 34.

52 Peter Dicken, 'Geographers and "Globalization": (Yet) Another Missed Boat?', *Transactions of the Institute of British Geographers* 29.1 (2004), p. 5. See also Warwick E. Murray, *Geographies of Globalization* (London and New York: Routledge, 2006), p. 355.

4

THE THIRD PILLAR OF GLOBAL STUDIES

Space and Time

The 'global village' is one of the earliest yet most enduring phrases marking the rise of the global imaginary. Coined in the early 1960s by Marshall McLuhan, the slogan reflected the growing public awareness of a rapidly shrinking world. However, what the Canadian literature and media scholar had in mind was a far more nuanced process than the one suggested by this popular slogan. Emphasizing the expanding reach of electricity-based communication technology, McLuhan sought to capture in a memorable phrase the complex and often uneven dynamics of spatial 'stretching' that made geographic distance much less of an obstacle in human interaction. Observing that the 'mechanical age' of the Industrial Revolution was rapidly receding, he predicted that the contemporary 'electric contraction' of space and time would eventually make the entire globe as open to instant and direct communication as small village communities in previous centuries had been. McLuhan opened his magisterial study on the globalization of the media by driving home his thesis in dramatic fashion: 'Today, after more than a century of electric technology, we have extended our central nervous system in a global embrace, abolishing both space and time as far as our planet is concerned'.[1] Leaving for our later discussion the question of whether the constraints of geography have indeed been overcome, McLuhan deserves much credit for recognizing already more than half a century ago the impact of globalizing modes of space and time.

This chapter explores the third pillar of global studies by highlighting the significance of what some observers have called the 'spatial turn' in the academic study of globalization.[2] After a brief consideration of 'globalization' as a spatial concept, we present a number of pertinent issues that have been debated by prominent global studies scholars. Starting with the influential thesis that humanity finds itself in the midst of a profound 'epochal transformation' from the 'Modern Age' to the 'Global Age', we discuss two opposing perspectives on the nature of the evolving relationship between modernity and globalization. Moving on to the ongoing debates in global studies on the nature and consequences of intensifying processes of 'deterritorialization', we consider conflicting perspectives on the fate of the conventional nation-state as it struggles to cope with the growing destabilization of sovereignty and territoriality in the Global Age. As we shall see, the contemporary transformation of territorial organizations has reoriented much globalization research toward an analysis of new spatial infrastructures and practices that have become visible in the emerging 'global cities' and 'network states' of the twenty-first century. Global studies scholars have offered new theories that explore how vertical spatial scales running from the local to the global are being flattened and rearranged in our globalizing world. We close the chapter with a brief look at the emerging field of 'global history' and its impact on global studies in the development of new historical periodization schemes. Indeed, human geographers, urban studies experts, and historians have been at the forefront of this growing tendency in global studies to pay closer attention to the spatio-temporal dynamics of globalization.

Globalization as a Spatial Concept

Globalization manifests in volatile dynamics of spatial integration and differentiation. These give rise to new temporal frameworks dominated by notions of 'instantaneity' and 'simultaneity' that assume ever-greater significance in academic investigations into the 'process of becoming worldwide'. Thus deeply resonating with spatio-temporal meanings, the keyword unites two semantic parts: 'global' and 'ization'. The primary emphasis is on 'global', which reflects people's growing awareness of the increasing significance of global-scale phenomena such as global economic institutions, transnational corporations, global civil society, the World Wide Web, global climate change, and so on. Indeed, the principal reason for why the term was coined in the first place had to do with people's recognition of intensifying spatial dynamics that occurred at the global scale. Global studies scholars have employed the terms 'deterritorialization' and 'denationalization' to indicate the growing significance of the highest rung on the conventional spatial ladder running from the global to the local. However, as we have noted previously and will discuss in more detail in this chapter, people's orientation toward what appeared to be explicitly global in scale does not mean that local, national, and regional scales were losing their significance in the Global Age. In fact, globalization processes create incessantly new geographies and complex spatial arrangements from within spaces and places that do not necessarily scale at the global level. This is especially true for the latest spatial frontier in human history: cyberspace. The 'glocal' dynamics of digital connectivity have shown themselves to be quite capable of pushing human interaction deep into the 'virtual reality' of a world in which geography is no longer a factor.

The second half of the keyword puts 'globalization' into the class of nouns that end in 'ization'—a suffix whose meaning is typically tied to the idea of change over time characterized as 'development' or 'unfolding'. Such dynamics infuse the 'global' with a kind of 'energy' that propel its movement forward. The trajectory occurs along discernible spatial patterns that are deeply embedded in progressive temporal logics. Regardless of whether such 'izations' occur quickly or slowly, they correspond to empirical processes of spatio-temporal change that have the potential to affect the wholesale transformation of existing social structures. For example, the related terms 'modernization' and 'industrialization' refer to a reconfiguration of space and time understood as the progressive transition from 'traditional' to 'modern' societies. But 'modernization' can also mean changing the physical appearance of lived space to meet the social tastes and expectations of current times—such as the 'modernization' of a kitchen. Similarly, 'globalization' has been associated with a progressive transition from 'modern' to 'postmodern' societies that also includes the 'updating' of existing social arrangements to meet contemporary standards.

In short, the concept 'globalization' signifies the transformation of spatial relations, thus emphasizing the active role of space and time in structuring human relations. Indeed, as French philosopher and sociologist Henri Lefebvre noted, space and time are interrelated dimensions of social existence:

> When we evoke 'space', we must immediately indicate what occupies that space and how it does so: the deployment of energy in relation to 'points' and within a time frame. When we evoke 'time', we must immediately say what it is that moves and changes therein. Space considered in isolation is an empty abstraction; likewise energy and time.[3]

Lefebvre's path-breaking analysis presented space as a changeable and embodied social category rather than an abstract and empty Euclidean category that equated it with a 'mental thing.' He suggested as early as 1984 that capitalism was subject to a spatial 'law of unevenness of growth and development' resulting in the 'globalization of a world market'. Understanding this spatial law made the analysis of the socially induced reconfigurations of space and time essential to what he saw as the first stirrings of an impending social transformation on a global scale: 'The creation (or production) of a planet-wide space as the social foundation of a transformed everyday life open to myriad possibilities—such is the dawn now beginning to break on the far horizon'.[4]

Several global studies pioneers linked the insights of Lefebvre and McLuhan to their own approaches to globalization, thus putting matters of time and space at the very core of their research projects. Consider, for example, Roland Robertson's snappy definition of globalization as 'the compression of the world into a single place'. It underpinned his efforts to develop a spatially sophisticated concept of 'glocalization' capable of counteracting the relative inattention paid to spatiality in the social sciences. Commenting on the remarkable fluidity of spatial scales in a globalizing world, Robertson focused on those complex and uneven processes 'in which the constraints of geography on social and cultural arrangements recede and in which people become increasingly aware that they are receding'.[5] Similarly, Arjun Appadurai developed subtle insights into what he called the 'global production of locality'—a new spatial dynamic that was occurring more frequently in 'a world that has become deterritorialized, diasporic, and transnational'.[6] Or recall David Harvey's influential inquiry into the spatial origins of contemporary cultural change which we discussed in Chapter 2. Centered on the uneven geographic development of capitalism, Harvey's innovative account generated new concepts that affirmed the centrality of spatio-temporal changes at the heart of neoliberal globalization and its associated postmodern cultural sensibilities: 'time–space compression'; 'the implosion of space and time'; 'subduing space'; 'the unreality of place'; 'the shrinkage of space'; 'the spatialization of time'; and, finally, 'the annihilation of space through time'.[7]

Modernity or Postmodernity?

Following on the heels of Harvey's reflections on 'time–space compression' and Robertson's analysis of 'glocalization', the most influential academic inquiry into the relationship between globalization and modernity flowed from the pen of a notable British sociologist who went on to become the Director of the London School of Economics and Political Science as well as a prominent advisor to British Prime Minister Tony Blair. Anthony Giddens opened his widely cited study *The Consequences of Modernity* (1990) with a rather controversial definition of modernity as 'modes of social life or organization, which emerged in Europe from about the seventeenth century onwards and which subsequently became more or less worldwide in their influence'. Seemingly comfortable with theorizing his subject within a Eurocentric framework, Giddens lost no time to advance his even more controversial thesis. Rejecting the notion of 'epochal change'—the popular view that humanity was standing at the threshold of a new era beyond modernity itself—he assured his readers that 'we are moving into one in which the consequences of modernity are becoming more radicalised and universalised than before.'[8]

In particular, Giddens opposed the influential perspective of poststructuralist thinkers like Jean-François Lyotard who had proclaimed the birth of a 'postmodern age' following the collapse of the foundational 'metanarratives' of Enlightenment rationality and its faith in progress.[9] For Giddens, however, such 'postmodern' propositions are based on the wholesale 'invention' of 'new terms like post-modernity and the rest' instead of an 'adequate analysis of modernity.' 'Postmodernism', Giddens sneered at his adversaries, was merely contributing to a growing sense of 'epistemological disorientation' in the social sciences. If the term was to mean anything at all, he argued, it should be banished from social scientific modes of inquiry and remain confined to 'aspects of aesthetic reflection of the nature of modernity' such as 'styles and movements within literature, painting, the plastic arts, and architecture'.[10]

In short, the author of *The Consequences of Modernity* refused to give up on the possibility of rational foundations that allowed for the production of generalizable knowledge about social life in the late twentieth century. He proceeded to build his case for the philosophical and historical continuity of modernity—albeit in its current 'radicalized' and 'universalized' form—around the core concept of 'time-space distanciation'.[11] Referring to the stretching of social systems across space and time, this novel dynamic constituted an intrinsic feature of modernity that had made it 'discontinuous' to earlier 'tribal' or 'traditional' social orders in which time had always been linked to a 'place' identified with regular but imprecise natural occurrences such as the cyclical movement of ocean tides or celestial objects. A unique period in human history, modernity had broken with tradition by instituting a radical separation of time and space expressed in a uniform dimension of 'empty' clock time and the corresponding uniformity in the social organization of time such as the standardization of calendars.

The modern reorganization of time and space involved both the 'speeding up' of time reflected in the accelerated pace of social change and the expansion of space that brought different areas of the globe into permanent intercourse with one another. Modernity's vital impulses—its 'restlessness' and 'inherent disposition to expand'—were most clearly on display in the major transformative forces shaping social life worldwide from the seventeenth century to today: rationalism, capitalism, and industrialism. Situated at the heart of modernity, 'time-space distanciation' worked hand in hand with 'disembedding mechanisms' like the modern state, media networks, or transnational corporations that lifted social relations out of their purely local interactions and then restructured them 'across large time-space distances'. Thus extending the scope of time-space distanciation, these disembedding institutions were able to 'connect the global and the local in ways which would have been unthinkable in more traditional societies and in so doing affect the lives of many millions of people'. Disembedding processes also facilitated 'reflexivity'—the production of systematic knowledge about social life that eventually extended across vast spans of time-space and challenged the fixities of traditional societies. Focusing his attention on the latest phase in this centuries-old expansionist dynamic, Giddens linked modernization to what would become the buzzword of the 1990s: 'We can interpret this process as one of *globalisation*, a term which must have a key position in the lexicon of the social sciences'.[12]

What, then, was the precise relationship between modernity and globalization? At this point in our discussion, we can already anticipate Giddens's answer: 'Modernity is inherently globalising'. In other words, the principal sources of the dynamism of modernity—time-space distanciation, disembedding, and reflexivity—and their corresponding systems and institutions—primarily capitalism and the nation-state system—were capable of 'tearing away' modernity from traditional social orders in ever-expanding and intensifying spatial movements. By the end of the twentieth century, the level of time-space distanciation dwarfed that of earlier stages of modernity as relations between local and distant social forms and events had been stretched to the point where different localities and regions had become networked across the entire globe. As Giddens observed, the globalizing tendencies of modernity were 'simultaneously extensional and intensional—they connect individuals to large-scale systems as part of complex dialectics of change at both local and global poles'.[13]

Finally, Giddens arrived at his influential definition of globalization: 'Globalization can thus be defined as the intensification of worldwide social relations which link distant localities in such a way that local happenings are shaped by events occurring many miles away and vice versa'.[14] This means that he saw globalization as the latest phase of modernization that had become so 'intensified' and 'extended' that it deserved its own qualifying terms: 'globalization' or 'globalizing' modernity. Rather than marking the end of modernity and the start of a new 'postmodern' era, globalization actually constituted one of the fundamental *consequences* of modernity. After all, globalization processes represented the apex of modernity's inherent tendencies to radically reorganize time and space. Having reached this conclusion, Giddens renewed his initial attack on 'postmodern' thinkers who had committed the error of 'mislabeling' various manifestations of globalizing modernity as phenomena portending a new and qualitatively distinct epoch in human history.[15]

Does this mean, as some of his critics charge, that Giddens's idea of globalization as the continuation of pre-established paths of modernity actually makes for a sophisticated theory of 'Westernization', which none-theless replicates all the problems associated with Eurocentrism?[16] Giddens's rejoinder comes in two parts. With respect to its *geographic origin* and its main organizational disembedding institutions such as capitalism and the nation-state system, modernity—and globalization—are indeed Western projects. At the same time, however, Giddens is extremely careful to point out that, by the end of the twentieth century, the expansionist dynamics of moder-nity had robbed the West of its exclusive hold on the phenomenon. From the standpoint of its *globalizing tendencies*, modernity is thus not particularly 'Western', because it pervades and motivates all regions and cultures of the planet.

While acknowledging the violent role of imperialism and colonialism in the process of globalizing modernity, Giddens nonetheless chose to empha-size its future-oriented, open-ended tendencies. Globalization generates incessantly new forms of 'world interdependence' and 'planetary conscious-ness' that must 'inevitably involve conceptions and strategies derived from non-Western settings'. Still, his view of modernity as universalizing—both in its global impact and in its generation of reflexive knowledge—locked the social thinker into the controversial position that 'universality' in the form of the scientific method or 'rational' argumentation ultimately over-rode cultural specificity. As he put it, 'Discursive argumentation, including that which is constitutive of natural science, involves criteria that override cultural differentiations'.[17]

Struggling to extricate himself fully from the charge of Eurocentrism, Giddens's thesis of globalization as a consequence of modernity clearly discounted competing theories of multiple paths of modernization.[18] The proponents of 'alternative modernities' had problematized Western development by insisting that all societies were capable of creating their own modernity. Pointing to the ongoing formation of new 'mélange modernities' that resulted from processes of globalization, increased communication, and enhanced mobility, the global studies scholar Jan

Nederveen Pieterse charged Giddens with failing to consider the creation of new hybrid combinations between 'traditional' and 'modern practices' in the Global Age.[19]

It should not surprise us that Giddens's understanding of globalization as the corollary of modernity incensed postmodern theorists or postcolonial thinkers like Pieterse. But it is less obvious that Giddens also alienated fellow 'universalists' like the British sociologist Martin Albrow, who shared his critique of postmodernism as 'philosophical relativism' parasitic upon the very concept—modernity—that it seeks to deconstruct. Still, Albrow rejected Giddens's thesis of globalizing modernity in the strongest terms possible and instead argued for an 'epochal shift' from the 'Modern Age' to the dawning 'Global Age'. Appropriately titled *The Global Age: State and Society Beyond Modernity* (1996), Albrow's seminal study opens with a criticism of the dominant view of modernity as a 'time without end'. In his view, this 'totalizing discourse' in the social sciences had reduced all forms of social change since the seventeenth century to mere manifestations of the 'Modern Age' and thus made it difficult to even imagine a future beyond modernity. For Albrow, however, modernity was running out of steam at the end of the twentieth century as a result of 'globalization'. He defined the key concept as a 'multi-dimensional and open-ended set of processes' powering today's comprehensive social transformation. Its outcome is not the apogee of the old but its end: a new historical epoch beyond modernity called the 'Global Age':

> Fundamentally, the Global Age involves the supplanting of modernity with globality and this means an overall change in the basis of action and social organization for individuals and groups. There are at least five major ways in which globality has taken us beyond the assumptions of modernity. These include the global environmental consequences of aggregate human activities; the globality of communication systems; the rise of a global economy; and the reflexivity of globalism, where people and groups of all kinds refer to the globe as the frame for their beliefs.[20]

Reversing Giddens's critique of the postmodernist understanding of modernity, Albrow reproaches his colleague for misreading what is actually a manifestation of 'rupture' and 'discontinuity' as the continuation of modernity's logic of expansion and intensification. Deemed as incapable of breaking out of the totalizing conceptual framework of modernity as 'time without end', Giddens stands accused of committing a number of serious conceptual errors. First, Albrow argues that his thesis of modernity as inherently globalizing is both deterministic and teleological. It treats an outcome (globalization) as a necessary product of a process (modernity)—as if modernity had fixed inner laws of development that set it on an inevitable course toward a predetermined goal. He also notes that Giddens's obsession with the supposed 'inner logic' of modernity prevents him from considering the emergence of new phenomena and circumstances that have the capacity of changing established modes in profound ways. What if modernity is actually an open-ended process capable of producing indeterminate outcomes that undermine its own tendencies? Might it then not be possible for human societies to move beyond modernity? Moreover, Albrow finds his colleague's attachment to continuity in the Modern Age especially troubling in light of Giddens's identification of *discontinuities* and *ruptures* that allegedly gave birth to modernity in the seventeenth century.[21]

Second, Albrow argues that Giddens's focus on 'expansion' eclipses the significance of contraction and limits under conditions of globalization. After all, forces of expansion associated with modernity run up against a systemic limit when the territory of the entire world is effectively enclosed. It is people's growing recognition of the dangers of expansionism that forces them to pay more attention to the material *finitude* of the globe. The necessity of honoring the ecological *limits* nature imposes on human activities become ever more obvious in a globalizing world subject to climate change. The seriousness of global environmental problems requires people to break with modernity's logic of expansion and intensification. As Albrow emphasizes, 'Globality promotes the recognition of the limits of the earth but is profoundly different from modernity in that there is no presumption of centrality of control. The unification of the world which was the outcome of the Modern Project generates the common recognition that it has ended'. Unlike the Modern Age, the Global Age becomes defined by central concerns of planetary finitude and human limits that arrest the dynamic of modernity. Hence, 'Globalization, far from being the end to which human beings have aspired, is the termination of modern ways of organizing life which they took for granted. The global shift is a transformation, not a culmination'.[22]

Accepting Albrow's thesis means that, far from being the latest stage of a long process of modern development, the Global Age actually constitutes a new era in history. It has arisen from a combination of different forces that have unexpectedly terminated the course of modernity by setting worldwide limits and creating alternatives to its supposedly 'inherent' tendencies and institutions. And these limits cannot be overcome from within the logic of modernity. Hence, Albrow's provocative inversion of Giddens's thesis: rather than embracing the idea that 'modernity is inherently globalizing',

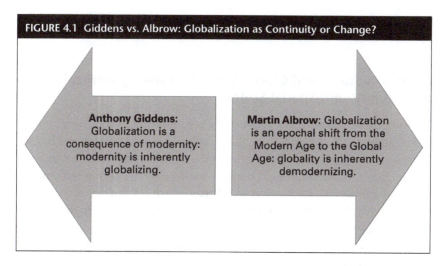

FIGURE 4.1 Giddens vs. Albrow: Globalization as Continuity or Change?

Anthony Giddens: Globalization is a consequence of modernity: modernity is inherently globalizing.

Martin Albrow: Globalization is an epochal shift from the Modern Age to the Global Age: globality is inherently demodernizing.

we should accept that 'globality is inherently demodernizing'.[23] The assumptions underlying Albrow's new formula of demodernizing globality also point to another flaw in Giddens's theory: the primacy of quantity over quality. Conceptualizing globalization in terms of 'expansion' and 'intensification' of existing modern social institutions and arrangements—primarily capitalism and the nation-state system—Giddens misses the significance of profound qualitative shifts reflected in newly emergent social forms and forces such as the rise of the digital network society or the transnationalization of capital that destabilizes the exclusive territoriality of the modern nation-state.

Regarding this point, Albrow's thesis of the Global Age received unexpected backing from critical political economists like William I. Robinson and Peter Dicken who distinguished between economic processes of 'internationalization' occurring within a modernist framework and those of 'transnationalization' associated with a qualitatively different context of globalization. 'Internationalization' refers to quantitative extensions of economic activities across national boundaries that lead to 'shallow' forms of social integration and thus keep intact the forms and functions of the modern nation-state system. 'Transnationalization' involves not merely the geographical extension of economic activity across national boundaries but also 'deep' functional integration that marks a qualitative shift from an 'international' to a 'transnational' or 'global' economy. Hence, Robinson and Dicken agree with Albrow that globalization has ushered in a new era beyond modernity whose defining features are the rise of transnational capital and the transcendence of the nation-state as a historically specific form of world social organization.[24] And it is to this crucial discussion of the dynamics of 'deterritorialization' that we now must turn.

Of Nation-States and Global Cities: Rethinking Territoriality, Sovereignty, and Spatial Scales

The concept of 'territoriality' refers to the use of territory for political, social, and economic ends. In modernity, the term has been associated with a largely successful strategy for establishing the exclusive jurisdiction implied by state 'sovereignty'.[25] State control of bounded 'national' terrain promised citizens living on the 'inside' the benefits of relative security and unity in exchange for their exclusive loyalty and allegiance to the nation-state. By the second half of the twentieth century, social existence in such relatively fixed spatial containers had gone on for such a long time that it struck most people as the universal mode of communal life in the world. However, the latest wave of globalization gathering momentum in the 1980s and 1990s unsettled the political and methodological territorialism underpinning this highly effective naturalization of territorial states. The intensifying dynamics of 'denationalization' and 'deterritorialization' exposed the artificiality of territoriality as a social construct and its historical role as a specific human technique for managing space and time in the interest of modern state power.

The impact of globalization on conventional forms of territoriality and the related changing nature of the 'international system' have raised major questions concerning the significance of the nation-state and the relevance of conventional notions of 'territory' and 'sovereignty' in analyzing the new spatial practices associated with globalization. This new spatial agenda also involves an important subset of issues pertaining to the proliferation and growing impact of non-state actors; the emergence of a 'global civil society' no longer confined within the borders of the territorial state; the prospects for 'global governance' understood as the norms and institutions that define and mediate relations between citizens, societies, markets, and states on a global scale; and the pluralization and hybridization of individual and collective identities. Various commentators have pointed to a growing gap between global space (where new problems arise) and national space, which proves increasingly inadequate for managing these transnational issues.[26] These mounting spatial incompatibilities combine with the increasing power of neoliberalism and the absence of effective institutions of global governance to produce interrelated crises of state legitimacy and economic equity that undermine democratic politics.

Although there is virtual agreement among global studies scholars that today's respatialization dynamics are profound and accelerating, there remain significant differences between a small band of thinkers comfortable with advancing an extreme thesis of deterritorialization and a much larger group holding more moderate views. Let us consider the conflicting 'absolutist' and 'relativist' views on deterritorialization by focusing on the arguments of influential representatives from each camp.

Deterritorialization Absolutists

Absolutist views rose to prominence during the Roaring Nineties when spectacular neoliberal market reforms seemed to diminish the role of the state in the economy. Market globalists like the Japanese business strategist Kenichi Ohmae embraced deterritorialization as an irreversible process intrinsically connected to the enlargement of the spatial reach of markets. Moreover, these neoliberal thinkers emphasized that market relations were increasingly mediated by computer technology and digital communication systems. Politics anchored in conventional forms of territoriality was losing out to a seemingly unstoppable techno–economic juggernaut that crushed conventional sovereignty understood as the state's exclusive control of strict and fixed territorial boundaries. The transnational practices of global capitalism were portrayed as ushering in a new phase in world history in which the state's survival in diminished form depended on its satisfactory performance of its new role as a handmaiden to global free-market forces, or, as global finance experts Lowell Bryan and Diana Farrell asserted, as 'a superconductor for global capitalism'.[27]

Envisioning the rise of a 'borderless world' where territory would eventually become obsolescent, Ohmae suggested that the deterritorializing effects of global capitalism were already robbing the nation-state of much of its former glory as the director and regulator-in-chief of the national economy. Territorial divisions and related sovereignty claims were becoming increasingly irrelevant to human society. States were less able to determine the direction of social life within their borders, thus suffering from a chronic legitimacy deficit that was bound to weaken people's feelings of national allegiance while strengthening their incipient transnational identities as 'global citizens'. For Ohmae, the workings of genuinely global capital markets dwarfed the ability of states to control exchange rates, protect their currency, or even stop cross-border migrants seeking economic betterment. Under the conditions of intensifying globalization, nation-states were increasingly subjected to 'market discipline' imposed by economic choices made elsewhere over which they had no significant control.

This dynamic extended to the global South where neoliberal development policies assumed the form of the dominant 'Washington Consensus'—a market-oriented form of conditional lending by powerful international financial institutions like the International Monetary Fund (IMF) and the World Bank that subjected poor countries to 'structural adjustment programs' anchored in the principles of austerity and fiscal conservatism. In the long run, Ohmae speculated, market-driven processes of denationalization would lead to the inevitable decline of state territory as a dominant framework for political and social life. Incapable of functioning along the lines of territorially-based units, the concrete forms of political order in the twenty-first century would be determined by regional economic spaces. These regions would be linked together in an almost seamless global web that operated in virtual space according to the ceaseless 24/7 rhythm of global financial markets. The core message of deterritorialization absolutists was loud and clear: brought on by globalization, the 'end of the nation-state' was at hand.[28]

Deterritorialization Relativists

While acknowledging the growing significance of deterritorialization dynamics in a globalizing world, relativists argued for the continued relevance of conventional territorial units, albeit in reconfigured forms. Proponents of this view come in two varieties. 'Strong relativists' focused on the global scale in stressing the significance of the increasingly 'transplanetary' and 'supraterritorial' nature of social relations. 'Weak relativists' highlighted the continued importance of subglobally scaled processes of 'reterritorializing' states and localities. A prominent representative of the former camp, the European global studies scholar Jan Aart Scholte asserted that globalization involves at its core 'strong' spatial processes of deterritorialization reflected in 'the large-scale spread of supraterritoriality'. Elevating the idea of globalization's compression of space and time to new historical heights in both quantitative and qualitative terms, Scholte's use of 'supraterritoriality' refers to global connections that substantially transcend territorial geography. These connections possess spatio-temporal qualities of 'transworld simultaneity'—extension anywhere across the planet at the same time—and 'transworld instantaneity'—movement anywhere on the planet in no time.[29]

For Scholte, such multiplying supraterritorial forms of globality were evident in 'countless facets of contemporary life' such as jet travel across any distance on the planet in twenty-four hours or less, telecommunications networks, the global mass media, global financial flows, the hybridization of human identities, and so on. In particular, he argued that the inadequacy of the nation-state to serve as the sole site for the governance of global relations was reflected in the growth of 'suprastate' or 'transworld' regimes that operated with significant autonomy from the state. In short, the principle of exclusive state sovereignty was giving way to 'pooled' or 'shared' forms of sovereignty.[30] The increasing inability of nation-states to manage the globalization processes forced them to change into what fellow strong relativist Manuel Castells called the 'network state', characterized by 'shared sovereignty and responsibility, flexibility of procedures of governance, and greater diversity in the relationships between governments and citizens in terms of time and space'.[31] In spite of their obvious affinities for a 'strong' version of deterritorialization relativism, Scholte and Castells carefully avoided absolutist predictions of the demise of the nation-state or the 'end of geography'. At the outset of the new century, sovereignty was still a mixed-spatial practice: 'Clearly, social space in today's world is *both* territorial *and* supraterritorial. Indeed, in social practice the two qualities always intersect. Supraterritoriality is only relatively deterritorialized, and contemporary territoriality is only partly supraterritorialized'.[32]

Elaborating on the deterritorialization theme, other 'strong relativists' like the political theorists Michael Hardt and Antonio Negri concurred with Scholte's thesis that the decline of nation-state sovereignty could not be equated with the decline of sovereignty as such. However, they insisted that sovereignty was rapidly transforming into a decentered and deterritorialized apparatus of rule they called 'Empire'. This radically new space of authority and control in the Global Age was composed of a hybrid series of national and supranational organisms that superseded old, nation-state-centered forms of sovereignty. For Hardt and Negri, 'Empire' was not merely a metaphor but an active 'political subject that effectively regulated these global exchanges, the sovereign power that governs the world'. Its single logic of globalization operated in all spheres of social life—perhaps most visibly in the regulation of human interaction, the formation of global markets, the creation of new technologies, the expansion of vast circuits of material and immaterial production, and the movement of gigantic cultural flows. No longer opposed by an extra-systemic 'outside', this new form of sovereignty constituted a regime that effectively encompassed the 'spatial totality' of the entire globe. Wielding enormous biopolitical powers, Empire could neither be reduced to particular nation-states nor to national imperialist projects. Establishing no territorial centers and relying on no fixed boundaries, it managed 'hybrid identities, flexible hierarchies, and plural exchanges through modulating networks of command. The distinct national colors of the imperialist map of the world have merged and blended in the imperial global rainbow'. Although Hardt and Negri placed stronger emphasis on the decline of national sovereignty than Scholte or Castells, they agreed with their colleagues that deterritorialization processes entailed spatial reconfigurations of sovereignty that involved primarily a process of 'up-scaling' from the national to the global.[33]

The proponents of 'weak' versions of deterritorialization relativism acknowledge the significance of global-scale dynamics. Still, they offer a different perspective. As we noted in Chapter 2, Saskia Sassen suggested that globalization involved not only the growth of supraterritoriality but also crucial processes and practices of 'down-scaling' that occur deep inside the local, national, and regional. To properly understand the full extent and impact of 'denationalization', Sassen cautioned, global studies researchers ought to pay careful attention to social processes that are localized in subglobal settings such as the formation of transboundary networks connecting multiple local *and* national processes and actors. Crucially, global economic networks were still relying heavily on localized control and command centers that completed the top-level financial, legal, managerial, and planning tasks necessary for the functioning of global organizations. Local and national spaces continued to play important roles in the

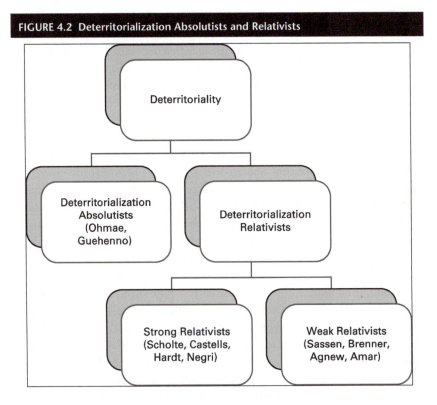

FIGURE 4.2 Deterritorialization Absolutists and Relativists

Deterritoriality

Deterritorialization Absolutists (Ohmae, Guehenno)

Deterritorialization Relativists

Strong Relativists (Scholte, Castells, Hardt, Negri)

Weak Relativists (Sassen, Brenner, Agnew, Amar)

globalization process. But what was still experienced as 'national' or 'local' had begun to shift away from the conventional manifestations of the national and local. As Sassen summarizes, 'An interpretation of the impact of globalization as creating a space economy that extends beyond the regulatory capacity of a single state is only half the story; the other half is that these central functions are disproportionately concentrated in the national territories of the highly developed countries'.[34] In addition to reconfiguring multiple geographic scales, the spatial dynamics of global modernity also require 'systemic expulsions'—socioeconomic and environmental dislocations—that cannot be fully understood in the usual economistic terms of poverty, growing inequality, and financial flows.[35]

The reason why globalization scholars like Sassen and urban studies expert Neil Brenner subscribe to a weak version of relativism is because they link deterritorialization to the *reterritorialization* of socioeconomic and political-institutional spaces occurring at multiple geographical scales.[36] Conceding that nation-states have lost their exclusive hold on sovereignty, weak relativists nonetheless insist that states remain central actors in the unfolding drama of globalization. In particular, states serve as important catalysts of globalization by enabling those major transformations of territorial organization that encourage the further extension and intensification of social relations. Perhaps the most critical of these spatial restructuring processes facilitated by states involves the localization of the 'control and command centers' of global capitalism in global cities. Conveying a deeply spatial understanding of globalization, Sassen's widely discussed 'global cities model' also theorized the spatial scales at which economic and political processes deterritorialize—but neither in absolutist terms as the end of the nation-state nor in strong relativist terms as the growth of supraterritoriality. Rather, she saw global cities as major forces in powerful 'rescaling' processes that entailed the 'glocalization' of conventional geographical scales.

As Sassen explained: 'Today we are seeing a partial unbundling of national space and the traditional hierarchies of scale centered on the national, with the city nested somewhere between the local and the region. This unbundling, even if partial, makes conceptualizing the city as nested in such hierarchies problematic'.[37] Neil Brenner concurred:

> The spatial scales of capitalist production, urbanization, and state regulation are today being radically reorganized, so dramatically that inherited geographical vocabularies for describing the nested hierarchy of scales that interlace world capitalism no longer provide adequate analytical tools for conceptualizing the multilayered, densely

interwoven, and highly contradictory character of contemporary spatial practices.[38]

Moreover, the thesis of the collapse of conventional vertical spatial scales impacts the symbolic production of meanings in new discursive environments. Paul James and Manfred Steger refer to these processes as 'condensation'—the production and engagement of discourses, symbols, ideas, spaces, performances, and images that compress and reconfigure familiar local, national, and regional tropes and scalings while orienting them toward the global imaginary. For example, almost all prominent US politicians are fond of the transnational construct of an 'American Pacific Century', which plays an important role in the semiotic integration of the entire Asia-Pacific region according to the American conceptual and ideological framework of neoliberal globalization. But a critical discourse analysis suggests that this new master narrative condenses a variety of meanings associated with subglobal spatial scales that are at odds with the imperatives of globality. The decoding of such processes of 'condensation'—such as those at work in the discursive production of 'America's Pacific Century'—yields critical insights into the formation of the rising global imaginary.[39]

Finally, new spatial insights into the destabilization of vertical, nested hierarchies of scale also have important consequences for mapping the analytical terrain of global studies. For example, they draw our attention to the increasingly complex, fluid, and multiple forms of association between sovereignty and territory. The idea that sovereignty is indeed neither inherently territorial nor invariably state-based but dispersed among a range of actors operating across overlapping geographical scales and spatial modalities challenges forms of methodological nationalism and methodological territorialism that imagine globalization primarily as the destabilization of homogenous spatial units of territorial states. For example, political geographer John Agnew and global studies scholar Paul Amar argue that an understanding of the spatially complex ways in which sovereignty works under conditions of intensifying globality should inspire global studies scholars to rethink deterritorialization as a productive force encouraging the creation of multiscalar 'sovereignty regimes' or 'security archipelagos'.

What Agnew has in mind are newly emerging systems of rule in which sovereignty 'is the emergent and contingent outcome of a myriad of transactions and governmentalities, only some of which need at any point in time be vested in a single centralized state authority'.[40] Writing in a similar vein, Amar offers perhaps one of the most innovative analyses of

IMAGES 4.1 AND 4.2 'Glocal' Dynamics Reflected in the Cityscapes of Shanghai and Seoul

Source: Tommaso Durante, The Visual Archive Project of the Global Imaginary, www.the-visual-archive-project-of-the-global-imaginary.com/visual-global-imaginary.

Reproduced with permission of Tommaso Durante

globalization's new 'securitization projects' and their multidimensional involvements in the reconfiguration of space. His creative metaphor of a transnational 'security archipelago'—referring to interlinked and highly dynamic 'hotspots' where the security-related activities of a multiplicity of state and non-state actors intersect with each other—brilliantly captures the complexity of the new spatial modalities of securitization in the Global Age.[41]

Thus, rethinking historically contingent categories of spatiality requires the construction of new theories and methodologies that are specifically designed to analyze not only global-scale formations like transnational financial institutions but globalization dynamics that occur often simultaneously on multiple scales. Examples for this multiscalar character of various globalization processes abound. Consider, for example, multiple cross-border networks of social activists engaged in localized struggles with an explicitly global agenda mediated by global information technologies or the global media story of Syrian migrants trying to reach Germany with the help of information gained from both digitally sophisticated devices and locally organized, transnational refugee trafficking networks raking in billions of dollars in the process. Such 'glocal' and 'hybrid' spatio-temporal dynamics highlight the need for academic inquiries into the new scalar politics of the Global Age.

Global History and the Challenge of Periodization

As our discussion of the third pillar of global studies has shown, the field owes much to the efforts of innovative human geographers and urban studies experts to develop new theoretical approaches that help us understand the changing spatial dynamics of our time. But global studies is equally indebted to the intellectual initiatives of sociologists and historians willing to rethink the conceptual frameworks governing the temporal record of human activity. Earlier in this chapter, we discussed the contribution of sociologists like Giddens and Albrow to the modernity/postmodernity debate. We now return to the theme of time by examining the emergence of 'global history' as one of the most promising academic endeavors in the necessary task of rethinking the past in light of current globalization dynamics.

As we indicated at the end of Chapter 2, this relatively new field of historiography focuses on the multibraided thread of globalization running from the past to the present. Thus, it explores why and how human communities have become more and more interconnected. Global history is based on the central premise that processes of globalization require more systemic historical treatments, and, therefore, the study of globalization deserves a more prominent place on the agenda of historical research.[42] Parting with narratives centered on the development of nations or Eurocentric 'world histories', global historians investigate the emergence of our globalized world as the result of exchanges, flows, and interactions involving many different cultures and societies—past and present. In short, they look backwards in time to identify the origins and trace the evolution of contemporary globalization. Recognizing the historical role of powerful drivers of globalization, many global studies scholars have integrated historical schemes in their study of intensifying human interactions across geographical, conceptual, and disciplinary boundaries.

In making their case for this new way of approaching history, global historians are careful to clarify their sometimes rather subtle differences with the related genres of 'universal history', 'world history', and 'big history'. As A. G. Hopkins emphasizes, these distinctions are rooted in the semantic difference between the terms 'universal' and 'global': 'A universal has to be global, but global phenomena are not necessarily universal because interactions among them may not be expressions of commonality'.[43] The impulse to write 'universal' histories can be traced back many centuries to the efforts of the Greek ancient philosopher Herodotus (484–425 BCE); the Hellenistic historian Polybius (200–118 BCE); the Chinese historian Sima Qian (145–90 BCE); the Persian chronicler Al-Tabari (839–923 CE); and the North African thinker Ibn Khaldun (1332–1406 CE), to mention but a few of these early pioneers. Hailing from different cultural backgrounds, they all used documents, testimonies, and artifacts to investigate stories, mythologies, and traditions that cut across what they perceived as 'cultures' or 'civilizations'. Revived in eighteenth-century Europe by Voltaire and other Enlightenment historians, such 'cosmopolitan' perspectives soon lost out to the more fashionable preoccupation with 'national history' that emerged out of early nineteenth-century Romanticism and the nationalistic fervor inspired by the Napoleonic Wars. Dominant for many decades, these nation-centered narratives were eventually challenged by a new generation of twentieth-century 'world historians'. Writing in the highly politicized context of the Cold War, they engaged in comparative investigations of 'world civilizations'—often narrated from a Western perspective that normalized the geopolitical, technological, economic, and cultural hegemony of the 'West' over the rest of the world.[44] Important exceptions to this rather biased approach included prominent world historians like William H. McNeill, J. R. McNeill, Jerry Bentley, Patrick Manning, and Arif Dirlik, who subscribed to a civilizational framework sensitive to the importance of mutual cultural borrowings and multidirectional diffusions. Concentrating their research on 'cross-cultural encounters', they encouraged historical investigations into patterns of social change reaching back much further than the (early) modern era—traditionally dated from the capture of the Americas by European colonizers.[45]

Reacting strongly against the Eurocentric bias inherent in most of the conventional world history approaches, these historians served as the catalysts for the birth of 'global history' as exemplified in the works of Bruce Mazlish, Akira Iriye, Nayan Chanda, Jürgen Osterhammel, A. G. Hopkins, Kenneth Pomeranz, and many others.[46] In addition to examining the historical movement of globalization, they also explore how studying historical events can be done from a global perspective. Global historians are eager to resurrect macrohistory and its associated 'grand narratives'—minus its previous tendencies toward determinism and Eurocentrism. To that end, they seek transdisciplinary collaboration in their exploration of multidimensional 'zones of interaction' that stretch across bounded spatial frameworks of all kinds.[47] Anchored in the comparative method and multicultural perspectives, they often engage their colleagues in the transdisciplinary field of global studies to produce valuable microhistories and mid-range historiographies of globalization. Global historians also interact regularly with the champions of the so-called 'big history' perspective concerned with interconnections and patterns of human and non-human change that stretch far back before the appearance of written documents.[48]

The growing appeal of global history is also reflected in the popularity of trade books written for general readers.[49] Today there exists a veritable cottage industry of accessible publications designed according to the winning formula: *X: A Global History*. 'X' can stand for commodities, activities, and concepts such as salt, cod, tobacco, cheese, chocolate, hot dogs, gold, diamonds, running, soccer, Christianity, Islam, international relations, non-violence, and climate change. And the list goes on.[50] To be sure, there is a strong appeal of global history beyond the walls of academia. After all, a general understanding of the historical trends reflected in the main dimensions of globalization has significant applied value for understanding how our world functions and how it could be made to work better. Hence, global history also holds much interest for professionals and policy makers committed to overcoming global problems and designing sustainable futures for the expanding population of our shrinking planet.

In trying to make sense of the past, historians of all sorts have always employed temporal indicators such as dates and periods to locate the origins of certain phenomena and trace their developments across time. The resulting 'periodization schemes' and 'time lines' give shape and structure to an otherwise incoherent and chaotic past. As Mazlish emphasizes, 'Periodization of any kind is central to the human effort to organize time (whether human or geological)'.[51] Perhaps the most pressing conceptual problem global historians encounter is that of reexamining and updating conventional periodization schemes such as the famous ancient-medieval-modern triptych. Their task is to craft new measures that are more capable of integrating historical phenomena under the overarching umbrella of 'globalization'. In the process of devising these new global periodization schemes, global historians confront two crucial conceptual challenges. The first is related to vertical integration: how to identify coherent patterns in the long sweep of past time. The second involves horizontal integration: how to connect in each era the broad range of human experiences around the world.[52]

But, as we noted in Chapter 2 with regard to Roland Robertson's pioneering periodization of globalization, each periodization scheme devised in response to these challenges must first tackle an even more fundamental question raised by global studies scholars in the last three decades: is globalization an 'old' or 'new' phenomenon?[53] Globalization research in the early 1990s tended to emphasize the novelty of the phenomenon, often dating its origins to the 1960s and 1970s. In recent years, however, the prevailing view on this question has shifted in a direction more weighted toward the longevity of globalization while at the same time recognizing that it has undergone dramatic changes and qualitative leaps at certain points in history. As a result, new periodization efforts have yielded much revised chronologies that tend to eschew conventional Eurocentric linear narratives and instead present globalization as a multinodal, multidirectional spatio-temporal dynamic full of unanticipated surprises, violent twists, sudden punctuations, and dramatic reversals. Let us briefly consider two contrasting periodization schemes devised by leading global historians.

David Northrup has put forward perhaps the most radical, yet incredibly simple, temporal model of global history.[54] He proposes that global history can be divided into just two periods: one dominated by dynamics of 'divergence' and the other by forces of 'convergence'. What Northrup calls the 'Age of Divergence' started nearly 100,000 years ago with early human communities in Africa and their 'diverging' migration from a single spatial origin to the rest of the world. Honing their survival skills by adapting physically and culturally to a multitude of different environments, humans lived in relative isolation from each other. Over millennia, they refined specialized technologies, worked out different belief systems and ways of reasoning, developed myriad languages and systems of writing, and devised distinctive styles of government, art, and architecture. At some point around 1000 CE, however, the gradually 'rising forces of convergence overtook those promoting ever-increasing diversity'. Northrup argues that expanding and universalizing 'forces of convergence' operating in economic, cultural, and political dimensions of increasingly complex societies drew people closer and closer: 'This "Great Convergence," as I shall call it, provides a useful framework for understanding the past thousand years of world history and the phenomena that in recent years have come to be called globalization'.[55]

Note how Northrup's periodization scheme manages to accommodate both temporal *and* spatial dynamics of globalization. Moreover, it responds quite effectively to the dual conceptual challenges of accounting for both vertical and horizontal forms of global integration. On the downside, however, his periodization model suffers from all the problems that come with devising measurement strategies that aim at capturing historical flux in the extreme long term (*la longue durée*). For example, periods encompassing many millennia favor explanations based on dynamics of continuity and gradualism that make it difficult to account for sudden social change as well as the immediate causal factors responsible for it.

By contrast, Bruce Mazlish's periodization scheme focuses on rupture and suddenness. While overcoming the problems of *la longue durée*, it loses the advantages that come with assembling a 'big picture' and a conceptual emphasis on continuity. Although he concedes that globalization is a long-term process that requires global historians to survey relevant developments in past centuries and millennia, Mazlish stresses the uniqueness of the current global era without being embroiled in the 'rather clamorous modern–postmodern debate' we discussed at the outset of this chapter:

> With the notion of global epoch, I am suggesting that we have an alternative way of revising, or renewing, our sense of history. In short the most useful, i.e., illuminating, successor to "modern" history as periodization rubric is, I believe, global or "new global history."' This emphasis on novelty is meant to 'set off the study of present-day globalization from previous manifestations of the process. . . . What matters is the recognition that something important has happened in the last fifty years or so, and as we head into the new millennium, this requires a new openness and a new mindset if we are to understand it well enough to grapple with it effectively.

In other words, Mazlish pushes the notion of a recent historical rupture that not only marks the beginning of a new global era, but also presents 'a profound shift in human consciousness, symbolic recognition and thus self-awareness of what has been taking place in real life'. Thus he affords the highest research priority to the most recent decades in human history characterized by the rise of the global imaginary. Mazlish's short-term periodization scheme introduces within the broader field of global history the innovative transdisciplinary initiative of 'new global history dedicated to the study of the new globalization that has emerged some time in the period after W W II'.[56]

In recent years, the transdisciplinary network linking the work of global historians to concrete research projects in global studies (and vice-versa) has further expanded and intensified. Perhaps the most impressive evidence for the power of these ongoing intellectual cross-fertilizations around shifting conceptions of time and the periodization of globalization can be gleaned in the pages of *Globalizations*, one of the leading academic journals in the field. As Barry Gills, its editor-in-chief, emphasized, the main task of the journal has been to 'attract key scholars who would bring to the table new critical understandings of the historicity of globalization and also its theoretical expansiveness'.[57] In fact, Gills represents the perfect hybrid of a global historian and global studies expert. A founding member of the World Systems Theory Group linked to the International Studies Association, he worked for many years with leading historians like Jerry Bentley and Andre Gunder Frank to illuminate the origins and development of globalization processes across the millennia. In addition to dedicating a special issue to the theme 'Globalization and Global History', *Globalizations* features regular articles examining various aspects of global history.[58]

Concluding Remarks

The variety of topics and themes covered in this chapter demonstrate the significance of the third pillar for global studies. Indeed, our definition of globalization as the extension and intensification of social relations and consciousness across world-space and world-time reflects the centrality of 'time-space compression' in the Global Age. We examined 'world-space' in terms of the historically variable ways that it has been practiced (objectively) and socially understood (subjectively) across changing world-time. Our definition thus recognizes the importance of both objective and subjective relations—practice and consciousness—in the spatio-temporal formation of globality.

In this context, the questions related to 'connectivity'—both in spatial and temporal terms—assume a central role in global studies.[59] But when used abstractly in the pertinent literature, the term 'connectivity' tends to be linked primarily to processes of communication and exchange, especially those related to mediated communication systems and financial exchange systems. This puts the focus of investigation on the delivery processes provided by information and communication technologies. But it only takes a moment to realize that the subjective experience of global connectivity and the feelings associated with it are as important as the 'objective' means of communication and exchange. Today, the subjective experience of 'global connectivity' is so obvious to people that it tends to be eclipsed by the objective structures of technological connection and innovation.

However, as we argued at the outset of this chapter, it was the growing *consciousness* of 'being (objectively) connected' that spawned Marshall McLuhan's 'global village' metaphor. Indeed, both subjective and objective dimensions of globalization must be united to allow for a full comprehension of the globality of space and time. This unity assumed visual form for the first time in human history in the extremely popular pictures of 'Earthrise' taken by Apollo 8 astronauts. Taken in 1968 from the orbit of the moon, these photographs of our half-shadowed planet did much to raise people's awareness of the actual globality of planetary space. But they fell short of presenting the complete, unobstructed view of Earth that is required for a full appreciation of 'space–time compression'.

Apollo 17 astronauts achieved this difficult feat four years later in their magnificent 1972 image of the unshadowed globe floating in the blackness of space. Given the number AS17-148-22727 by NASA, the picture quickly achieved the status of the most widely reproduced photograph in history. To this day, it is the sharpest of only four whole round Earth pictures snapped by a human being. With Earth nearing winter solstice at the time, Apollo's optical lens revealed a brilliantly white South Pole tilting sunward. White clouds over Antarctica were swirling north across the Great Southern Ocean, penetrating as far as to the middle of the magnificent African continent and to the tiniest visible slivers of Australia and South America. The deserts of Arabia and the Horn of Africa take up the top of the earthly sphere and the vista reaches its limits at the barely visible small oval of the Mediterranean basin. This famous 'Blue Marble Shot' reveals to the human eye the full panorama of our terrestrial home in blue-brown-white hues without political boundaries or a privileged Western geographical center. Most importantly, by giving concreteness to McLuhan's 'global village', the photo provided a tremendous boost to the emerging discourse of globalization configured around circulation, connectivity, and communication. As the human geographer Denis Cosgrove points out, 'It is a universalist, progressive, and mobile discourse in which the image of the globe signifies the potential, if not actual, equality of all locations networked across frictionless space'.[60]

The tremendous global impact of the Blue Marble Shot demonstrates that space and time are *ontological* categories, that is, are patterned ways of *being* in the world that are lived and experienced across all levels of consciousness as

IMAGE 4.3 'Blue Marble Shot', Taken from Apollo 17, 1972

Source: NASA, www.nasa.gov/sites/default/files/images/135918main_bm1_high.jpg

the grounding or existential conditions of the social. For example, modern ontologies of linear time, territorial space, and individualized embodiment frame the way in which we walk about the modern city. It is only within a modern sense of time that the ideologies of progress or economic growth can make sense. Historically constituted in the structures of human inter-relations, ontological categories of human existence such as space and time are always talked about, yet rarely interrogated, analyzed, or historically contextualized except by philosophers and social theorists.

Global studies scholars focus primarily on space, since globalization is obviously a spatial process and includes dynamics cutting across all spatial scales. The academic observation that to globalize means to compress time and space and enhance connectivity has long been part of public discourse.

However, to be more historically specific, contemporary globalization is predominantly lived through a modern conception of spatiality linked to an abstracted geometry of compressed territories and sovereignties. Modern space tends to subsume rather than replace traditional cosmological senses of time held together by God or some other generalized Supreme Being. Different spatial formations are interconnected in specific relations of dominance rather than moving in a simple epochal shift from an older form of temporality. Modern spaces overlay older forms with networks of interchange and movement. For example, wireless technologies have bound the virtual and physical worlds together in ways that make geographic space part of cyberspace and vice-versa. Such hybrid 'geographies of cyberspace' sustain new forms of social interaction in which online interactions are not divorced from those offline, but rather are contextualized by them.[61] Consider, for example, the growing role of major social media platforms like Facebook, Twitter, or Instagram that offer personal and instant ways of connecting to others around people's physical, concrete life-worlds of day-to-day existence. This rise of 'new spaces' accords with our transdisciplinary discussion of contemporary globalization as generating multiple forms of complexity across all dimensions of social life.

In this context, it might be useful to recall our discussion of Manuel Castells's point about how globalization facilitates the slide of modern spatialities into 'networked' global formations. But the Spanish sociologist insisted that these spatial dynamics are intrinsically linked to corresponding reconfigurations of time. Hence, he linked his central analytic category of 'space of flows' to that of 'timeless time'.[62] Timeless time breaks with the logic of 'sequence' as the only basis of ordering temporality, which is the hallmark of modern time as the demarcated, linear, and empty time of the calendar and clock. It is the time of change, progress, and development, which connects people and events on a single time-line of history. But this ontological sense that time moves 'forward' one-second-per-second is a modern convention rather than being an intrinsically natural measure. 'Timeless time' is a 'mix of multiple temporalities' in which the mode reorganizing events into instances without meaningful sequence has become dominant. Driven by a seemingly perennial ICT revolution, today's shift toward timeless time becomes a mundane occurrence in digitally mediated activities such as the recording and retrieving of events for later action or the instantaneous electronic purchase in the globalized marketplace. Such global reconfigurations of space and time enable the billions of transactions on Wall Street just as much as they impose a non-regressive discipline on the millions of bidders on eBay, at a local real estate auction, or waiting at a motion-sensitive red traffic light. And yet, both modern and traditional modalities of space and time have become overlaid by the 'space of flows' and 'timeless time' without erasing them. Instantaneity and proximity have become the cutting-edge spatio-temporal modes in the Global Age, but they continue to cohabit our globalizing world with older forms of space and time.

NOTES

1 Marshall McLuhan, *Understanding Media: The Extension of Man*, reprint ed. (Cambridge, MA: MIT Press, 1994 [1964]), p. 3.
2 Barrie Axford, *Theories of Globalization* (Cambridge, UK: Polity Press, 2013), p. 69.
3 Henri Lefebvre, *The Production of Space* (Oxford: Blackwell, 1991), p. 12.
4 Ibid., pp. 335, 422.
5 Robertson, *Globalization*, pp. 6–7; and Roland Robertson, 'The Conceptual Promise of Glocalization: Commonality and Diversity', *Art-e-Fact: Strategies of Resistance* 4 (2005); http://artefact.mi2.hr/_a04/lang_en/theory_robertson_en.htm. Accessed 29 November 2015.
6 Appadurai, *Modernity at Large*, p. 188.
7 Harvey, *The Condition of Postmodernity*, pp. 137, 265, 270–3, 293.
8 Giddens, *The Consequences of Modernity*, pp. 1–3.
9 Jean-François Lyotard, *The Postmodern Condition: A Report on Knowledge* (Minneapolis, MN: The University of Minnesota Press, 1984), p. 3.
10 Giddens, *The Consequences of Modernity*, p. 45.
11 Ibid., p. 20.
12 Ibid., pp. 52–3.
13 Ibid., p. 177.
14 Ibid., p. 64.
15 Ibid., p. 177.
16 See, for example, Jan Nederveen Pieterse, *Globalization and Culture: Global Mélange*, 3rd ed. (Lanham, MD: Rowman & Littlefield, 2015), p. 69.
17 Giddens, *The Consequences of Modernity*, pp. 175–6.
18 See, for example, Shmuel N. Eisenstadt, ed., *Multiple Modernities* (New Brunswick, NJ: Transaction Books, 2002).
19 Pieterse, *Globalization and Culture*, p. 172.
20 Martin Albrow, *The Global Age: State and Society Beyond Modernity* (Stanford: Stanford University Press, 1996), p. 4.
21 Ibid., pp. 99–101.
22 Ibid., pp. 100, 192.
23 Ibid., p. 99.
24 William I. Robinson, *A Theory of Global Capitalism: Production, Class, and State in a Transnational World* (Baltimore, MD: Johns Hopkins University Press, 2004), pp. 14, 142; and Peter Dicken, *Global Shift: Mapping the Changing Contours of the World Economy*, 7th ed. (New York and London: The Guilford Press, 2015), pp. 1–6.
25 John Agnew, *Globalization & Sovereignty* (Lanham, MD: Rowman & Littlefield, 2009), p. 6.
26 See, for example, Manuel Castells, 'The New Public Sphere: Global Civil Society, Communication Networks, and Global Governance', *Annals of the American Academy of Political and Social Science* 616.1 (March 2008), p. 82; and

Ramesh Thakur and Thomas G. Weiss, *Thinking About Global Governance: Why People and Ideas Matter* (London and New York: Routledge, 2011).

27 Lowell Bryan and Diana Farrell, *Market Unbound: Unleashing Global Capitalism* (New York: Wiley, 1996), p. 187.

28 Kenichi Ohmae, *The End of the Nation State: The Rise of Regional Economies* (New York: Free Press, 1995); and *The Borderless World: Power and Strategy in the Interlinked World Economy* (New York: Harper Business, 1990). See also Richard O'Brien, *Global Financial Integration: The End of Geography* (London: Pinter, 1992); Jean-Marie Guéhenno, *The End of the Nation-State* (Minneapolis, MN: University of Minnesota Press, 1995); and Richard Rosecrance, 'The Obsolescence of Territory', *New Perspectives Quarterly* 12.1 (1995), pp. 44–50.

29 Jan Aart Scholte, *Globalization: A Critical Introduction*, 2nd ed. (Houndmills, UK: Palgrave Macmillan, 2005), p. 61.

30 Ibid., pp. 190–1.

31 Castells, 'The New Public Sphere: Global Civil Society, Communication Networks, and Global Governance', p. 88.

32 Scholte, *Globalization*, p. 77.

33 Michael Hardt and Antonio Negri, 'Preface', in *Empire* (Cambridge, MA: Harvard University Press, 2000), pp. xi–xvi.

34 Saskia Sassen, 'The Places and Spaces of the Global: An Expanded Analytic Terrain', in David Held and Anthony McGrew, eds., *Globalization Theory: Approaches and Controversies* (Cambridge, UK: Polity Press, 2007), p. 86; and Saskia Sassen, 'Globalization or Denationalization?', *Review of International Political Economy* 10.1 (2003), p. 3.

35 Saskia Sassen, *Expulsions: Brutality and Complexity in the Global Economy* (Cambridge, MA: Harvard University Press, 2014).

36 Neil Brenner, 'Globalisation as Reterritorialisation: The Re-Scaling of Urban Governance in the European Union', *Urban Studies* 36.3 (1999), p. 432.

37 Sassen, *Territory, Authority, Rights*, p. 345; and Saskia Sassen, *A Sociology of Globalization* (New York: Norton, 2007), p. 102.

38 Brenner, 'Globalisation as Reterritorialisation: The Re-Scaling of Urban Governance in the European Union', p. 447.

39 James and Steger, 'A Genealogy of "Globalization": The Career of a Concept', p. 424.

40 Agnew, *Globalization & Sovereignty*, pp. 9–10.

41 Paul Amar, *The Security Archipelago: Human-Security States, Sexuality Politics, and the End of Neoliberalism* (Durham and London: Duke University Press, 2013).

42 See A. G. Hopkins, 'Globalization—An Agenda for Historians', in A. G. Hopkins, ed., *Globalization in World History* (New York: Norton, 2002), p. 2; and William Gervase Clarence-Smith, Kenneth Pomeranz, and Peer Vries, 'Editorial', *Journal of Global History* 1.1 (2006), p. 1.

43 A. G. Hopkins, 'Introduction: Interactions Between the Universal and Local', in A. G. Hopkins, ed., *Global History: Interactions between the Universal and the Local* (Houndmills, UK: Palgrave Macmillan, 2006), p. 7.

44 See, for example, Arnold Toynbee, *A Study of History*. 12 vols. (Oxford: Oxford University Press, 1934–61).

45 See Jerry H. Bentley, *Old World Encounters: Cross-Cultural Contacts and Exchanges in the Pre-Modern Times* (Oxford: Oxford University Press, 1993); J. R. McNeill and William H. McNeill, *The Human Web: A Bird's-Eye View of World History.* (New York: Norton, 2003); and Patrick Manning, *Navigating World History: Historians Create a Global Past* (Houndmills, UK: Palgrave MacMillan,

2003); and Arif Dirlik, 'Performing the World: Reality and Representation in the Making of World Histor(ies)', *Journal of World History* 16.4 (2005), pp. 391–410.

46 Bruce Mazlish and Akira Iriye, eds., *The Global History Reader* (London and New York: Routledge, 2005); Akira Iriye, *Global and Transnational History: The Past, Present, and Future* (New York: Palgrave, 2012); Nayan Chanda, *How Traders, Preachers, Adventurers and Warriors Shaped Globalization* (New Haven, CT: Yale University Press, 2007); Kenneth Pomeranz, *The Great Divergence: China, Europe, and the Making of the World Economy* (Princeton, NJ: Princeton University Press, 2000); Robbie Robertson, *Three Waves of Globalization* (London: Zed Books, 2003); Jürgen Osterhammel and Niels P. Petersson, trans. Donna Geyer. *Globalization: A Short History* (Princeton, NJ: Princeton University Press, 2005); and Alex MacGillivray, *A Brief History of Globalization: The Untold Story of our Incredibly Shrinking Planet* (New York: Running Press, 2006); Peter N. Stearns, *Globalization in World History* (London and New York: Routledge, 2010); and Dominic Sachsenmaier, *Global Perspectives on Global History: Theories and Approaches in a Connected World* (Cambridge, UK: Cambridge University Press, 2011).

47 Patrick O'Brien, 'Historiographic Traditions and Modern Imperatives for the Restoration of Global History', *Journal of History* 1.1 (2006), pp. 3–39.

48 See, for example, Clarence-Smith, Pomeranz, and Vries, 'Editorial', p. 2. David Christian, *Maps of Time: An Introduction to Big History* (Berkeley, CA: University of California Press, 2004); Cynthia Stokes Brown, *Big History: From the Big Bang to the Present* (New York: Free Press, 2007); and Heikki Patomäki and Manfred B. Steger, 'Social Imaginaries and Big History: Towards a New Planetary Consciousness?', *Futures: A Journal of Policy, Planning, and Future Studies* 42.8 (2010), pp. 1056–63.

49 See, for example, John E. Wills Jr., *1688: A Global History* (New York: W. W. Norton, 2002); and Sven Beckert, *Empire of Cotton: A Global History* (New York: Vintage, 2015).

50 See, for example, Michael F. Suarez and H. R. Woudhuysen, *The Book: A Global History* (Oxford: Oxford University Press, 2014); and Helen Saberi, *Tea: Global History* (London: Reaktion Books, 2010).

51 Bruce Mazlish, *The New Global History* (London and New York: Routledge, 2006), p. 18. See also Mazlish and Iriye, *The Global History Reader*, p. 7.

52 David Northrup, 'Globalization and the Great Convergence: Rethinking World History in the Long Term', *Journal of World History* 16.3 (2005), p. 249.

53 See, for example, William H. McNeill, 'Globalization: Long Term Process or New Era in Human Affairs?', *New Global Studies* 2.1 (2008), pp. 1–9; Alex MacGillivray, *A Brief History of Globalization: The Untold Story of our Incredibly Shrinking Planet* (New York: Running Press, 2006); Jürgen Osterhammel and Niels P. Petersson, *Globalization: A Short History* (Princeton, NJ: Princeton University Press, 2005); and Robbie Robertson, *Three Waves of Globalization* (London: Zed Books, 2003).

54 Northrup, 'Globalization and the Great Convergence: Rethinking World History in the Long Term'; and Pamela Kyle Crossley, *What is Global History* (Cambridge, UK: Polity Press, 2008).

55 Northrup, 'Globalization and the Great Convergence: Rethinking World History in the Long Term', p. 251. For an insightful discussion of 'divergence' and 'convergence' as analytical concepts and narrative strategies that have

defined global studies, see Pamela Kyle Crossley, *What is Global Studies?* (Cambridge, UK: Polity Press, 2008), Chapters 2 and 3.

56 Bruce Mazlish, *The New Global History* (London and New York: Routledge, 2006), pp. 12–13, 18. Staking out a middle ground between Mazlish and Northrup, A. G. Hopkins and his collaborators developed a periodization sequence of globalization based on four stages or categories: (1) archaic globalization (pre-1500s CE.); (2) proto-globalization (1600–1800); (3) modern globalization (1800–1950s); and (4) postcolonial globalization (1950s-present). See Hopkins, *Globalization in World History*, pp. 3–10.

57 Barry Gills, 'Interview', in Manfred Steger and Paul James, eds., *Globalization: The Career of a Concept* (London and New York: Routledge, 2015), p. 141.

58 See, for example, Barry K. Gills and William R. Thompson, eds., *Globalization and Global History* (London and New York, Routledge: 2006); and Andre Gunder Frank and Barry K. Gills, *The World System: Five Hundred Years or Five Thousand?* (London and New York, Routledge, 1994).

59 See Paul James and Manfred B. Steger, 'Globalization and Global Consciousness: Layers of Connectivity' in Roland Robertson and Didem Buhari-Gulmez eds., *Global Culture: Consciousness and Connectivity?* (Aldershot, UK: Ashgate, 2016), pp. 21–39.

60 Denis Cosgrove, *Apollo's Eye: A Geographic Genealogy of the Earth in the Western Imagination* (Baltimore, MD: Johns Hopkins University Press, 2001), p. 263. For the informative story behind NASA image AS17-148-22727, see Al Reinert, 'The Blue Marble Shot: Our First Complete Photograph of Earth', *The Atlantic* (12 April 2011); www.theatlantic.com/technology/archive/2011/04/the-blue-marble-shot-our-first-complete-photograph-of-earth/237167/. Accessed 13 November 2015.

61 See Warwick E. Murray, *Geographies of Globalization* (London and New York: Routledge, 2006), pp. 26–7.

62 Castells, *The Rise of the Network Society,* Vol. 1, pp. xl–xli.

5

THE FOURTH PILLAR OF GLOBAL STUDIES

Critical Thinking

Few global studies scholars would object to our proposition that their field is significantly framed by 'critical thinking'. As we emphasized throughout this book, global studies constitutes an academic space of tension that generates *critical* investigations into our age as one shaped by the intensifying forces of globalization. The young field both embraces and exudes the global imaginary—those largely prereflexive convocations of the social whole within which the very problematic of globalization is continuously produced and contested. But if global studies scholars claim to analyze globalization processes through a *critical* prism, then they need to be prepared to respond to a number of obvious questions regarding the nature of their critical enterprise. How, exactly, is 'critical thinking' linked to global studies? Do globalization scholars favor specific forms of critical thinking? If so, which types have been adopted and for what purposes? Finally, what forms of internal and external criticism have been leveled against the field and how have these objections been dealt with? These four questions provide the guiding conceptual framework for this final chapter of our book. It seeks to provide both a conceptual orientation and the thematic overview indispensable for a full appreciation of the significance of critical thinking in the field. But let us pave the way for our ensuing discussion of this fourth pillar of global studies by first offering a brief reflection on various understandings of critical thinking.

Critical Thinking: Analytical *and* Ethico-Political

The term 'critical' derives from the ancient Greek verb *krinein*, which translates in various ways as 'to judge', 'to discern', 'to separate', and 'to decide'. The compound 'critical thinking', then, signifies a discerning mode of thought capable of judging the quality of a thing or a person by separating its essence from mere attributes. While modern social thinkers have postulated a strong philosophical affinity between 'critical' and 'thinking', the conceptual connection between these terms goes back for millennia. Both Western and Eastern cultural traditions have celebrated the ethical virtues of critical thinking as epitomized in such heroic figures as Plato's beloved teacher Socrates, or Arjuna, the *Bhagavad Gita*'s courageous royal warrior. Indeed, most philosophical traditions do not understand critical thinking solely in analytic terms as a 'value-free' operation of our discerning mind. Socrates, for example, famously called conventional wisdom into question by subjecting the opinions of his fellow Athenian citizens to rational scrutiny. His dialectical mode of analytic thinking was inseparable from his ethico-political concerns with the existing social order in his native Greek city-state. Similarly, just prior to leading his troops into the epic battle at Kurukshetra, Arjuna engaged Krishna, his divine charioteer, in a deeply political dialogue over the nature of his moral duties toward family members and friends fighting in both armies. For both Socrates and Arjuna, critical thinking entailed a normative commitment to social justice along the reflective process of coming to rational decisions about worldly matters.

But these vital ethical dimensions and political implications of rational thought were given short shrift in the 'critical thinking' framework created by leading Anglo-American educators during the second half of the twentieth century. Turning a philosophical ideal into a popular educational catch phrase, these influential pedagogues elevated the program of 'enabling students to think critically' to the universal goal of schooling. A teachable method of self-directed reasoning, such critical thinking expressed itself in cognitive operations like 'seeing both sides of an issue, being open to new evidence that disconfirms your ideas, reasoning dispassionately, demanding that claims be backed by evidence, deducing and inferring conclusions from available facts, solving problems, and so forth'.[1] However, the well-meaning efforts of these pedagogues to enhance the educational effectiveness of their vocation remained largely unconcerned with political and ethical reflexivity, thereby reducing the activity of critical thinking to a mere analytical 'skill'. Indeed, their presentation of critical activity as a form of cognitive dexterity betrayed their rather impoverished social and ethical imagination. After all, confined to its 'neutral' analytic framework, critical thinking connected to the life-world only in rather instrumental ways. For example, it resonated with the exhortations of business leaders who demanded from schools to improve their students' 'critical thinking skills' in the hope of taking material advantage of a 'well-educated workforce'. Other than making more profitable work-related judgments, however, the notion of 'well-educated' in this neoliberal context had no explicit ethico-political connection to the social world. Rather, it referred to economic efficiency, productivity, flexibility, and other instrumental skills highly valued in advanced capitalist societies.

Even those few academic critical thinking experts who were willing to admit that the process of 'looking at an issue from multiple perspectives' never operated in a normative vacuum, were reluctant to spell out what critical thinking meant in concrete social contexts. But their explicit concession that critical thought processes were always intertwined with an object of thought provided at least a small opening for more ethico-political interpretations of the catch phrase.[2] After all, once it was conceded that critical thought needed to relate to an empirical referent—in this case, concrete 'content knowledge' (usually understood as disciplinary knowledge of the world)—then it was possible to point to the crucial link between thinking and its social consequences. Since thought processes cannot be

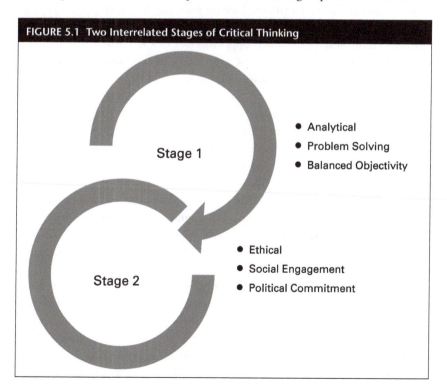

FIGURE 5.1 Two Interrelated Stages of Critical Thinking

Stage 1
- Analytical
- Problem Solving
- Balanced Objectivity

Stage 2
- Ethical
- Social Engagement
- Political Commitment

isolated from the entire spectrum of the human experience, we ought to think of critical thinking encompassing the two interconnected dimensions of the analytical and the ethical. This conclusion brings us back to the holistic insights expressed by the ancient philosophers: critical thinking inevitably contains a socio-political imperative. It was not enough to engage things merely in terms of how they are but also how they might be and should be. And to be mindful of the social dimensions of thinking also meant to be aware of the connection between contemplation and action, between analytical and ethical critical thinking.

Critical Theory: Old and New

This emphasis on the crucial link between theory and practice has served as common ground for various socially engaged currents of critical thinking that have openly associated themselves with 'critical theory'. Originally used in the singular and upper case, 'Critical Theory' was closely associated with mid-twentieth-century articulations of 'Western Marxism' as developed by Max Horkheimer, Theodor Adorno, Herbert Marcuse, Walter Benjamin, and other prominent members of the famous Institute for Social Research in Frankfurt, Germany. Fleeing political and racial persecution in Hitler's Germany, many of these first-generation 'Frankfurt School' social thinkers found new professional opportunities in the United States in the 1930s. While rejecting the Marxist orthodoxy of economic determinism, they retained a social democratic understanding of the emancipatory role of 'critique' in the class struggle for social justice and against new forms of alienation, commodification, and conformity generated in advanced capitalist societies. Analyzing modern 'mass society' by giving the spheres of political economy and culture equal consideration, Critical Theory was as much a constructive enterprise committed to progressive social activism, as it was a descriptive denunciation of the persistence of asymmetrical power relations in society. Frankfurt School scholar Stephen Eric Bronner aptly summarizes the self-understanding of this influential intellectual tradition: 'Critical Theory insists that thought must respond to the new problems and the new possibilities for liberation that arise from changing historical circumstances'.[3]

In recent decades, the Critical Theory tradition carried forward by three successive generations of Frankfurt School thinkers has been subsumed under the pluralized framework of 'critical theories'—in the plural and in lower case. In his recent efforts to offer a global cartography of these contemporary critical theories, the French social thinker Razmig Keucheyan argues that they represent the contemporary inheritors of Western Marxism.[4]

At the same time, however, critical theories have multiplied and now stretch across an extremely wide intellectual terrain. Covering conventional class-based perspectives, they also include more contemporary identity-centered enunciations of social critique ranging from feminist theory and queer theory to psychoanalytic theory, from poststructuralism and postcolonialism to indigenous thought, and from literary criticism and critical legal studies to critical race theory. In spite of their tremendous methodological diversity and philosophical eclecticism, today's critical theorists take as their common point of departure the historical specificity of existing social arrangements. They also share a vital concern with analyzing the causes of current forms of domination, exploitation, and injustice. Committed to the integration of theory and practice, critical theorists offer explicit and comprehensive challenges to what they consider to be unjust social arrangements. In short, their critical acts of problematizing dominant social orders always contain a political dimension.

How, then, are these new forms of critical theory linked to global studies? As we discussed previously, dominant neoliberal modes of globalization

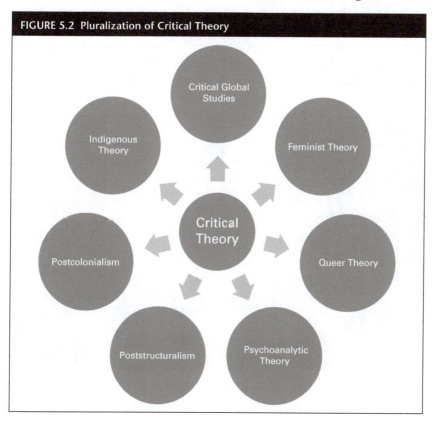

FIGURE 5.2 Pluralization of Critical Theory

have produced growing disparities in wealth and wellbeing within and among societies. They have also led to an acceleration of ecological degradation, new forms of militarism and digitalized surveillance, previously unthinkable levels of inequality, and a chilling advance of consumerism and cultural commodification. As we briefly touched upon in Chapter 2, the negative consequences of such a corporate-led 'globalization-from-above' became subject to democratic contestation in the 1990s and impacted the evolution of critical theory in at least two major ways. First, they created fertile conditions for the emergence of powerful social movements advocating a people-led 'globalization-from-below'. These transnational activist networks, in turn, served as catalysts for the proliferation of 'new' critical theories developing within the novel framework of globalization.

As we discuss in more detail below, many of these new critical theorists were inspired by local forms of social resistance to neoliberalism such as the 1994 Zapatista uprising in Chiapas, Mexico, the 1995 strikes in France and other parts of Europe, and the powerful series of protests in major cities around the world following in the wake of the iconic 1999 anti-WTO demonstration in Seattle. Critical intellectuals interacted with the participants of these alter-globalization movements at these large-scale protest events or at the massive meetings of the newly founded World Social Forum in the 2000s. They developed and advanced their critiques of market globalism in tandem with constructive visions for alternative global futures.

IMAGE 5.1 Anti-WTO Protests in Seattle, 1999

Source: Eric Draper/Associated Press, AP Photo ID 99113001850

As a Zapatista manifesto puts it, 'If this world does not have a place for us, then another world must be made. . . . What is missing is yet to come'.[5]

The second impact of corporate-led 'globalization-from-above' on the evolution of critical theory is closely related to the first. Since the struggles over the meanings and manifestations of globalization occurred in interlinked local settings around the world, they signified a significant alteration in the geography of critical thinking. Keucheyan has emphasized that the academic center of gravity of these new forms of critical thinking was shifting from the traditional centers of learning located in 'old Europe' to the top universities of the New World.[6] The United States, in particular, served as a powerful economic magnet for job-seeking academics from around the globe while also posing as the obvious hegemonic target of their criticisms. Indeed, during the last quarter century, America has managed to attract a large number of talented postcolonial critical theorists to its highly reputed and well-paying universities and colleges. A significant number of these politically progressive recruits, in turn, promptly put their newly acquired positions of academic privilege into the service of their socially engaged ideologies, which resulted in a vastly more effective production and worldwide dissemination of their critical publications. Moreover, the global struggle against neoliberalism heating up in the 1990s and 2000s also contributed significantly to the heightened international exposure of cutting-edge critical theorists located in the vast 'postcolonial' terrains of Asia, Latin America, and Africa. In particular, the permanent digital communication revolution centered on the World Wide Web and the new social media made it easier for these voices of the global South to be heard in the dominant North. In fact, as Keucheyan points out, the 'globalization of critical thinking' culminated in the formation of a 'world republic of critical theories'.[7] Although this worldwide community of critical thinkers is far from homogenous in their perspectives and continues to be subjected to considerable geographic and social inequalities, it has had a profound influence on the evolution of global studies.

Still, we need to be careful not to exaggerate the extent to which such 'critical theories' pervade the field. Our discussion of the developing links between the post-1989 'new wave' of critical theories and critical globalization studies should not seduce us into assuming that *all* global studies scholars support radical or even moderate socially engaged perspectives on what constitutes their field and what it should accomplish. After all, global thinking is not inherently 'critical' in our second, socially engaged, use of the term. An informal perusal of influential globalization literature produced during the last fifteen years suggests that nearly all authors express some appreciation for 'critical thinking' understood in our first sense as a cognitive ability to 'see multiple sides of an issue' (in this case, the issue is 'globalization'). But only about two-thirds of well-published globalization scholars take their understanding of 'critical' beyond the social-scientific ideal of 'balanced objectivity' and 'value-free research' and thus challenge in writing the dominant social arrangements of our time and/or promote emancipatory social change.[8] This locates the remaining one third of globalization authors within a conceptual framework that transnational sociologist William Robinson has provocatively characterized as 'noncritical globalization studies'.[9] Obviously, global studies scholars relegated to this category would object to Robinson's classification on the basis of their differing understanding of what 'critical thinking' entails.

The Basics of Critical Global Studies and the Responsibility of Intellectuals

By the early 2000s, a growing number of globalization scholars were willing to adopt a socially engaged approach to their subject that became variously known as 'critical globalization studies', 'critical global studies', and 'critical theories of globalization'.[10] Most globalization researchers used the related terms 'global studies' and 'globalization studies' loosely, interchangeably, and without much system-building ambition in the pursuit of their transdisciplinary globalization projects. In fact, the empirical referent of both 'global studies' and 'globalization studies' is the same global network of scholars dedicated to the transdisciplinary study of globalization. Richard Appelbaum and William Robinson, two UCSB-affiliated global studies faculty and highly influential proponents of critical approaches to the study of globalization, called on like-minded scholars from around the world to produce the kind of research that could easily be identified as exercising 'a preferential option for the subordinate majority of emergent global society'. Their comprehensive overview of the collective project of 'critical global studies' (CGS) first appeared in 2005 in their substantive editorial introduction to their *Critical Globalization Studies* anthology. Including the contributions of nearly forty globalization scholars from around the world, the volume was based on an understanding of critical thinking that linked analytical operations of the mind to concrete ethico-political applications in the globalizing world of the twenty-first century.

Regarding matters of conceptual analysis, Appelbaum and Robinson emphasized that CGS should be broad enough to house a diversity of methods and epistemologies. Yet, they were equally clear in their conviction that operating within the conceptual framework of globalization committed global studies scholars to putting forward a cogent critique of the social dynamics and impacts of global capitalism. In their view, asymmetrical power relations derived from the capital-labor relation still represented the central logic responsible for the systemic reproduction of unjust social structures worldwide. At the same time, however, they argued that capitalism was undergoing tremendous change. The current phase of globalization presented an 'epochal shift' from the 'nation-state phase of world capitalism' to the 'transnational phase of global capitalism' characterized by the globalization of the production of goods and services and the forging of so-called 'flexible' capital-labor relations. Moreover, global capitalism generated novel organizational forms such as decentralized management techniques, subcontracting and outsourcing, and transnational business alliances. Hence, a proper understanding of emergent global society required sophisticated forms of political economy analyses capable of explaining the emergence of new transnational structures—most importantly the social formation of a 'transnational capitalist class' and its political expression, the 'transnational state'.[11]

Yet, Appelbaum and Robinson rejected the orthodox Marxist emphasis on the economic mode of production as the determining factor of various forms of culture, ideology, law, and other aspects located in the 'ideological superstructure'. Instead, they adopted a 'dialectical' form of critical thinking as developed by Antonio Gramsci. The Italian interwar socialist philosopher had rejected the separation of political economy analysis from cultural investigations as a false dualism that obscures rather than elucidates the complex reality of society. His dialectical approach suggested that the different dimensions of social reality did not possess an independent status but were internally related and thus the mutually constitutive factors of the larger social 'totality'. For Gramsci, it was the role of 'organic intellectuals' to utilize their critical analysis of capitalist society on behalf of the oppressed and exploited against hegemonic power blocs. In particular, their task was to produce a new culture and diffuse a new, more just, conception of the world.[12] Following the Italian philosopher's suggestion, Robinson's analysis of the role of culture in the global capitalist system focused, therefore, on consumerism, individualism, and competition as structurally interdependent processes linking economic and cultural globalization.[13]

Similarly, fellow neo-Gramscian global studies scholar Leslie Sklair employed a judicial mix of conceptual argument and empirical analysis to explore the formation of the transnational capitalist class. His 'global system theory' suggested that the new transnational practices of global capitalism operated simultaneously in three interrelated spheres: the economic, the political, and cultural-ideological. Concentrated in transnational corporations, the transnational capitalist class was assuming ever more control of the processes of globalization. Following his philosophical mentor, Sklair insisted that the forces driving the globalization of capitalism could not be properly appreciated within the narrow parameters of a political economy analysis. A holistic 'Gramscian' understanding of the reproduction of the economic system required, therefore, a close examination of the 'profit-driven culture-ideology of consumerism'. Sklair concluded that, at that moment, no social movement appeared even remotely capable of disrupting the relatively smooth running of global capitalism. Still, he concurred with Appelbaum and Robinson's thesis of the special responsibility of critical intellectuals to challenge the culture-ideology of consumerism produced and disseminated by the hegemonic transnational capitalist class.[14]

Perhaps the most lucid contribution to the subject of intellectual responsibility in the Global Age flowed from the pen of the celebrated French sociologist Pierre Bourdieu who had become intensely involved with the global justice movement in the last years before his untimely death in 2002. Titled 'For a Scholarship with Commitment', his televised 1999 keynote address for the Modern Language Association Meeting in Chicago, invoked French novelist Émile Zola's role as an engaged 'public intellectual' during the infamous Dreyfus Affair in late nineteenth-century France. Like Zola, who accused his government of hiding its anti-Semitic bias behind the veil of 'patriotism' and 'judicial objectivity', Bourdieu argued that today's intellectuals 'must engage in a permanent critique of all the abuses of power or authority committed in the name of intellectual authority'. For Bourdieu, such critical thinking was especially important in a globalizing world where 'scholars have a decisive role to play in the struggle against the new neoliberal doxa [opinion] and the purely formal cosmopolitanism of those obsessed with words such as "globalization" and "global competitiveness"'. Accepting their ethical responsibility meant that academics had to breach the 'sacred boundary' inscribed in their minds that separated scholarship from social commitment. As Bourdieu emphasizes, 'Today's researchers must innovate an improbable but indispensable combination: *scholarship with commitment*, that is, a collective politics of intervention in the political field that follows, as much as possible, the rules that govern the scientific field'. It is important to note that Bourdieu's willingness to follow, as much as possible, the scientific logic of 'objectivity' of science showed a proper respect for the analytical dimension of critical thinking. However, Bourdieu was equally clear that academics ought not remain in such politically neutral territory, but had to be prepared to take the second step in critical thinking: the acceptance of their ethico-political obligation as 'public intellectuals' to contest all forms of domination and exploitation by the powerful. Ultimately, Bourdieu likened scholarly intervention in the social world on behalf of the powerless to an indispensable act of giving symbolic force to critical ideas and analyses.[15]

Whether applied by Bourdieu's 'public intellectuals' or Gramsci's 'organic intellectuals', the dialectical method at the heart of critical global studies serves to connect rational analysis with social commitment. As Appelbaum and Robinson emphasize, the ultimate goal of this process is 'self-knowledge of global society through active theorizing and political work'.[16] Elaborating on their critical epistemological issues, James Mittelman offered an important contribution to the methodological framework of CGS. Responding to the related questions, 'what do critical globalization scholars really want to find out?' and 'what is their desired knowledge?', the prominent globalization theorist set out to identify commonalities among the proliferating critical knowledge sets produced by the 'counterhegemonic historical bloc' of globalization scholars from around the world. Mittelman's careful investigation of pertinent CGS literature yielded what he called a 'coherent complex of critical knowledge' consisting of the following five interacting components.[17]

Reflexivity, the first element of CGS, connotes an awareness of the relationship between knowledge and specific material and political conditions. Mittelman insists that to be reflexive means to probe the historical context and power interests embedded in various globalization perspectives. This critical emphasis on often-conflicting historical perspectives also relates to Mittelman's second component—historicism—which incorporates the time dimension in global studies. As we discussed in the previous chapter, rigorous historical thinking has the potential to correct abstract views portraying specific forms of globalization—such as the global integration of markets—as the inevitable outcome of a benign capitalist process. Mittelman refers to the third component of CGS as 'decentering', which involved the production of myriad perspectives and forms of knowledge of globalization from both its epicenters and the margins. Such a 'decentered lens' provides the necessary peripheral vision that enabled critics to see globalization from multiple angles and spatial locations—especially from the point of view of the marginalized regions of the global South. Mittelman characterizes transdisciplinarity, the fourth element of CGS, as the ability to forge 'crossovers' between the social sciences and complementary branches of knowledge. Key to a critical understanding of globalization, crossovers encourage scholars to break through disciplinary barriers in their holistic pursuit of real-world problems. Strategic transformations, the final component of Mittelman's version of critical global studies, involve a willingness to present ongoing challenges to the hegemonic power interests of the incipient global

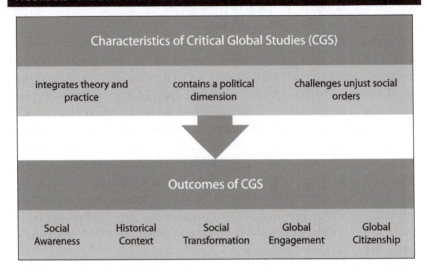

FIGURE 5.3   Characteristics and Outcomes of Critical Global Studies

society. For Mittelman, the organic intellectuals behind these strategic maneuvers develop emancipatory visions that have practical purposes for the formation of more democratic forms of globalization. As he emphasizes, 'The goal is to inculcate a new moral order in lieu of the dominant ethos—currently an ethos of efficiency, competition, individualism, and consumption inscribed in neoliberalism'.[18]

Echoing the overlapping social concerns of Gramsci and Bourdieu, Mittelman's 'complex of critical knowledge' can be seen as a research agenda for public intellectuals committed to generating a 'new common sense' about the negative consequences of neoliberal globalization. By linking their object of analysis to the production of a socially empowering pedagogy, such engaged academics would feed the 'creative mills of critical globalization studies' that would produce alternative knowledge and powerful visions of an egalitarian global future. Bourdieu calls them 'realistic utopias' and Mittelman refers to them in a similar manner as 'grounded utopias'. Most importantly, Mittelman's relentless emphasis on the importance of producing critical epistemologies reminds socially engaged researchers not to underestimate the significance of studying the subjective dimensions of globalization: scrutinizing the language used to frame globalizing processes, revealing the institutions in which knowledge and ideology are created, locating an analysis within definite cultural contexts, listening to different voices, and engaging in embodied and lived experiences in concrete social contexts.[19]

Critical Global Studies and Global Activist Thinking

Having dealt sufficiently with the first guiding question posed at the outset of this chapter—'How, exactly, is critical thinking linked to global studies?'—let us now tackle questions number two and three: 'Do globalization scholars favor specific forms of critical thinking?' and, 'If so, which types have been adopted and for what purposes?' Given the obvious spatial limitations of this chapter, we confine our discussion to what we call 'global activist thinking'—the dominant form of critical thinking utilized by influential CGS public intellectuals. While this 'activist' style of criticism engages a large number of themes associated with the main domains of globalization, this section concentrates on just a few significant issues: the connection between 'global civil society' and 'global citizenship', the tremendous impact of the global justice movement on the evolution of CGS, and growing critique of unsustainable ecological practices linked to neoliberal globalization-from-above.

As the previous section has made clear, the dialectical approach embraced by critical global studies scholars like Appelbaum, Robinson, Sklair, and Mittelman allows for an analysis of the 'totality' of emergent global society. It makes possible not only an investigation of crucial cultural dynamics within the related framework of global capitalism, but also sheds light on the connection of theoretical reflection with practical issues of social justice. As Appelbaum and Robinson observe, such forms of reflexivity inspire a style of critical global thinking that is 'deeply informed by our political activism'. Explicitly committed to 'building bridges between this field and the global justice movement', they emphasize their moral obligation 'as scholars to place an understanding of the multifaceted processes of globalization in the service of those individuals and organizations that are dedicated to fighting its harsh edges'. Indeed, one of the most important achievements of their *Critical Globalization Studies* anthology consists in the skill of its contributors to provide their critical assessment of contemporary globalization dynamics in a language accessible to both socially engaged scholars and non-academic movement activists. The editors describe the style of critical thinking that informs their understanding of CGS in the following way:

> We believe that the dual objectives of understanding globalization and engaging in global social activism can best be expressed in the idea of a critical globalization studies. We believe as scholars it is incumbent upon us to explore the relevance of academic research to the burning political issues and social struggles of our epoch, and to the many

conflicts, hardships, and hopes bound up with globalization, more directly stated, we are not indifferent observers studying globalization as a sort of detached academic exercise. Rather, we are passionately concerned with the adverse impact of globalization on billions of people as well as on our increasingly stressed planetary ecology.[20]

This 'dual objective' of CGS to produce globalization theory that is useful to emancipatory global social movements animates 'global activist thinking'. Articulated by dozens of scholar-activists hailing from different disciplines, this style of critical thinking also addresses the important spatial concerns of connecting local or national grievances to the larger normative ideals located at the global scale such as 'global justice', 'global equality', and 'solidarity with the global South'. Indeed, most of the globalization scholars engaged in global activist thinking could be characterized as 'rooted cosmopolitans' who remain embedded in their local environments while at the same time cultivating a global consciousness as a result of their vastly enhanced contacts to like-minded academics and social organizations across national borders. Their social activism co-evolved with an emergent 'global civil society'—a space of uncoerced human association that was no longer confined to the borders of the territorial state. The British social scientist Mary Kaldor, one of the earliest analysts of the globalization of civil society, demonstrated in her work how this worldwide network of social activists advocating 'globalization-from-below' was also linked to anti-war movements and other NGOs concerned with minimizing violence in social relations.[21] Kaldor's research convinced many public intellectuals that the building of an egalitarian global civil society was not just about the struggle to rectify economic inequities created by global capitalism, but also about building world peace and finding innovative, transnational forms of conflict resolution. As it turned out, Kaldor's thematic focus on creating global alternatives to war became especially important in a post-9/11 world plagued by new manifestations of 'global insecurity' such as the prolonged 'Global War on Terror', intrusive systems of digital surveillance, and proliferating strategies of 'cyber-warfare'.

Stimulated by the vitality of emergent global civil society, CGS scholar-activists thought of new ways of making their intellectual activities in the 'ivory tower' relevant to the happenings in the global public sphere. These novel permutations of global activist thinking manifested themselves in two interconnected projects. The first involved the linking of critical educational activities directed to the cultivation of what was increasingly referred to as 'global citizenship'. Absorbing these new civic values, the second project sought to produce emancipatory knowledge that could be used directly in the ongoing struggle of the global justice movement against the dominant forces of globalization-from-above. To illustrate these two variations on the theme of global critical thinking, let us engage the relevant ideas of some CGS scholar-activists.

Educating for Global Citizenship

Based at Yonsei University in Seoul, South Korea, Hans Schattle has emerged as one of the principal authorities on 'global citizenship'. As he has pointed out, the term is linked to the classical cosmopolitan traditions of ancient Greece and Rome that regarded each human as worthy of equal respect and concern, regardless of the legal and political boundaries of any government jurisdictions.[22] But it was not until the latest wave of globalization starting in the 1990s that the term leapt into the modern public discourse. In the twenty-first century, 'global citizenship' has been embraced by educational institutions, transnational corporations, advocacy groups, community service organizations, and even some national governments. Although the phrase means different things to different social groups, it has increasingly been associated with educational initiatives seeking to inspire young people to grow into morally responsible, intellectually competent, and culturally perceptive global citizens. For example, in September 2012, UN Secretary General Ban Ki-moon released his educational initiative 'Global Education First', which aimed to make a major contribution to the global movement for education. The thirty-two-page initiative features as its 'Priority Area 3' the objective to 'foster global citizenship'. Noting that the interconnected global challenges of the twenty-first century call for far-reaching changes in how people think and act for the dignity of their fellow human beings, the document describes the crucial relationship between global education and global citizenship in the following way:

> Education must be transformative and bring shared values to life. It must cultivate an active care for the world and for those with whom we share it . . . . Education must fully assume its central role in helping people to forge more just, peaceful, tolerant and inclusive societies. . . . We now face the much greater challenge of raising global citizens. Promoting respect and responsibility across cultures, countries and regions has not been at the centre of education. Global citizenship is just taking root and changing traditional ways of doing things always brings about resistance.[23]

As Schattle notes, the promotion of global citizenship in the educational arena involves a number of elements: the cultivation of thinking beyond

IMAGE 5.2 Global Citizenship Poster at RMIT University, 2015

Source: Tommaso Durante, The Visual Archive Project of the Global Imaginary at: www.the-visual-archive-project-of-the-global-imaginary.com/visual-global-imaginary/

Reproduced with permission of Tommaso Durante

one's imagined physical boundaries toward a global consciousness of planetary interdependence, a sense of one's global responsibility and shared moral obligations across humankind, and the strengthening of democratic ideals of democratic empowerment and participation.[24] Recently, the Seoul-based global studies scholar has taken his analysis a step further by suggesting that the process of globalization and the 'global' form of citizenship can be viewed as compatible, interactive categories. If so, then the study of globalization itself represents an educational path to global citizenship that calls for a 'critical way of thinking and living within new geographical, intellectual, and moral horizons'.[25]

Echoing some points of Schattle's typology, educational psychologists Duarte Morais and Anthony C. Ogden present global citizenship as a multi-dimensional construct consisting of three factors: (1) *Social responsibility* understood as students' perception of global interdependence and a social concern for other individuals, societies as a whole, and the environment; (2) *Global competence* defined as students' openness to cultural difference, an interest in world issues, and an awareness of their own cultural biases and

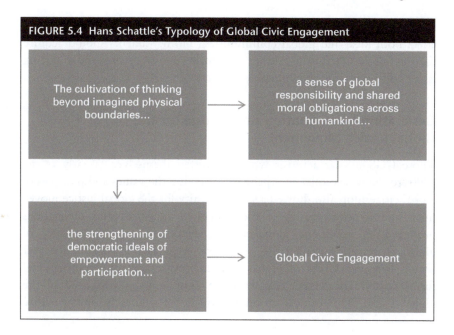

FIGURE 5.4 Hans Schattle's Typology of Global Civic Engagement

limitations, which strengthens a commitment to multiculturalism; and (3) *Global civic engagement* expressed in students' understanding of local, national, and global issues and their involvement in social volunteerism, political activism, and community service.[26]

Global studies pioneer Mark Juergensmeyer adds another element by linking 'global citizenship' to specific educational efforts to create 'global literacy'—the ability of students to see themselves as active 'citizens of the world', capable of critical examinations of specific aspects of diverse cultures and economic practices as well as influential global trends and patterns.[27] This emphasis on the critical interpretation of globalizing dynamics dovetails with innovative projects like the Global Learning Value Rubric, an educational matrix developed by teams of faculty experts representing colleges and universities across the United States. Commissioned by the Association of American Colleges and Universities, this performance assessment tool defines 'global learning' as the 'critical analysis of and an engagement with complex, interdependent global systems and legacies (such as natural, physical, social, cultural, economic, and political) and their implications for people's lives and the earth's sustainability'. Constituting a serious attempt to link the analytical and ethico-political dimensions of critical thinking, this educational framework lists three desired global learning outcomes. First, students should become informed, open-minded, and responsible people who are attentive to diversity across the spectrum of differences. Second, they should be able to understand how their actions affect both local and global communities. Third, students should acquire the interest and facility to address the world's most pressing and enduring issues collaboratively and equitably.[28]

Generating Emancipatory Knowledge for the Global Justice Movement

Those CGS scholar-activists who committed themselves as early as the 1990s to the educational enterprise of advancing the values and practices of global citizenship also showed a strong affinity for the global justice movement and its contestation of the enormous injustices and inequalities produced by neoliberal globalization. Hence, their understanding of global citizenship entailed the search for emancipatory knowledge that would help the forces of global civil society to generate transnational forms of solidarity, especially with the poor and disadvantaged in the global South. This critical grounding of global studies in emancipatory

IMAGE 5.3 'Occupy Wall Street' Camp in Washington, DC, 2012

Source: Tommaso Durante, The Visual Archive Project of the Global Imaginary at: www.the-visual-archive-project-of-the-global-imaginary.com/visual-global-imaginary/

Reproduced with permission of Tommaso Durante

practice connects the educational mission of public intellectuals to more explicit efforts to generate emancipatory knowledge in support of the struggles of the global justice movement (GJM)—and, more recently, the global Occupy Movement.[29] A large number of these social movement-oriented scholar-activists have acknowledged the galvanizing impact of the 'Zapatistas' in the mid-1990s on the evolution of their global activist thinking.

On January 1, 1994, the day the North American Free Trade Agreement (NAFTA) took effect, a relatively small group of guerillas calling themselves the Zapatista Army of National Liberation launched an uprising in their native province of Chiapas in Southern Mexico. Drawing on an eclectic set of beliefs and values linked to Ché Guevara, Emiliano Zapata, indigenous Mayan culture, and Catholic Liberation Theology, the Zapatistas had stitched together an interpretive framework that presented their rebellion as an act of popular resistance against their government's neoliberal free-trade policies. Engaging in effective global framing, their leader Subcomandante Marcos announced to the world that the local struggle in Chiapas was of global significance: '[W]e will make a collective network of all our particular struggles and resistances: an intercontinental network of resistance against neoliberalism, an intercontinental network of resistance for humanity'.[30] Keeping their promise, the Zapatistas ultimately proved to be immensely successful in transmitting their message to other progressive civil society networks around the world. Their efforts led to the organization of the First Intercontinental Gathering for Humanity and Against Neoliberalism, held in 1996 in in the jungles of Chiapas. Attended by more than four thousand participants from nearly thirty countries, the conference set into motion further globalization-from-below initiatives that sensitized scores of scholars and activists to the suffering of poor peasants in the global South caused by market-globalist policies such as the IMF's lending practices of requiring developing countries to implement neoliberal 'structural adjustment programs'. Ultimately, the creation of the global 'Zapatista solidarity network' exerted a profound influence on the founding and evolution of the World Social Forum (WSF).

The WSF was established in 2001 as an alternative progressive forum to the market-globalist World Economic Forum (WEF) in Davos, Switzerland. Designed as an 'open meeting place', the WSF encouraged and facilitated a free exchange of ideas among scholars and activists dedicated to challenging the neoliberal framework of globalization-from-above. In particular, the WSF sought to accomplish two fundamental tasks. The first was ideological, reflected in concerted efforts to undermine the premises of the reigning market-globalist worldview. WSF member organizations constructed and

IMAGE 5.4 Zapatista Gathering in Chiapas, Mexico, 1994

Source: Marco Ugarte/Associated Press, AP Photo ID 9410150172

disseminated alternative articulations of the global imaginary based on the core principles of the WSF: equality, global social justice, diversity, democracy, non-violence, solidarity, ecological sustainability, and planetary citizenship. The second task was political, manifested in the attempt to realize these principles by means of mass mobilizations and non-violent direct action aimed at transforming the core structures of market globalism: international economic institutions like the WTO and the IMF, transnational corporations and affiliated NGOs, and large industry federations and lobbies.[31]

To illustrate what GJM-connected global activist thinking means, let us briefly consider the critical perspectives of Susan George and Naomi Klein, two leading public intellectuals connected to the WSF and frequent lecturers at universities around the world. An American-born political activist living in France with deep roots in the anti-Vietnam War movement, George has been a prolific writer on global social justice. An active participant in most alter-globalization demonstrations in the 1990s and 2000s, she has produced a steady stream of essays critical of what she calls 'corporate-led globalization'. She has held key offices in prominent transnational justice networks and her widely read articles and books have earned her the reputation as one of the premier 'idea persons' of the GJM. In the 2000s, George presented the main principles, values, and demands of the global justice movement in exceptionally clear and condensed language in a monograph, which employed in its title the official slogan of the WSF: *Another World Is Possible If. . . .*[32]

At the core of George's extensive critique of market globalism lies her unshakable conviction that the liberalization and global integration of markets has led to greater social inequalities, environmental destruction, the escalation of global conflicts and violence, the weakening of participatory forms of democracy, the proliferation of self-interest and consumerism, and the further marginalization of the powerless around the world. In order to contest more effectively the powerful worldview behind the creation of these social pathologies, she emphasizes the significance of the ongoing ideological struggle over the meaning and direction of globalization. Yet, she insists that the aim of uncovering the 'real meaning' of the world's increasing connectivity can only occur *indirectly* by means of exposing the underlying economic dynamics of global capitalism. Hence, she uses 'globalization' as a signifier that contains both a negative and positive meaning. The former becomes visible in the distorted market-globalist articulation of the global imaginary. George's insistence on putting the qualifiers 'finance-driven' or 'corporate-led' in front of the term 'globalization' represents, therefore, an act of discursive resistance to the dominant neoliberal narrative. The positive meaning of globalization highlights the possibility of an undistorted translation of the global imaginary as 'people-led globalization' that serves the interest of all humanity, not just a powerful few.

Although George reaffirms the GJM's commitment to 'fight capitalism', she rejects Marxism's radical anti-market rhetoric: 'The issue as I see it is not to abolish markets. . . . Trying to ban markets would rather be like banning rain. One can, however, enforce strict limitations on what is and is not governed by market rules and make sure that everyone can participate in exchange'. Indeed, George shows no hesitation to dispense with Marxism's traditional agent of social change—'the international working class'—as 'more wishful thinking than reality'. The revolutionary expectation of the inevitable collapse of capitalism strikes her as a 'global accident' unlikely to occur. Even if such a doomsday scenario were to occur, it should not be cheerfully welcomed for it would entail 'massive unemployment, wiped-out savings, pensions and insurance; societal breakdown, looting, crime, misery, scapegoating and repression, most certainly followed by fascism, or at the very least, military takeovers'. George connects her rejection of orthodox Marxist thinking with a criticism of both the Soviet-style systems of state-socialism and the naïve political schemes of the New Left in the 1960s. While acknowledging their far-reaching cultural and social influence, she reminds readers that the political and ideational foundation of the New Left was not strong enough to withstand the 'neoliberal onslaught of the Reagan-Thatcher years'.[33]

George contributed the lead chapter to Appelbaum and Robinson's *Critical Globalization Studies* anthology affirming the 'positive role of academia and intellectuals' in the GJM. At the same time, she makes clear that the movement has no anointed 'leaders' or a 'cadre' empowered to give binding marching orders to the masses or prescribe rigid ideological injunctions. The GJM's decentralized nature means that the impact of social activism on theory formation is just as significant for affiliated public intellectuals as the more conventional dynamics of theory guiding practice—in this case the generation of conceptual blueprints that might help the GJM 'attain its goals through the tools of scholarship'. In such a spirit of mutual collaboration and experimentation, George offers scholar-activists four concrete pieces of advice for the advancement of critical global studies.

First, she warns against the concentration of research efforts on the conditions of the world's poor and disadvantaged: 'Those who genuinely want to help the [global justice] movement should study the rich and powerful, not the poor and powerless'. Her rationale for this unusual suggestion is rather striking: 'The poor and powerless already know what is wrong with their lives and those who want to help them should analyze the forces that keep them poor and powerless. Better a sociology of the Pentagon or the Houston country club than of single mothers or L.A. gangs'. Second, she makes a strong case for the significance of transdisciplinarity as the mode of critical thinking *par excellence*: 'One should also take as a given that, just as rules are made to be broken, disciplinary boundaries are made to be crossed'. Third, she urges public intellectuals eager to contribute to the GJM that they have to be more rigorous than their mainstream colleagues. 'If you're in the academic minority, you must assume that the majority will be out to get you and you'll need high-quality body armor to be unassailable. One way to do this is to use the adversary's own words'.[34] Fond of citing that 'ideas have consequences'—the 1950s slogan of American conservatives—George reminds CGS scholar-activists of the importance of creating permanent 'think tanks' and effective intellectual networks committed to the spread of global critical thinking.

George's last point deserves some additional elaboration. While the GJM has not been able to endow major left-leaning think tanks that rival conservative institutions like the Adam Smith Institute in London or the Heritage Foundation in Washington, DC, there has been considerable progress in the expansion of intellectual networks linking globalization scholars and movement activists. In addition to the WSF and its multiple affiliated regional social forums, there has been a proliferation of smaller academic networks dedicated to the direct support of counter-hegemonic globalization movements. For example, the Global Studies Association (GSA) was founded in 2000 at Manchester Metropolitan University, UK, and is now based at the Centre for Global and Transnational Politics at Royal Holloway, University of London. Its purpose is to bring together and advance the efforts of critical scholars and activists interested in promoting the creation and dissemination of transdisciplinary knowledge in the social and human sciences concerning globalization. Its sister organization, the GSA North America, was established two years later under the leadership of its organizational secretary Jerry Harris. A CGS scholar-activist and labor historian affiliated with DeVry University in Chicago, Harris has been actively involved in many alter-globalization struggles and edited a comprehensive study on the global Occupy Movement.[35] Most recently, the International Network of Scholar Activists (INoSA) has been organized by Jackie Smith, a prominent scholar of global social movements based at the University of Pittsburgh, and other like-minded public intellectuals from around the world. INoSA is a fast-growing network of teachers and scholars from many disciplines committed to advancing social movements and radical democracy—both within and outside academia. The organization supports scholarship and educational work related to these efforts, especially within the World Social Forum process. Indeed, Jackie Smith has published a steady stream of influential work on the WSF and its pivotal role in the effort to define an alternative course of globalization.[36]

As our final example of global activist thinkers who seek to generate emancipatory knowledge for the GJM and related global civil society networks, let us consider Naomi Klein, a tremendously influential voice in the GJM's struggle against the neoliberal forces of globalization-from-above. The Canadian journalist, filmmaker, and university lecturer emerged in the wake of the 1999 anti-WTO protests as the best-selling author of *No Logo: Taking Aim at Brand Bullies*. The book soon became one of GJM's 'required texts'. Blasting the sweat labor practices of powerful transnational corporations (TNCs) like Nike in so-called 'export producing zones' in the global South as well as their worldwide promotion of an uncritical, brand-conscious consumer culture, Klein suggested that giant corporations such as Shell and McDonald's were controlling major political institutions and thus actively undermining the core values of democracy. Adjusting the Frankfurt School's central themes of commodification and alienation to the globalizing world of the twenty-first century, the scholar-activist argued that the unholy alliance of TNCs and neoliberal governments aimed at nothing less than 'the privatization of every aspect of life, the transformation of every activity and value into a commodity'. But she also noted that the market-globalist policy package of 'cutting taxes, privatizing services, liberalizing regulations, busting unions' had the unanticipated effect of 'sowing the seeds of a genuine alternative to corporate rule' by encouraging the formation of a multi-issue, transnational network of global civil society actors. Hence, in the final part of the book, Klein calls upon her readers to engage in this struggle and resist the advance of corporate rule through a variety of actions ranging from educational sit-ins and shareholder lobbying to mass demonstrations and anti-brand campaigns and boycotts.[37]

As Klein's message was finding tremendous resonance in the global public sphere—especially among students at college campuses in the global North—she was already busy expanding her global critical thinking in the context of 9/11 and its impact on the GJM. In particular, she connected her critique of global capitalism and its supportive political framework to the exploding issues of militarization, security, and surveillance. Realizing both the dangers and opportunities in a post-9/11 world, Klein suggested a change in movement strategy: 'After 9-11, the task is even clearer: the challenge is to shift a discourse around the vague notion of globalization into a specific debate about democracy'.[38] Her goal was to link thousands of local movements fighting neoliberal globalization to the rapidly growing anti-Iraq War movement. The resulting new 'movement of movements' would cohere around demands for distributive justice, global peace, and democratic accountability. Klein continued her line of critical inquiries into the capitalism-militarism nexus in her next best-selling study. *The Shock Doctrine* investigated the links between the ideological evolution of neoliberal economics and its practical application as a 'disaster capitalism' in various global contexts: Augusto Pinochet's authoritarian Chile in the 1970s, Margaret Thatcher's United Kingdom and Ronald Reagan's conservative America in the 1980s, post-1989 liberalizing China and post-Soviet transitional Eastern Europe in the 1990s, and the post-9/11 Middle East region ravaged by George W. Bush's 'Global War on Terror'. Klein's critical analysis suggested that the Iraq War served as a model for the global export of 'privatized war and reconstruction'—a 'package deal' securing profits of billions of dollars for TNCs.[39]

Still, Klein's critical thinking kept evolving. Her most recent investigation into the social and political causes of global warming—yet another bestselling book—represents a striking example of what might be the most significant and promising trend in global activist thinking in recent years: the marriage of 'red' and 'green' traditions of critical theory. Explaining the current global climate change crisis as yet another consequence of the neoliberal policies of 'disaster capitalism', the Canadian scholar–activist sees the core obstacle in the way of a transition into a more sustainable future as the stranglehold that market logic has secured over public life. The media power and worldwide reach of market-globalist propaganda is making the most direct and large-scale responses seem politically heretical. Challenging this ideological dominance of neoliberal 'common sense' on 'securing jobs' and 'exploiting natural resources', *This Changes Everything: Capitalism vs. The Climate* tries to achieve two goals: offering a critique of the status quo capable of changing the public discourse and providing an attractive alternative vision that might encourage direct social action on a mass scale.

As for the first objective, the author seeks to demonstrate how 'unfettered corporate power' driving the process of globalization-from-above has posed a 'grave threat to the habitability of the planet'. As she states ironically, '[T]he liberation of world markets, a process powered by the liberation of unprecedented amounts of fossil fuels from earth, has dramatically sped up the same process that is liberating Artic ice from existence'. With regard to the second goal, Klein provides numerous uplifting examples and concrete illustrations of globally connected, local activist networks that have joined the battle between capitalism and the environment on the side of our planet. Posing climate change as the 'ultimate, all-encompassing global crisis', Klein calls especially on scholar-activists to develop an alternative-energy 'Marshall Plan for the Earth' that includes concrete suggestions of how to secure 'financing and technology transfer on scales never seen before'. As she makes abundantly clear, however, without a massive wave of popular mobilization that coincides with the promotion of such globally-coordinated environmental policies, it is unlikely that governments will embark on a green energy path anytime soon: 'Put another way, only mass social movements can save us now'.[40] In other words, the GJM must merge with the global climate movement without jettisoning its dialectical critique of global capitalism and its neoliberal ideology.

Indeed, Naomi Klein's global activist thinking resonated most with scholar-activists whose intellectual contributions evolved in the context of the global struggle against market globalism. These public intellectuals are the indispensable catalysts for the rapid convergence of critical 'red' thinking challenging the dynamics of global capitalism and critical 'green' thinking seeking to reverse our planet's ecological degradation.[41] Ultimately, then, the critical thinking framing of global studies encourages forms of social engagement that link educational engagement and the production of emancipatory knowledge for social movements to political projects committed to advancing social justice on a global level.

Concluding Remarks: Critiques of Global Studies

As this chapter—and, indeed, our book—draws to a close, the only subject left to consider is the capacity of global studies for self-criticism as expressed in our final guiding question: What forms of internal and external criticism have been leveled against global studies and how have these objections been dealt with? Obviously, the critical thinking frame creates a special obligation for all scholars working in the field to listen to and take seriously internal and external criticisms with the intention of correcting existing shortcomings, illuminating blind spots, and avoiding theoretical pitfalls and dead ends. As is the case for any newcomer bold enough to be entering today's crowded and competitive arena of academia, global studies, too, has been subjected to a wide range of criticisms ranging from constructive interventions to ferocious attacks. Since previous chapters have already covered some of the reproaches and objections raised by globalization rejectionists, skeptics, world-systems theorists, IR experts, and other critics, we will limit our discussion in this concluding section to a brief overview of two influential critiques of the field.

The first criticism concerns the intellectual scope of global studies as well as its current status in various academic settings around the world. Perhaps the most polished formulation of this criticism comes from Jan Nederveen Pieterse, a discerning internal critic hailing from UCSB's Global Studies Department—the most successful of its kind in the United States. Much to his credit, Pieterse's privileged position of being affiliated with the first full-fledged global studies PhD program in the country does not prevent him from engaging in constructive self-criticism. In his recent assessment of the field, he presents a rather bleak picture of 'actual global studies as it is researched and taught at universities around the world'. For Pieterse, the crux of the problem lies with the field's immaturity and lack of focus: it has, intellectually, 'barely developed' beyond a discipline-based study of globalization. Moreover, he alleges that currently existing global studies programs and conferences are still relatively rare and haphazard; they resemble 'scaffolding without a roof'. Finally, the global studies scholar bemoans the dearth of intellectual innovators willing and able to provide necessary 'programmatic perspectives on global studies' framed by 'multicentered and multilevel thinking' capable of 'adding value' to the field.[42]

Pieterse's intervention is important for a number of reasons. For one, it provides a necessary corrective to the idealized and romanticized accounts that often accompany the rise of a new academic endeavor. In fact, the authors of the present study could probably be found guilty of this charge more than once in the preceding chapters of their work. Moreover, Pieterse is certainly right in pointing to the current childhood stage of global studies as, in many respects, a serious affliction plaguing this inexperienced academic initiative. Incidentally, most academic fields deemed 'barely developed' are prone to display, paradoxically, a certain kind of youthful arrogance expressed in exaggerated aspirations to 'set things straight' and brash proclamations of serving as bastions of intellectual innovation. Global studies is no stranger to such boastful behavior. At times, its invidious airs of superiority displayed toward 'conventional disciplines' have given just cause for consternation as have some of its hubristic and ultimately unproven claims to novelty and universality. As James Mittelman has pointed out, there lies a severe risk 'in any attempt to encapsulate all phenomena in a single, totalizing framework, irrespective of whether it is named "global" or "globalization" studies'.[43]

To be sure, there is nothing wrong with sincere aspirations to universality. But, as IR critic Justin Rosenberg's important, yet somewhat dated, appraisal of globalization theory points out, the 'grand theory' claims of some thinkers have not been substantiated. He charges that 'globalization studies' has set itself up as a field capable of generating a new 'general social theory' in which 'globalization' serves as both the evolving outcome and the explanatory category for social change in the contemporary world. The result has been the new field's lamentable tendency to indulge in 'a conceptual inflation of the "spatial," which is both difficult to justify ontologically and liable to produce not explanations but reifications'.[44] Although most of Rosenberg's early broadsides against 'globalization theory' have been effectively countered in subsequent years, we share his distaste for the overblown intellectual ambitions of some global studies scholars.[45]

Finally, Pieterse's criticism hits the nail on its head when he points to the often shocking discrepancy between the rich conceptual promise of the field—as, we hope, has been laid out in this study—and the poor design and execution of 'actual global studies as it is researched and taught at universities around the world'. As we noted in the Introduction of this book, there is some truth to the complaints of some external critics that a good number of 'actually existing' global studies programs lack focus and specificity, which makes the field appear to be a rather nebulous study of 'everything global'. Like most of the other interdisciplinary efforts originating in the 1990s, global studies programs sometimes invite the impression of a rather confusing combination of wildly different approaches reifying the global level of analysis.

But perhaps the most troubling development we have observed in recent years is that 'global studies' has been increasingly used as a convenient catch phrase by 'academic entrepreneurs' eager to 'cash in' on its popularity with students. Thus, its desirable label has become attached to a growing number of conventional area studies curricula, international studies offerings, and diplomacy and foreign affairs programs—primarily for the purpose of boosting their intellectual and instructional appeal without having to make substantive changes to the familiar teaching and research agenda attached to such programs. Unfortunately, these vacuous and instrumental appropriations have not only caused much damage to the existing global studies 'brand' but also cast an ominous shadow on the future of the field.

In spite of its obvious insights, however, Pieterse's critique of 'actually existing global studies' strikes us as unbalanced. Much of the empirical data presented in the appendix and supplemental online resources of this study shows that there are promising pedagogical and research efforts underway in the field. These initiatives suggest that Pieterse's instructive pessimism must be matched by cautious optimism. To be sure, our empirical examination of the field shows global studies as a project that is still very much in the making. Yet, its tender age and relative inexperience should not deter globalization scholars from acknowledging the field's considerable intellectual achievements and growing institutional infrastructure. As we have endeavored to demonstrate in our discussion of its four pillars, global studies 'as it actually exists' has come a long way from its rather modest and eclectic origins in the 1990s. Of course, there can never be enough global studies conferences and workshops, but it simply defies reality to blow off the current choices of pertinent academic programs and professional gatherings as 'scaffolding without a roof'. For example, the regular meetings of the Global Studies Associations (UK and North America) and the annual convention of the Global Studies Consortium provide ample networking opportunities for globalization scholars from around the world. In fact, Pieterse himself is a founding member of the Global Studies Knowledge Community, a very active global studies organization holding large conferences and publishing a refereed scholarly journal devoted to mapping and interpreting past and emerging trends and patterns in globalization.[46]

In addition, our discussion of the growing global studies literature has revealed, contra Pieterse, the existence and ongoing emergence of profound intellectual innovators. Equipped with the necessary intellectual hard and software, they are furnishing those trailblazing 'programmatic perspectives' that contain 'multicentered thinking', 'multilevel thinking', and many other favorable features Pieterse deems essential for the evolution toward a 'value-added' global studies. Many global studies teaching programs and research centers around the world already incorporate a good number of the desired qualities we have identified in this book. As discussed in Chapters 2 to 5, global studies scholars are developing serious initiatives to recenter the social sciences toward global systemic dynamics and incorporate multilevel analyses. They are rethinking existing analytical frameworks that expand critical reflexivity and methodologies unafraid of mixing various research strategies. In short, the very rationale for writing this book—the delineation of global studies as a reasonably coherent, transdisciplinary 'space of tension' dedicated to the exploration of globalization processes and framed by both disagreements *and* agreements—yields a more complex and accurate picture of the young field. 'Actually existing' global studies appears to be in far better shape than Pieterse would have us believe. Where he sees intellectual underdevelopment and scaffolding without a roof, we also observe intellectual innovation, cutting-edge research, and thriving teaching programs. Our guarded optimism notwithstanding, however, we appreciate the critical interventions of global studies insiders and agree that there is plenty of room for further improvement.

The second criticism we discuss in this concluding section comes from 'postcolonial' thinkers located both within and without the field of global studies. As Robert Young explains, postcolonial theory is a related set of perspectives and principles that involves a conceptual reorientation toward the perspectives of knowledges developed outside the West—in Asia, Africa, Oceania, and Latin America. By seeking to insert alternative knowledges into the dominant power structures of the West as well as the non-West, postcolonial theorists attempt to 'change the way people think, the way they behave, to produce a more just and equitable relation between the different people of the world'. Emphasizing the connection between theory and practice, postcolonial intellectuals consider themselves critical thinkers challenging the alleged superiority of Western cultures, racism and other forms of ethnic bias, economic inequality separating the global North from the South, and the persistence of 'Orientalism'—a discriminatory, Europe-derived mindset so brilliantly dissected by late postcolonial theorist Edward Said.[47] Thus, Young concludes, postcolonialism is a socially engaged form of critical thinking 'about a changing world, a world that has been changed by struggle and which its practitioners intend to change further'.[48]

A good number of postcolonial and indigenous theorists have examined the connections between globalization and postcolonialism.[49] While many have expressed both their appreciation and affinity for much of what global studies stands for, they have also offered incisive critiques of what they see as the field's troubling geographic, ethnic, and epistemic location within the hegemonic Western framework. The noted ethnic studies scholar Ramón

Grosfoguel, for example, offers a clear and comprehensive summary of such postcolonial concerns: 'Globalization studies, with a few exceptions, have not derived the epistemological and theoretical implications of the epistemic critique coming from subaltern locations in the colonial divide and expressed in academia through ethnic studies and women studies. We still continue to produce a knowledge from the Western man "point zero" god's-eye view'.[50]

Some postcolonial thinkers, like the WSF-connected scholar-activist Boaventura de Sousa Santos, have taken their epistemic criticism beyond the confines of global studies in their indictment of the hegemonic academic framework as failing to recognize the different ways of knowing by which people across the globe provide meaning to their existence. In fact, his charge of 'cognitive injustice' moves far beyond conventional academic approaches and methodologies, deeply penetrating into the supposedly 'counter-hegemonic' territory of most of the 'critical theories' we discussed in this chapter. De Sousa Santos argues that 'genuine radicalism seems no longer possible in the global North', because 'Western, Eurocentric critical theory' has lost the capacity to learn from the experiences of the world. Haunted by a 'sense of exhaustion', he charges, the tradition of critical theory has lapsed into irrelevance, inadequacy, impotence, stagnation, and paralysis. Hence, his ideal of 'epistemological justice' contains the radical demand to end what he calls 'epistemicide', that is, the suppression and marginalization of epistemologies of the South by the dominant critical theories of the North. De Sousa Santos concludes that if the critical impulse is to survive in the twenty-first century, it is imperative for radical thinkers around the world to distance themselves from the Eurocentric critical tradition that has provided only weak answers for the strong questions confronting us in the Global Age.[51]

Postcolonial critics like Grosfoguel and De Sousa Santos provide an invaluable service to global studies by highlighting the conceptual parochialism behind its allegedly 'global' theoretical and practical concerns. Indeed, their intervention suggests that global studies thinkers have not paid enough attention to the postcolonial imperative of contesting the dominant Western ways of seeing and knowing. They also force all scholars working in the field to confront questions that are often relegated to the margins of intellectual inquiry. Is critical theory sufficiently global to represent the diverse voices of the multitude and speak to the diverse experiences of disempowered people around the world? What sort of new and innovative ideas have been produced by public intellectuals who do not necessarily travel along the theoretical and geographical paths frequented by Western critical thinkers? Are there pressing issues and promising intellectual approaches that have been neglected in critical global studies? Some of these questions also point to the central role of the English language in global studies. With English expanding its status as the academic lingua franca, thinkers embedded in Western universities still hold the monopoly on the production of critical theories. Important contributions from the global South in languages other than English often fall through the cracks or only register in translated form on the radar of the supposedly 'global' academic publishing network years after their original publication.

At the same time, however, it is essential to acknowledge the progress that has been made in global studies to expand its 'space of tension' by welcoming and incorporating global South perspectives. As early as 2005, for example, a quarter of the contributions featured in Appelbaum and Robinson's *Critical Globalizations Studies* anthology came from authors located in Africa, Asia, and Latin America. Since then, pertinent criticisms from within that demanded the inclusion of multiple voices and perspectives from around the world have proliferated. Consider, for example, Eve Darian-Smith's recent condemnation of taken-for-granted assumptions on the part of Western scholars to speak for others in the global South.[52] Moreover, scores of public intellectuals hailing from the global South such as Samir Amin, Ibrahim Aoudé, Arjun Appadurai, Mohammed Bamyeh, Walden Bello, Nestor Garcia Canclini, Enrique Dussel, Wang Hui, Liu Kang, Sankaran Krishna, Álvaro Garcia Linero, Achille Mbembe, Eduardo Mendieta, Walter Mignolo, Jamal R. Nassar, Norani Othman, Anibal Quijano, Arundhati Roy, Saskia Sassen, Vandana Shiva, Supriya Singh, Nevzat Soguk, Ramesh Thakur, Chico Whitaker, and Paul Tiyambe Zeleza have not only produced influential studies on globalization, but also have stood in solidarity with movement activists struggling against the forces of globalization-from-above.

Finally, we must not forget that it was the Mexican Zapatista movement—mostly composed of indigenous *campesinos* in the region—that confronted globalization-from-above with a resounding ¡*Ya basta!*, thus inaugurating what eventually became the global justice movement. In this context, it is important to remember the point we made earlier in this chapter about the role of the West, and the United States in particular, as a magnet for postcolonial scholars from around the world. As Keucheyan has emphasized, 'For today's critical theorists, U.S. universities constitute a site of recognition comparable to Paris for writers in the first half of the twentieth century'.[53] Still, with regard to the postcolonial criticism of global studies, we come to the same conclusion as in the previous charge related to the field's underdeveloped scope and status. We appreciate and take seriously the postcolonial interventions and agree that there is still plenty of room for further improvement.

Looking back at the stated purpose of this study, we hope to have supplied readers with an adequate delineation of global studies in terms of its four 'pillars' or 'framings': globalization, transdisciplinarity, space and time, and critical thinking. Most of all, this book has sought to pay tribute to the growing significance of global studies and its many affiliated scholars and students who appreciate its importance as an unorthodox academic 'space of tension' linking the arts, sciences, and humanities.

But let us end with the tiniest of speculations about the future of global studies. Perhaps its most pressing task for the next decade is to keep chipping away at the disciplinary walls that still divide the academic landscape today. Animated by an ethical imperative to 'globalize knowledge', such transdisciplinary efforts have the potential to reconfigure our discipline-oriented academic infrastructure around issues of global public responsibility.[54] This integrative endeavor must be undertaken steadily and tirelessly—but also carefully and with the proper understanding that diverse and multiple forms of knowledge are sorely needed to educate a global public. The necessary appreciation for the interplay between 'specialists' and 'generalists' must contain a proper respect for the crucial contributions of the conventional disciplines to our growing understanding of globalization. But the time has come to take the next step. The rising global imaginary demands nothing less from students and faculty hailing from all disciplines and fields of inquiry. Let us approach our core activities of learning, teaching, and research with the innovative openness and cosmopolitan intellectuality befitting the interdependent world of the twenty-first century.

NOTES

1 Daniel T. Willingham, 'Critical Thinking: Why Is It So Hard to Teach?', *Arts Education Policy Review* 109.4(2008), p. 8.
2 Ibid., pp. 8–10, 17. See also Richard Paul and Linda Elder, *The Miniature Guide to Critical Thinking Concepts and Tools,* (Tomales, CA: Foundation for Critical Thinking Press, 2008).
3 See Stephen Eric Bronner, *Critical Theory: A Very Short Introduction* (Oxford: Oxford University Press, 2011), p. 7.
4 Razmig Keucheyan, Gregory Elliott, trans. *The Left Hemisphere: Mapping Critical Theory Today* (London and New York: Verso, 2013), p. 12.
5 *Ejercito Zapatista de Liberación Nacional* (2008), cited in Charles Lindblom and José Pedro Zúquete, *The Struggle for the World: Liberation Movements for the 21st Century* (Stanford: Stanford University Press, 2010), p. 2.
6 Keucheyan, *The Left Hemisphere*, p. 3.
7 Ibid., pp. 20–1.
8 See Steger, *Globalisms*, Chapter 2.
9 Robinson, 'What Is a Critical Globalization Studies? Intellectual Labor and Global Society', in Appelbaum and Robinson, *Critical Globalization Studies*, p. 12.

10 See, for example, Richard P. Appelbaum and William I. Robinson, eds., *Critical Globalization Studies* (London and New York: Routledge, 2005); and Chamsy El-Ojeili and Patrick Hayden, eds., *Critical Theories of Globalization: An Introduction* (Houndmills, UK: Palgrave Macmillan, 2006). See also the *Critical Global Studies* Book Series edited by R. A. Dello Buono (The Hague: Brill):. www.brill.com/publications/critical-global-studies. Accessed 1 June 2016.

11 Robinson, *A Theory of Global Capitalism*, pp. 17, 32.

12 Antonio Gramsci, *Selections from the Prison Notebooks of Antonio Gramsci*, eds. Quentin Hoare and Geoffrey Nowell-Smith (London: Lawrence and Wisehart, 1971), pp. 3–8.

13 Robinson, *A Theory of Global Capitalism*, p. 84. See also William I. Robinson, *Global Capitalism and the Crisis of Humanity* (Cambridge, UK: Cambridge University Press, 2014).

14 Leslie Sklair, *The Transnational Capitalist Class* (Oxford: Blackwell, 2001), p. 296. See also Leslie Sklair, *Globalization: Capitalism and Its Alternatives* (Oxford: Oxford University Press, 2002).

15 Pierre Bourdieu, 'For a Scholarship With Commitment' in *Firing Back: Against the Tyranny of the Market 2* (New York: The New Press, 2003), pp. 24–5.

16 Robinson, 'What Is a Critical Globalization Studies? Intellectual Labor and Global Society', in Appelbaum and Robinson, *Critical Globalization Studies*, pp. 14–17.

17 James H. Mittelman, 'What Is a Critical Globalization Studies?' in Appelbaum and Robinson, *Critical Globalization Studies*, pp. 19, 24–5. See also Mittelman, *Whither Globalization?*

18 Mittelman, 'What Is a Critical Globalization Studies?', pp. 24–5.

19 Mittelman, *Whither Globalization?*, p. 98.

20 Appelbaum and Robinson, 'Introduction', in Appelbaum and Robinson, *Critical Globalization Studies*, pp. xii–xiii.

21 Mary Kaldor, *Global Civil Society: An Answer to War* (Cambridge, UK: Polity Press, 2003).

22 Hans Schattle, *The Practices of Global Citizenship* (Lanham, MD: Rowman & Littlefield, 2008), p. 2.

23 Ban Ki-moon, *Global Education First Initiative: An Initiative of the United Nations Secretary General* (2012), p. 20: www.globaleducationfirst.org/files/GEFI_White_Brochure_UPDATED.pdf. Accessed 1 June 2016.

24 Ibid., pp. 44–5.

25 Hans Schattle, *Globalization and Citizenship* (Lanham, MD: Rowman & Littlefield, 2012), p. 14.

26 Duarte B. Morais and Anthony C. Ogden, 'Initial Development and Validation of the Global Citizenship Scale', *Journal of Studies in International Education* 15.5 (2011), pp. 445–466.

27 Mark Juergensmeyer, 'What Is Global Studies', *global-e: A Global Studies Journal* 5 (2012), global-ejournal.org/2011/05/06/what-is-global-studies-3/. Accessed 1 June 2016.

28 See www.aacu.org/value/rubrics/global-learning.

29 For a recent assessment of the connections and continuities between the GJM and the Occupy Movement, see Helma G. E. de Vries-Jordan, 'The Global Justice Movement and Occupy Wall Street: Spillover, Spillout, or Coalescence?', *Global Discourse* 4.2/3 (2014), pp. 1–21.

30 Subcomandante Marcos, 'First Declaration of La Realidad', 3 August 1996: http://flag.blackened.net/revolt/mexico/ezln/ccri_1st_dec_real.html. Accessed 1 June 2016.

31 See Manfred B. Steger, James Goodman, and Erin K. Wilson, *Justice Globalism: Ideology, Crises, Policy* (London and Thousand Oaks: SAGE, 2013); and see www.routledge.com/cw/steger

32 Susan George, *Another World Is Possible If . . .* (London and New York: Verso, 2004).

33 Ibid., pp. 90–6.

34 Susan George, 'If You Want To Be Relevant: Advice to the Academic from a Scholar-Activist', in Appelbaum and Robinson, *Critical Globalization Studies*, p. 8.

35 See, for example, Jerry Harris, ed., Special Issue, 'Dystopia and Global Rebellion', *Perspectives on Global Development and Technology* 12.1–2 (2013).

36 See, for example, Jackie Smith, *Social Movements for Global Democracy* (Baltimore, MD: Johns Hopkins University Press, 2008); and Jackie Smith, *Global Democracy and the World Social Forums* (Boulder: Paradigm Publishers, 2008). For more information on the GSA North America, see: www.net4dem.org/mayglobal/contact.html
For more information on INoSA, see: http://inosa.wikispaces.com/home
See also the appendix in this study.

37 Naomi Klein, *No Logo: Taking Aim at Brand Bullies* (New York: Flamingo, 2000), pp. xxi, 325–40, and 'Reclaiming the Commons', *New Left Review* 9 (May-June 2001), pp. 81–9.

38 Naomi Klein, *Fences and Windows: Dispatches from the Front Lines of the Globalization Debate* (New York: Picador, 2002), p. 243.

39 Naomi Klein, *The Shock Doctrine: The Rise of Disaster Capitalism* (New York: Picador, 2008). See also Jones, *Globalization*, pp. 179–80.

40 Naomi Klein, *This Changes Everything: Capitalism vs. The Climate* (New York: Simon & Schuster, 2014), pp. 5, 19–20, 450.

41 For a systematic analysis of the relationship between globalization and the environment from the early modern period to the present, see Peter Christoff and Robyn Eckersley, *Globalization and The Environment* (Lanham, MD: Rowman & Littlefield, 2013).

42 Pieterse, 'What is Global Studies'.

43 James H. Mittelman, 'What's in a Name? Global, International, and Regional Studies', *Globalizations* 10.4 (2013), p. 516.

44 Justin Rosenberg, *The Follies of Globalisation Theory: Polemical Essays* (London and New York: Verso, 2000), p. 13. For a later iteration of essentially the same criticism, see Justin Rosenberg, 'Globalization Theory: A Post Mortem', *International Politics* 42.1 (2005), pp. 2–74.

45 For an insightful summary of counter-arguments to Rosenberg's critique of globalization theory, see Axford, *Theories of Globalization*, pp. 17–20, 183–88.

46 See http://onglobalization.com/about

47 Edward W. Said, *Orientalism* (New York: Vintage, 1979).

48 Robert J. C. Young, *Postcolonialism: A Very Short Introduction* (Oxford: Oxford University Press, 2003), pp. 6–7.

49 See, for example, Sankaran Krishna, *Globalization and Postcolonialism: Hegemony and Resistance in the Twenty-First Century* (Lanham, MD: Rowman & Littlefield, 2009).

50 Ramón Grosfoguel, 'The Implications of Subaltern Epistemologies for Global

Capitalism: Transmodernity, Border Thinking, and Global Coloniality', in Appelbaum and Robinson, *Critical Globalization Studies* (London and New York: Routledge, 2005) p. 284.

51 Boaventura de Sousa Santos, *Epistemologies of the South: Justice Against Epistemicide* (Boulder: Paradigm Publishers, 2014).

52 Darian-Smith, 'Global Studies—The Handmaiden of Neoliberalism?'

53 Keucheyan, *The Left Hemisphere*, p. 73.

54 See Michael Kennedy, *Globalizing Knowledge: Intellectuals, Universities, and Publics in Transformation* (Stanford: Stanford University Press, 2015), p. xv.

APPENDIX: GLOBAL STUDIES RESOURCES

Journals, Academic Programs, Professional Global Studies Associations, and Academic and Intellectual Networks

Journals

1. *Globalizations*: www.tandfonline.com/toc/rglo20/current#.Vc0fNLU0_Sg. *Globalizations* is the premier global studies journal. The journal seeks to publish research that explores new meanings of globalization, brings fresh ideas to the concept, broadens its scope, and contributes to shaping the debates of the future. It is peer-reviewed and transdisciplinary.

2. *Journal of Critical Globalisation Studies:* www.criticalglobalisation.com/JCGS-about.htm. This journal is the partner journal of the Global Studies Association. It publishes peer-reviewed research that emphasizes the contested nature of the concept of globalization.

3. *global-e*: http://globalstudiesconsortium.org/global-e. This journal is the partner journal of the Global Studies Consortium. *global-e* is a forum for practitioners seeking to create a more just globalization and scholars interested in global events, processes, and issues. The articles published are all brief but seek to stimulate discussion among the global studies community.

4. *Global Studies Journal*: http://onglobalization.com/journal. *The Global Studies Journal* is peer-reviewed and publishes research that seeks to advance understanding of globalization in terms of the past and future directions of globalization. It seeks to do this by showcasing research linking theory and practice.

5. *Glocalism: Journal of Culture, Politics, and Innovation*: www.glocalismjournal.net. *Glocalism* is a peer-reviewed, open-access, and cross-disciplinary journal that publishes research around the new dynamics that characterize the global-local, or 'glocal', reality.

6. *New Global Studies*: www.degruyter.com/view/j/ngs. *New Global Studies* publishes peer-reviewed research on topics including but not limited to: the patterns and local effects of economic globalization, global media networks, preservation of the global environment, transnational manifestations of culture, and the methodology of global studies itself.

7. *Global Networks*: http://onlinelibrary.wiley.com/journal/10.1111/%28 ISSN%291471-0374/homepage/ProductInformation.html. *Global Networks* is a peer-reviewed academic journal that publishes research related to global networks, transnational affairs and practices, and their relation to wider theories of globalization. This journal also serves as a location for wide-ranging debate and discussion on new ideas in the field of global studies.

8. *Journal of Global History:* http://journals.cambridge.org/action/displayJournal?jid=JGH. *Journal of Global History* publishes peer-reviewed research that tells the multiple histories of globalization along with the main problems of global change over time.

9. *Transcience: A Journal of Global Studies*: www.transcience-journal.org. *Transcience* promotes global and transdisciplinary studies. It does this by publishing peer-reviewed research in global studies that crosses or extends geographical and disciplinary boundaries.

10. *Global Social Policy*: http://gsp.sagepub.com. This peer-reviewed journal publishes research that seeks to advance understandings of social policy from a global perspective.

11. *Global Studies Law Review*: http://openscholarship.wustl.edu/law_ globalstudies. This journal publishes articles, book reviews, essays, and notes from academics, practitioners, and students that expand the global community's knowledge and understanding of real-world issues related to globalization.

12. *Globalization and Health*: http://globalizationandhealth.biomedcentral. com. This transdisciplinary journal focuses on public health and well-being situated within the dynamic forces of global development. It publishes peer-reviewed research and debate on globalization and its positive and negative effects on public health.

13. *Identities: Global Studies in Culture and Power*: www.tandfonline.com/ action/journalInformation?show=aimsScope&journalCode=gide20#. VnXA7Fmhv04. *Identities* publishes theoretically informed empirical research and critical analysis that opens up questions of race, ethnicity, and culture.

14. *Indiana Journal of Global Legal Studies*: http://ijgls.indiana.edu. This journal publishes peer-reviewed research dealing with the intersections

of global and domestic legal regimes, markets, politics, technologies, and cultures.

15. *Journal of International and Global Studies*: www.lindenwood.edu/jigs/about.cfm. This journal provides a peer-reviewed multidisciplinary forum for the critical discussion of and reflections on the consequences of globalization throughout the world.

16. *Journal of World History*: www.uhpress.hawaii.edu/t-journal-of-world-history.aspx. This journal publishes peer-reviewed historical analysis from a global perspective.

17. *YaleGlobal Online*: http://yaleglobal.yale.edu/content/about-yaleglobal. *YaleGlobal Online* is a journal that seeks to analyze and promote debate on all aspects of globalization through publishing original articles and multimedia presentations.

Online Resources

1. *Globalisation Café*: http://globalisationcafe.com/about. This website offers political and economic analysis gathered from around the web, though some articles are original and written especially for *Globalisation Café*. The website's mission is to bridge the gap between theory and practice through critical thought and dynamic pedagogy.

2. *Mapping Globalization*: www.princeton.edu/~mapglobe/HTML/home.html. Housed at Princeton University, the main goal of the website is to make empirical work on globalization as widely accessible as possible.

3. *KOF Index of Globalization*: http://globalization.kof.ethz.ch. The KOF Index of Globalization measures the economic, social, and political dimensions of globalization.

4. *Women's Environment and Development Organization (WEDO)*: http://wedo.org. WEDO is an organization focused on ensuring that women are included in global policy making. It works to connect women's organizations with human rights groups, development activists, environmental groups, governments, and intergovernmental organizations.

5. *Focus on the Global South*: www.focusweb.org. Founded as a direct response to neoliberal globalization in 1995, *Focus on the Global South* is a network and resource clearinghouse for activists fighting against neoliberalism, militarism, and corporate-driven globalization. Recently, *Focus* has adopted a 'deglobalization' approach to address the climate crisis.

6. *International Forum on Globalization*: www.ifg.org. The *International Forum on Globalization* is a research, advocacy, and action organization. Founded in 1994, it is focused on the impacts of dominant economic and geopolitical policies.

7. *Global Justice Now:* www.globaljustice.org.uk. This United Kingdom-based social justice organization works to promote solidarity actions with those fighting injustice around the world, but especially in the global South. A variety of information related to global justice can be found on this website.

8. *Library of Congress Business and Economics Research Advisor on Globalization*: www.loc.gov/rr/business/BERA/issue1/history.html. The *Library of Congress Business and Economics Research Advisor on Globalization* presents literature that examines the historical aspects of globalization by looking at its origins, the history of international economics and trade, and the history of international finance, exchange, and global markets.

9. *United Nations Human Development Reports*: http://hdr.undp.org/en. The Annual UN Human Development Report, commissioned by the United Nations Development Program, focuses the global debate on key development issues, providing new measurement tools, innovative analysis, and often controversial policy proposals.

10. *World History Matters*: http://worldhistorymatters.org. Housed in the Roy Rosenzweig Center for History and New Media at George Mason University, *World History Matters* serves as a clearinghouse of world history websites.

11. *350.org*: http://350.org. *350.org* is an NGO committed to building a global grassroots movement to solve the climate crisis.

12. *Big Future*: https://bigfuture.collegeboard.org/college-search. *Big Future* is a college search website that allows users to conduct searches by different majors. Nearly 300 US universities and colleges have developed global studies majors. This website allows for a variety of college searches by major.

13. *Start Class*: www.startclass.com. *Start Class* is a college search website that allows searches by academic major for those interested in undergraduate and graduate education. It also lists nearly 300 schools offering majors in global studies in the United States.

Academic Programs

1. *Department of Global Studies at the University of California Santa Barbara:* www.global.ucsb.edu. The Department of Global Studies at the University of California Santa Barbara is one of the first global studies programs in the world and offers bachelor's, master's, and doctoral degrees in global studies. In 2014 it became the first Tier-1 research university in the United States to offer a PhD in global studies.

2. *Centre for Global Research, RMIT University, Australia*: www.rmit.edu. au/research/research-institutes-centres-and-groups/research-centres/ centre-for-global-research/about. Founded in 2002 as the Globalism Institute, the Centre for Global Research is committed to rethinking the relationship between the global and the local. Its primary intellectual task is to understand the processes of change and continuity and to think through political-cultural questions about how people can live in ways that are sustainable and meaningful to them. In particular, it seeks to facilitate and enhance activities of political and cultural dialogue across the continuing and positive boundaries of cultural diversity in the world today.

3. *School of Global, Urban and Social Studies (GUSS) at RMIT University*: www. rmit.edu.au/about/our-education/academic-schools/global-urban-and-social-studies/about. This school is based at the Royal Melbourne Institute of Technology (RMIT), another pioneering program, and also offers bachelor's, master's, and doctoral degrees in global studies.

4. *University of North Carolina at Chapel Hill*: http://globalstudies.unc.edu. This pioneering global studies program supports numerous institutes and degree programs at the undergraduate and graduate level. It specifically offers a curriculum in global studies at the undergraduate and master's level.

5. *Centre for International Studies and Diplomacy (CISD) at the University of London*:   www.soas.ac.uk/cisd/programmes/research-degree.   This program offers a doctoral degree in global studies that specifically focuses on the study of globalization itself. CISD encourages multidisciplinary research that is both theoretically rich and policy relevant, focusing on the nature and evolution of contemporary globalization and on globally-shared issues.

6. *Institute for the Study of Global Issues at Hitotsubashi University Japan*: http://133.46.124.5:8080/isgi/about-isgi. The institute's home is at Hitotsubashi University in Japan. It is the first graduate program in the world to offer degrees in global studies.

7. *Division of Global Affairs at Rutgers University-Newark*: http://dga.rutgers. edu/index.php/about-global-affairs. This program offers master's and doctoral degrees in global affairs.

8. *Graduate School of Global Studies at Sophia University, Japan*: www.sophia. ac.jp/eng/program/graduate_p/G_GS. This Japanese university offers master's and doctoral degrees in global studies.

9. *Graduate Program in Global Studies at Sophia University, Japan*: http:// gpgs.fla.sophia.ac.jp/about. The graduate program in global studies (GPGS) offers instruction in English and the curriculum is thematically

organized around interdisciplinary global studies, theories and methodologies, and cross-cultural understanding.

10. *European Master in Global Studies*: http://gesi.sozphil.uni-leipzig.de/joint-projects/emgs. This program allows students to study at two different European universities, each for one academic year.

11. *International and Global Studies at Middlebury College*: www.middlebury.edu/academics/igs. Middlebury College in Middlebury, Vermont began offering its BA in International and Global Studies in 1996. The major draws from faculty and resources cross-disciplinarily. Students taking global studies as a major must become proficient in a second language, study abroad for at least one semester, and are encouraged to think critically about a range of questions related to global studies.

12. *Department of Global Studies, St. Lawrence University, New York*: www.stlawu.edu/global-studies. This department offers undergraduate degrees in global studies. It highlights an interdisciplinary approach to the study of numerous global topics.

13. *Buffett Institute for Global Studies at Northwestern University:* http://buffett.northwestern.edu/about/index.html. The Buffett Institute at Northwestern University works in conjunction with a variety of other globally-focused programs to promote global studies research, training, and awareness both at Northwestern University and throughout the world. Most recently the institute has launched three new research programs: Global Capitalism and Law, Global Politics and Religion, and the Global Humanities Initiative.

14. *University of Montana's Global Leadership Initiative*: www.umt.edu/gli/about/default.php. This initiative seeks to infuse students across traditional disciplines with a global perspective. Instead of promoting a specific global studies major, student fellows are encouraged and supported in conducting research and participating in opportunities with a global focus.

15. *Global Awareness Through Education (GATE)-University of Texas at Tyler*: www.uttyler.edu/gate/gateoverview.php. The GATE program at the University of Texas at Tyler is designed to introduce students from different disciplines to globally-relevant issues, problems, and potential solutions. Although not a degree, GATE students take 'globalized' core classes that have been designed with a global focus, attend cultural activities on and off campus, and participate in a five-week study abroad experience during the summer after their sophomore year. GATE seeks to offer freshman and sophomore students the knowledge, skills, and ways of thinking that are necessary to succeed in an increasingly global community.

16. *Global Studies Initiative at Whitman College*: www.whitman.edu/academics/signature-programs/global-studies-initiative. This liberal

arts college in Walla Walla, Washington, offers a campus-wide global studies curriculum that includes sending over half of its student body abroad during their course of study. Noting that 'a good liberal arts education must include global education', Whitman College has recently won grants to fund their Global Studies Initiative.

Professional Global Studies Associations

1. *Global Studies Consortium*: http://globalstudiesconsortium.org. The Global Studies Consortium, which hosts the journal *global-e,* serves as a gathering point for academic programs responding to the forces of globalization in creative ways. It strives to promote and facilitate graduate teaching programs in global studies and to foster cooperation among them.

2. *Global Studies Association (GSA)*: https://globalstudiesassoc.wordpress. com. The GSA is based in the Centre for Global and Transnational Politics at Royal Holloway, University of London. This multidisciplinary scholarly association was developed in order to address the vast social, political, and economic transformations of global scope that are impacting the world today. The GSA provides a forum for scholars to collaborate and explore shared responses to such phenomena, particularly in the context of globalization. Committed to multidisciplinarity and to the global context, it aims to offer its members contacts and connections. In addition, the thematic approach of the GSA allows interests not easily accommodated in single-disciplinary associations to be fully recognized and encouraged.

3. *Asia Association for Global Studies (AAGS)*: www.aags.org. The AAGS strives to promote innovative research and alternative perspectives on issues of international significance. It particularly encourages cross-disciplinary and transnational theoretical approaches that dissolve traditional academic boundaries and relate local events to wider global processes. The association also seeks to function as an open forum for the expression of regional opinions and viewpoints that might otherwise go unheard in the English-speaking world.

4. *Global Studies Association-North America* (GSA-NA): www.net4dem. org/mayglobal. The Global Studies Association and the Global Studies Association-North America are sister organizations. Both are multidisciplinary scholarly associations. Thus, GSA-NA is supported by a group of scholars worldwide who wish to collaborate in order to better understand vast global transformations. Membership includes academics and activists from Canada, the United States, Mexico, and Central America.

5. *Globalization Studies Network (GSN):* http://gsnetwork.igloogroups.org. Founded in 2004 as a network of globalization research centers, the GSN is a collaborative and interdisciplinary effort. At its first meeting more than eighty centers and institutions from around the world participated. Membership is comprised of three categories: (1) research centers and institutes; (2) non-academic organizations, government agencies, and funders interested in the results of globalization studies research; and (3) academics not associated with institutes or centers but focus their own research on globalization studies.

6. *International Network of Scholar Activists* (INoSA): http://inosa. wikispaces.com/home. This network specifically encourages a critical view of globalization. Its membership is comprised of teachers and activists who are committed to furthering the aims of the World Social Forum. It seeks to do this in three ways: (1) resisting neoliberalism on college and university campuses; (2) defending the knowledge commons; and (3) supporting social movements and radical democracy.

Academic and Intellectual Networks

1. *Globalization and World Cities Research Network (GaAWC):* www. lboro.ac.uk/gawc. Created in the Geography Department at Loughborough University (UK), this network focuses on research regarding the external relations of world cities. Their frequently published bulletins offer analysis on cutting-edge topics connected to world cities.

2. *Global Cities Research Institute (GCRI)*: http://global-cities.info. The GCRI was inaugurated in 2006 to bring together researchers at RMIT University (Australia), working on understanding the complexity of globalizing urban settings from provincial centers to megacities.

3. *Centre for the Study of Globalisation and Regionalisation (CSGR)*: www2. warwick.ac.uk/fac/soc/pais/research/researchcentres/csgr. CSGR hosts conferences, roundtables, research, publications, working papers, and a globalization index that covers the period 1982 to 2004. Founded at the University of Warwick (UK) in 1997, its titular mission has evolved to include topics of global governance and global order and global civil society. It is explicitly interdisciplinary in nature.

4. *Global Studies Knowledge Community:* http://onglobalization.com. Founded in 2008, the Global Studies Knowledge Community supports the mapping and interpreting of past and emerging trends in globalization. To this end, the community hosts an annual conference, sponsors a journal, *The Global Studies Journal*, and a book imprint.

5. *International Studies Association (ISA)*: www.isanet.org. This association is the premier scholarly association for the field of international studies. Its members sponsor, through the organization, six journals and numerous academic conferences around the world. Founded in 1959, ISA cooperates with fifty-seven international studies organizations in over thirty countries.

6. *British International Studies Association (BISA)*: www.bisa.ac.uk. This association includes members interested in global studies, international studies, international relations, and international politics. Membership is diverse and includes scholars and practitioners. It also hosts an annual conference that provides scholars and practitioners an opportunity to present and discuss their research.

7. *British Sociological Association (BSA)*: www.britsoc.co.uk/the-bsa.aspx. The BSA is a network of academics trained in sociology but includes members in and out of the profession. BSA members have created groups dedicated to understanding topics related to global studies, including: climate change, citizenship, diaspora, migration, transnationalism, cities, and many more.

8. *Transnational Institute (TNI)*: www.tni.org/en. TNI serves as a network for engaged scholars and activists seeking to create a more just world. TNI's mission is to help strengthen international social movements with rigorous research, reliable information, sound analysis, and constructive proposals that advance progressive, democratic policy change, and common solutions to global problems. A wide range of publications can be found on TNI's website.

9. *Toda Institute for Global Peace and Policy Research*: www.toda.org/index.html. This institute focuses on global peace research. Its main activities to this end include the organization of conferences, the publication of books, and the publication of its yearly journal, *Peace & Policy*.

10. *The Centre on Migration, Policy, and Society (COMPAS)*: www.compas.ox.ac.uk. COMPAS research covers a spectrum of global migration processes and phenomena, from conditions in places of migrant origins, through to institutions and activities affecting mobility, to social and economic effects in receiving contexts. The website includes links to original research and other resources related to global migration.

11. *Institute for Research on World-Systems (IROWS)*: http://irows.ucr.edu. Located at the University of California-Riverside, the Institute for Research on World-Systems organizes collaborative research among social and physical scientists on long-term, large-scale social change and its ecological, geographical, and epidemiological causes and effects.

BIBLIOGRAPHY

Agnew, John A. *Globalization and Sovereignty*. Lanham, MD: Rowman & Littlefield, 2009.

Albrow, Martin. *The Global Age: State and Society Beyond Modernity*. Stanford: Stanford University Press, 1996.

Alvargonzález, David. 'Multidisciplinarity, Interdisciplinarity, Transdisciplinarity, and the Sciences'. *International Studies in the Philosophy of Science* 25, no. 4 (2011): 387–403.

Amar, Paul. *The Security Archipelago: Human-Security States, Sexuality Politics, and the End of Neoliberalism*. Durham and London: Duke University Press, 2013.

Amin, Ash. 'Placing Globalization'. *Theory, Culture & Society* 14, no. 2 (1997): 123–38.

Anonymous. 'European Communities'. *International Organization* 13, no. 1 (1959): 174–78.

Appadurai, Arjun. *Modernity at Large: Cultural Dimensions of Globalization*. Minneapolis, MN: University of Minnesota Press, 1996.

Appelbaum, Richard P., and William I. Robinson, eds. *Critical Globalization Studies*. London and New York: Routledge, 2005.

Arendt, Hannah. *The Human Condition*. Chicago: University of Chicago Press, 1958.

Arrighi, Giovanni. *The Long Twentieth Century: Money, Power, and the Origins of Our Times*. London and New York: Verso, 1994.

Axford, Barrie. *Theories of Globalization*. Cambridge, UK: Polity Press, 2013.

Bamyeh, Mohammed A. *The Ends of Globalization*. Minneapolis, MN: University of Minnesota Press, 2000.

Barber, Benjamin R. *Jihad Vs. McWorld*. New York: Crown, 1995.

Barney, Darin. *The Network Society*. Cambridge, UK: Polity Press, 2004.

Bauman, Zygmunt. *Liquid Modernity*. Cambridge, UK: Polity Press, 2000.

Beck, Ulrich. *What Is Globalization?* Cambridge, UK: Polity Press, 2000.

———. 'Toward a New Critical Theory with a Cosmopolitan Intent'. *Constellations* 10, no. 4 (2003): 453–68.

Beckert, Sven. *Empire of Cotton: A Global History*. New York: Vintage, 2015.

Benedikter, Roland. 'Understanding Contemporary Change. What is the "Global Systemic Shift" of our Days and How Does it Work? A Seven-Dimensional Approach of Reconstruction, Analysis, and Foresight to Address "Post-Ideological," "Post-9/11," and "Post-Empire" Complexity', *Transcience* 4, no. 1 (2013): 20–35.

Bentley, Jerry H. *Old World Encounters: Cross-Cultural Contacts and Exchanges in Pre-Modern Times*. Oxford: Oxford University Press, 1993.

Berger, Peter L., and Samuel P. Huntington. *Many Globalizations: Cultural Diversity in the Contemporary World*. Oxford: Oxford University Press, 2002.

Berlin, Jeffrey. 'Beyond Intercultural Competence: Global Citizenship and a Critical Study Abroad'. PhD Dissertation, University of Hawai'i-Mānoa, 2015.

Bin Laden, Osama. *Messages to the World: The Statements of Osama Bin Laden*. Edited by Bruce B. Lawrence. Translated by James Howarth. London and New York: Verso, 2005.

Bourdieu, Pierre. *Firing Back: Against the Tyranny of the Market 2*. New York: New Press, 2003.

Boyd, William. *The History of Western Education*. 3rd ed. London: A & C Black, 1932.

Boyd, William, and Muriel M. Mackenzie. *Towards a New Education*. New York: A. Knopf, 1930.

Braudel, Fernand. *On History*. Translated by Sarah Mathews. Chicago: University of Chicago Press, 1982.

Brenner, Neil. 'Beyond State-Centrism? Space, Territoriality, and Geographical Scale in Globalization Studies'. *Theory and Society* 28, no. 1 (1999): 39–78.

———. 'Globalisation as Reterritorialisation: The Re-Scaling of Urban Governance in the European Union'. *Urban Studies* 36, no. 3 (1999): 431–51.

Bronner, Stephen Eric. *Critical Theory: A Very Short Introduction*. Oxford: Oxford University Press, 2011.

Brown, Cynthia Stokes. *Big History: From the Big Bang to the Present*. New York: Free Press, 2007.

Bryan, Lowell, and Diana Farrell. *Market Unbound: Unleashing Global Capitalism*. London and New York: Wiley, 1996.

Brysk, Alison, ed. *Globalization and Human Rights*. Berkeley, CA: University of California Press, 2002.

Burtless, Gary T., Robert Z. Lawrence, Robert E. Litan, and Robert J. Shapiro. *Globaphobia: Confronting Fears about Open Trade*. Washington, DC: Brookings Institution Press, 1998.

Cameron, Angus, and Ronen Palan. *The Imagined Economies of Globalization*. London and Thousand Oaks: SAGE, 2004.

Campbell, Patricia J., Aran S. MacKinnon, and Christy Stevens. *An Introduction to Global Studies*. Chichester, UK: John Wiley, 2010.

Cantwell, Brendan, Ilkka Kauppinen and Sheila Slaughter, eds. *Academic Capitalism in the Age of Globalization*. Baltimore, MD: John Hopkins University Press, 2014.

Castells, Manuel. *The Rise of the Network Society*. The Information Age: Economy, Society, and Culture. 3 vols. Vol. 1, Malden, Mass.: Blackwell Publishers, 1996.

———. *The Power of Identity*. The Information Age: Economy, Society, and Culture. 3 vols. Vol. 2, Malden, Mass.: Blackwell, 1997.

———. *End of Millennium*. The Information Age: Economy, Society, and Culture. 3 vols. Vol. 3, Malden, MA: Blackwell Publishers, 1998.

———. 'Materials for an Exploratory Theory of the Network Society'. *British Journal of Sociology* 51, no. 1 (2000): 5–24.

———. 'The New Public Sphere: Global Civil Society, Communication Networks, and Global Governance'. *Annals of the American Academy of Political and Social Science* 616, no. 1 (2008): 78–93.

———. *Communication Power*. Oxford: Oxford University Press, 2009.

———. *End of Millennium*. The Information Age: Economy, Society, and Culture. 2nd ed. 3 vols. Vol. 3, Malden, MA: Wiley-Blackwell, 2010.

———. *The Power of Identity*. The Information Age: Economy, Society, and Culture. 2nd ed. 3 vols. Vol. 2. Malden, MA: Wiley-Blackwell, 2010.

———. *The Rise of the Network Society*. The Information Age: Economy, Society, and Culture. 2nd ed. 3 vols. Vol. 1, Malden, MA: Wiley-Blackwell, 2010.

———. *Networks of Outrage and Hope: Social Movements in the Internet Age*. Cambridge, UK: Polity Press, 2012.

———. *Communication Power*. 2nd ed. Oxford: Oxford University Press, 2013.

Chan, Sucheng. *Asian Americans: An Interpretive History*. Farmington Hills, MI: Twayne Publishers, 1991.

Chanda, Nayan. *Bound Together: How Traders, Preachers, Adventurers, and Warriors Shaped Globalization*. New Haven: Yale University Press, 2007.

Chase-Dunn, Christopher K. *Global Formation: Structures of the World-Economy*. Lanham, MD: Rowman & Littlefield, 1998.

Choi, Bernard C. K., and Anita W. P. Pak. 'Multidisciplinarity, Interdisciplinarity, and Transdisciplinarity in Health Research, Services, Education and Policy: Definitions, Objectives, and Evidence of Effectiveness'. *Clinical & Investigative Medicine* 29, no. 6 (2006): 351–64.

Christian, David. *Maps of Time: An Introduction to Big History*. Berkeley, CA: University of California Press, 2004.

Christoff, Peter, and Robyn Eckersley. *Globalization and the Environment*. Lanham: Rowman & Littlefield, 2013.

Clarence-Smith, William Gervase, Kenneth Pomeranz, and Peer Vries. 'Editorial'. *Journal of Global History* 1, no. 1 (2006): 1–2.

Claude, Inis L. 'Implications and Questions for the Future'. *International Organization* 19, no. 3 (Summer 1965): 835–46.

Corbin, Juliet M., and Anselm L. Strauss. *Basics of Qualitative Research: Techniques and Procedures for Developing Grounded Theory*. 3rd ed. London and Thousand Oaks: SAGE, 2008.

Cosgrove, Denis E. *Apollo's Eye: A Cartographic Genealogy of the Earth in the Western Imagination*. Baltimore, MD: Johns Hopkins University Press, 2001.

Crossley, Pamela Kyle. *What Is Global History?* Cambridge, UK: Polity Press, 2008.

Darian-Smith, Eve. 'Global Studies—the Handmaiden of Neoliberalism?' *Globalizations* 12, no. 2 (2015): 164–68.

de Vries-Jordan, Helma G. E. 'The Global Justice Movement and Occupy Wall Street: Spillover, Spillout, or Coalescence?' *Global Discourse* 4, no. 2–3 (2014): 182–202.

Decroly, Ovide. *La Fonction De Globalisation Et L'Enseignement,* Brussels: Lamertin, 1929.

Dello Buono, R. A., ed., *Critical Global Studies Book Series.* Accessed 1 June 2016. The Hague: Brill. www.brill.com/publications/critical-global-studies.

Devji, Faisal. *Landscapes of the Jihad: Militancy, Morality, Modernity.* Ithaca, NY: Cornell University Press, 2005.

———. 'Osama Bin Laden's Message to the World'. *OpenDemocracy* (December 2005). Accessed 1 June 2016. www.opendemocracy.net/conflict-terrorism/osama_3140.jsp.

Dicken, Peter. 'Geographers and "Globalization": (yet) Another Missed Boat?' *Transactions of the Institute of British Geographers* 29, no. 1 (2004): 5–26.

———. *Global Shift: Mapping the Changing Contours of the World Economy.* 7th ed. New York and London: Guilford Press, 2015.

Dirlik, Arif. 'Performing the World: Reality and Representation in the Making of World Histor(ies)'. *Journal of World History* 16, no. 4 (2005): 391–410.

Douglass, Mike, and John Friedmann, eds. *Cities for Citizens: Planning and the Rise of Civil Society in a Global Age.* New York: John Wiley, 1998.

Dufoix, Stéphane, 'Between Scylla and Charybdis: French Social Science Faces Globalization'. Unpublished Manuscript.

Editorial. 'What Is Global Studies?' *Globalizations* 10, no. 4 (2013): 497–98.

Eisenstadt, Shmuel N., ed. *Multiple Modernities.* New Brunswick, NJ: Transaction Books, 2002.

El-Ojeili, Chamsy, and Patrick Hayden, eds. *Critical Theories of Globalization: An Introduction.* Houndmills, UK: Palgrave Macmillan, 2006.

Engle, Lilli, and John Engle. 'Study Abroad Levels: Toward a Classification of Program Types'. *Frontiers: The Interdisciplinary Journal of Study Abroad* 9 (2003): 1–20.

Fairclough, Norman. *Language and Globalization.* London and New York: Routledge, 2007.

Featherstone, Mike, ed. *Global Culture: Nationalism, Globalization, and Modernity.* London and Thousand Oaks: SAGE, 1990.

Foucault, Michel. *Discipline and Punish: The Birth of the Prison.* New York: Vintage Books, 1995.

Frank, Andre Gunder. *ReORIENT: Global Economy in the Asian Age.* Berkeley, CA: University of California Press, 1998.

Frank, Andre Gunder, and Barry K. Gills. *The World System: Five Hundred Years or Five Thousand?* London and New York: Routledge, 1994.

Freeden, Michael. *Ideologies and Political Theory: A Conceptual Approach.* Oxford: Clarendon Press, 1996.

Friedman, Thomas L. *The Lexus and the Olive Tree: Understanding Globalization.* New York: Anchor Books, 1999.

——. *The World Is Flat 3.0: A Brief History of the Twenty-First Century.* New York: Picador, 2007.

George, Susan. *Another World Is Possible If . . .* London and New York: Verso, 2004.

——. 'If You Want to Be Relevant: Advice to the Academic from a Scholar-Activist'. In *Critical Globalization Studies*, edited by Richard P. Appelbaum and William I. Robinson, 3–10. London and New York: Routledge, 2005.

Gerges, Fawaz A. *The Far Enemy: Why Jihad Went Global* 2nd ed. Cambridge, UK: Cambridge University Press, 2009.

Giddens, Anthony. *The Consequences of Modernity.* Stanford: Stanford University Press, 1990.

Gills, Barry K. ed. *Globalization and the Politics of Resistance.* Houndmills, UK: Palgrave Macmillan, 2002.

Gills, Barry K., and William R. Thompson. *Globalization and Global History.* London and New York: Routledge, 2006.

Gilpin, Robert. *The Challenge of Global Capitalism: The World Economy in the 21st Century.* Princeton, NJ: Princeton University Press, 2000.

Gramsci, Antonio. *Selections from the Prison Notebooks of Antonio Gramsci.* Edited and translated by Quintin Hoare and Geoffrey Nowell-Smith. London: Lawrence and Wisehart, 1971.

Grosfoguel, Ramón. 'The Implications of Subaltern Epistemologies for Global Capitalism: Transmodernity, Border Thinking, and Global Coloniality'. In *Critical Globalization Studies.* Edited by Richard P. Appelbaum and William I. Robinson, 283–92. London and New York: Routledge, 2005.

Guéhenno, Jean-Marie. *The End of the Nation-State.* Minneapolis, MN: University of Minnesota Press, 1995.

Gunn, Giles. *The Culture of Criticism and the Criticism of Culture.* Oxford: Oxford University Press, 1988.

——. *Beyond Solidarity: Pragmatism and Difference in a Globalizing World.* Chicago: University of Chicago Press, 2001.

——. *Ideas to Die For: The Cosmopolitan Challenge.* London and New York: Routledge, 2013.

Hannerz, Ulf. *Cultural Complexity: Studies in the Social Organization of Meaning.* New York: Columbia University Press, 1992.

——. *Transnational Connections: Culture, People, Places.* London and New York: Routledge, 1996.

Hardt, Michael, and Antonio Negri. *Empire.* Cambridge, MA: Harvard University Press, 2000.

Harper, Lucius C. 'He Is Rich in the Spirit of Spreading Hatred'. *Chicago Defender*, 15 January 1944.

Harris, Jerry. ed., 'Dystopia and Global Rebellion', Special Issue, *Perspectives on Global Development and Technology* 12, no 1–2 (2013).

Harvey, David. *The Condition of Postmodernity: An Enquiry into the Origins of Cultural Change.* Oxford: Blackwell, 1989.

——. 'Globalization in Question'. *Rethinking Marxism* 8, no. 4 (Winter 1995): 1–17.

Held, David, and Anthony G. McGrew. *Globalization/Anti-Globalization.* Cambridge, UK: Polity Press, 2002.

Held, David, Anthony McGrew, David Goldblatt, and Jonathan Perraton. *Global Transformations: Politics, Economics, and Culture.* Stanford: Stanford University Press, 1999.

Hirst, Paul, and Grahame Thompson. *Globalization in Question: The International Economy and the Possibilities of Governance.* 2nd ed. Cambridge, UK: Polity Press, 1999.

Holton, Robert. *Global Networks.* Houndmills, UK: Palgrave Macmillan, 2008.

Hopkins, A. G., ed. *Globalization in World History.* New York: Norton, 2002.

———. ed. *Global History: Interactions between the Universal and the Local.* Houndmills, UK: Palgrave Macmillan, 2006.

Iriye, Akira. *Global and Transnational History: The Past, Present, and Future.* New York: Palgrave, 2012.

James, Paul. *Nation Formation: Towards a Theory of Abstract Community.* London and Thousand Oaks: SAGE, 1996.

———. 'What is Globalism?' *Globalism Institute RMIT Annual Report.* January 2002–January 2003.

———. 'Globalization, Approaches To'. In *Encyclopedia of Global Studies*, Vol. 2. Edited by Helmut K. Anheier and Mark Juergensmeyer, 753–57. London and Thousand Oaks: SAGE, 2012.

———. 'Globalization, Phenomenon Of'. In *Encyclopedia of Global Studies*. Vol. 2. Edited by Helmut K. Anheier and Mark Juergensmeyer, 761–65. London and Thousand Oaks: SAGE, 2012.

James, Paul, and Manfred B. Steger. 'A Genealogy of "Globalization": The Career of a Concept'. *Globalizations* 11, no. 4 (2014): 417–34.

———. 'A Genealogy of "Globalization": The Career of a Concept'. *Globalizations.* Special Issue. www.tandfonline.com/toc/rglo20/11/4.

———. 'Globalization and Global Consciousness: Layers of Connectivity'. In *Global Culture: Consciousness and Connectivity.* Edited by Roland Robertson and Didem Buhari-Gulmez, 21–39. Aldershot, UK: Ashgate, 2016.

James, Paul (with Liam Magee, Andy Scerri, and Manfred B. Steger). *Urban Sustainability in Theory and Practice: Circles of Sustainability.* London and New York: Routledge, 2015.

Jameson, Fredric. 'Preface'. In *The Cultures of Globalization.* Fredric Jameson and Masao Miyoshi, eds. Durham and London: Duke University Press, 1998.

Jameson, Fredric, and Masao Miyoshi, eds. *The Cultures of Globalization.* Post-Contemporary Interventions. Durham and London: Duke University Press, 1998.

Jones, Andrew. *Globalization: Key Thinkers.* Cambridge, UK: Polity Press, 2010.

Juergensmeyer, Mark. *The New Cold War? Religious Nationalism Confronts the Secular State.* Berkeley, CA: University of California Press, 1993.

———. 'What Is Global Studies?' *global-e: A Global Studies Journal* 5 (2012). Accessed 1 June 2016. http://global-ejournal.org/2011/05/06/what-is-global-studies-3/.

———. 'Interview Mark Juergensmeyer'. *Globalizations* 11, no. 4 (2014): 539–47.

———. *Thinking Globally: A Global Studies Reader.* Berkeley, CA: University of California Press, 2014.

Kaldor, Mary. *Global Civil Society: An Answer to War.* Cambridge, UK: Polity Press, 2003.

Kaldor, Mary, Henrietta L. Moore, and Sabine Selchow, eds. *Global Civil Society 2012: Ten Years of Critical Reflection.* Houndmills, UK: Palgrave Macmillan, 2012.

Kamola, Isaac A. *Producing the Global Imaginary: Academic Knowledge, Globalization and the Making of the World.* PhD Dissertation, University of Minnesota, May 2010.

———. 'US Universities and the Production of the Global Imaginary'. *British Journal of Politics & International Relations* 16, no. 3 (2014): 515–33.

Keane, John. *Global Civil Society?* Cambridge, UK: Cambridge University Press, 2003.

Kennedy, Michael. *Globalizing Knowledge: Intellectuals, Universities, and Publics in Transformation.* Stanford: Stanford University Press, 2015.

Kenway, Jane, and Johannah Fahey, eds. *Globalizing the Research Imagination.* London and New York: Routledge, 2009.

Keohane, Robert O. *After Hegemony: Cooperation and Discord in the World Political Economy.* Princeton, NJ: Princeton University Press, 1984.

Kepel, Gilles, and Jean-Pierre Milelli, eds. *Al Qaeda in Its Own Words.* Cambridge, MA: Belknap Press of Harvard University Press, 2008.

Keucheyan, Razmig. *Left Hemisphere: Mapping Critical Theory Today.* Translated by Gregory Elliott. London and New York: Verso, 2013.

Khondker, Habibul Haque. 'Globalization, Glocalization, or Global Studies: What's in a Name?' *Globalizations* 10, no. 4 (2013): 527–31.

Ki-moon, Ban. *Global Education First Initiative: An Initiative of the United Nations Secretary General.* 2012. Accessed 1 June 2016. www.globaleducationfirst.org/files/GEFI_White_Brochure_UPDATED.pdf.

Klein, Julie Thompson. *Interdisciplinarity: History, Theory, and Practice.* Detroit: Wayne State University Press, 1990.

Klein, Naomi. *No Logo: Taking Aim at the Brand Bullies.* New York: Flamingo, 2000.

———. *Fences and Windows: Dispatches from the Front Lines of the Globalization Debate.* New York: Picador, 2002.

———. 'Reclaiming the Commons'. *New Left Review*, no. 9 (May–June 2001): 81–89.

———. *The Shock Doctrine: The Rise of Disaster Capitalism.* New York: Picador, 2008.

———. *This Changes Everything: Capitalism vs. The Climate.* New York: Simon & Schuster, 2014.

Krishna, Sankaran. *Globalization and Postcolonialism: Hegemony and Resistance in the Twenty-First Century.* Lanham, MD: Rowman & Littlefield, 2009.

Krishnan, Armin. 'What Are Academic Disciplines? Some Observations on the Disciplinarity vs. Interdisciplinarity Debate'. ESRC National Centre for Research Methods, NCRM Working Paper Series, January 2009.

Kuhn, Thomas. *The Structure of Scientific Revolutions.* Chicago: University of Chicago Press, 1962.

Lawrence, Bruce B. 'Introduction'. In *Messages to the World: The Statements of Osama Bin Laden,* Edited by Bruce B. Lawrence. Translated by James Howarth. London and New York: Verso, 2005

Lawrence, Roderick J., and Carole Després. 'Futures of Transdisciplinarity'. *Futures* 36, no. 4 (2004): 397–405.

Lefebvre, Henri. *The Production of Space*. Oxford: Blackwell, 1991.

Levitt, Theodore. 'The Globalization of Markets'. *Harvard Business Review* 61, no. 3 (May/Jun 1983): 92–102.

Lie, John. 'Asian Studies/Global Studies: Transcending Area Studies and Social Sciences'. *Cross-Currents: East Asian History and Culture Review* no. 2 (March 2012): 1–23. Accessed 22 January 2016. https://cross-currents.berkeley.edu/e-journal/issue-2.

Lindholm, Charles, and José Pedro Zúquete. *The Struggle for the World: Liberation Movements for the 21st Century*. Stanford: Stanford University Press, 2010.

Lyotard, Jean-François. *The Postmodern Condition: A Report on Knowledge*. Minneapolis, MN: University of Minnesota Press, 1984.

McCarty, Philip C. 'Communicating Global Perspectives'. *Basel Papers in European Global Studies* 105 (2014): 27–37. Accessed 16 February 2015. https://europa.unibas.ch/fileadmin/europa/redaktion/PDF_Basler_Schriften/BS105.pdf.

———. 'Globalizing Legal History'. *Rechtsgeschichte/Legal History* 22 (2014): 283–91.

MacGillivray, Alex. *A Brief History of Globalization: The Untold Story of Our Incredible Shrinking Planet*. New York: Running Press, 2006.

McLuhan, Marshall. *Understanding Media: The Extensions of Man*. Cambridge, MA: MIT Press, 1994 [1964].

McNeill, John Robert, and William H. McNeill. *The Human Web: A Bird's-Eye View of World History*. New York: Norton, 2003.

McNeill, William H. 'Globalization: Long Term Process or New Era in Human Affairs?' *New Global Studies* 2, no. 1 (2008): 1–9.

Manning, Patrick. *Navigating World History: Historians Create a Global Past*. Houndmills, UK: Palgrave Macmillan, 2003.

Marcos, Subcomandante. 'First Declaration of La Realidad', 3 August 1996. Accessed 1 June 2016. http://flag.blackened.net/revolt/mexico/ezln/ccri_1st_dec_real.html.

Martens, Pim, Marco Caselli, Philippe De Lombaerde, Lukas Figge, and Jan Aart Scholte. 'New Directions in Globalization Indices'. *Globalizations* 12, no. 2 (2015): 217–28.

Max-Neef, Manfred A. 'Foundations of Transdisciplinarity'. *Ecological Economics* 53, no. 1 (2005): 5–16.

Mazlish, Bruce. *The New Global History*. London and New York: Routledge, 2006.

Mazlish, Bruce, and Akira Iriye, eds. *The Global History Reader*. London and New York: Routledge, 2005.

Meadows, Paul. 'Culture Theory and Industrial Analysis'. *Annals of the American Academy of Political and Social Science* 274 (1951): 9–16.

Mertes, Tom, Walden Bello, Bernard Cassen and Jose Bove. *A Movement of Movements: Is Another World Really Possible?* London and New York: Verso, 2004.

Middell, Matthias. 'What Is Global Studies All About?' *Basel Papers on Europe in a Global Perspective* 105 (2014): 38–49. Accessed 16 February 2015. https://europa.unibas.ch/fileadmin/europa/redaktion/PDF_Basler_Schriften/BS105.pdf.

Mignolo, Walter. *Local Histories/Global Designs: Coloniality, Subaltern Knowledges, and Border Thinking*. Princeton, NJ: Princeton University Press, 2000.

Mittelman, James H. *Globalization: Critical Reflections*. Boulder: Lynne Rienner Publishers, 1996.

———. *The Globalization Syndrome: Transformation and Resistance*. Princeton, NJ: Princeton University Press, 2000.

———. 'Globalization: An Ascendant Paradigm?' *International Studies Perspectives* 3, no. 1 (2002): 1–14.

———. *Whither Globalization? The Vortex of Knowledge and Ideology*. London and New York: Routledge, 2004.

———. 'What Is a Critical Globalization Studies?' In *Critical Globalization Studies*, edited by Richard P. Appelbaum and William I. Robinson, 19–32. London and New York: Routledge, 2005.

———. 'What's in a Name? Global, International, and Regional Studies'. *Globalizations* 10, no. 4 (2013): 515–19.

Modelski, George. 'Communism and the Globalization of Politics'. *International Studies Quarterly* 12, no. 4 (1968): 380–93.

Morais, Duarte B., and Anthony C. Ogden. 'Initial Development and Validation of the Global Citizenship Scale'. *Journal of Studies in International Education* 15, no. 5 (2011): 445–66.

Moran, Joe. *Interdisciplinarity*. London and New York: Routledge, 2002.

Murray, Warwick E. *Geographies of Globalization*. London and New York: Routledge, 2006.

Nairn, Tom. *Faces of Nationalism: Janus Revisited*. London and New York: Verso, 1997.

Neubauer, Deane E., ed. *The Emergent Knowledge Society and the Future of Higher Education: Asian Perspectives*. London and New York: Routledge, 2013.

Northrup, David. 'Globalization and the Great Convergence: Rethinking World History in the Long Term'. *Journal of World History* 16, no. 3 (2005): 249–67.

O'Brien, Patrick. 'Historiographical Traditions and Modern Imperatives for the Restoration of Global History'. *Journal of Global History* 1, no. 01 (2006): 3–39.

O'Brien, Richard. *Global Financial Integration: The End of Geography*. London: Pinter, 1992.

O'Byrne, Darren J., and Alexander Hensby. *Theorizing Global Studies*. Houndmills, UK: Palgrave Macmillan, 2011.

Odin, Jaishree Kak, and Peter T. Manicas, eds. *Globalization and Higher Education*. Honolulu: University of Hawai'i Press, 2004.

Ohmae, Kenichi. *The Borderless World: Power and Strategy in the Interlinked Economy*. New York: Harper Business, 1990.

———. *The End of the Nation State: The Rise of Regional Economies*. New York: Free Press, 1995.

Osterhammel, Jürgen, and Niels P. Petersson. *Globalization: A Short History*. Translated by Dona Geyer. Princeton, NJ: Princeton University Press, 2005.

Paige, R. Michael, and Michael Vande Berg. 'Why Students Are and Are Not Learning Abroad: A Review of Recent Research'. In *Student Learning Abroad: What Our Students Are Learning, What They're Not, and What We Can Do About*

It. Edited by R. Michael Paige, Michael Vande Berg, and Kris Hemming Lou, 29–60. Sterling, VA: Stylus Publishing, 2012.

Paige, R. Michael, Michael Vande Berg, and Kris Hemming Lou, eds. *Student Learning Abroad: What Our Students Are Learning, What They're Not, and What We Can Do About It.* Sterling, VA: Stylus Publishing, 2012.

Patomäki, Heikki, and Manfred B. Steger. 'Social Imaginaries and Big History: Towards a New Planetary Consciousness?' *Futures: A Journal of Policy, Planning, and Futures Studies* 42, no. 8 (2010): 1056–63.

Paul, Richard, and Linda Elder. *The Miniature Guide to Critical Thinking Concepts and Tools.* Tomales, CA: Foundation for Critical Thinking Press, 2008.

Perroux, Francois, and Therese Jaeger. 'The Conquest of Space and National Sovereignty'. *Diogenes* 10, no. 39 (1962): 1–16.

Pieterse, Jan Nederveen. 'What Is Global Studies?' *Globalizations* 10, no. 4 (2013): 499–514.

———. *Globalization and Culture: Global Mélange.* 3rd ed. Lanham, MD: Rowman & Littlefield, 2015.

Pohl, Christian. 'From Transdisciplinarity to Transdisciplinary Research'. *Transdisciplinary Journal of Engineering & Science* 1, no. 1 (2010): 65–73.

Pohl, Christian, and Gertrude Hirsch Hadorn. 'Methodological Challenges of Transdisciplinary Research'. *Natures Sciences Sociétés* 16, no. 2 (2008): 111–21.

Pomeranz, Kenneth. *The Great Divergence: China, Europe, and the Making of the Modern World Economy.* Princeton, NJ: Princeton University Press, 2000.

Reinert, Al. 'The Blue Marble Shot: Our First Complete Photograph of Earth'. *The Atlantic,* 12 April 2011. Accessed 13 November 2015. http://www. theatlantic.com/technology/archive/2011/04/the-blue-marble-shot-our-first-complete-photograph-of-earth/237167/.

Repko, Allen F. *Interdisciplinary Research: Process and Theory.* 2nd ed. London and Thousand Oaks: SAGE, 2011.

Ritzer, George. *The McDonaldization of Society.* London and Thousand Oaks: SAGE, 1992.

Robertson, Robbie. *The Three Waves of Globalization: A History of a Developing Global Consciousness.* London: Zed Books, 2003.

Robertson, Roland. *Globalization: Social Theory and Global Culture.* London and Thousand Oaks: SAGE, 1992.

———. 'Globalisation or Glocalisation?' *The Journal of International Communication* 1, no. 1 (1994): 33–52.

———. 'The Conceptual Promise of Glocalization: Commonality and Diversity'. *ART-e-FACT: Strategies of Resistance* 4 (2005). Accessed 29 November 2015. http://artefact.mi2.hr/_a04/lang_en/theory_robertson_en.htm.

———. 'Interview Roland Robertson'. *Globalizations* 11, no. 4 (2014): 447–59.

Robinson, William I. *A Theory of Global Capitalism: Production, Class, and State in a Transnational World.* Baltimore, MD: Johns Hopkins University Press, 2004.

———. 'What Is a Critical Globalization Studies? Intellectual Labor and Global Society'. In *Critical Globalization Studies.* Edited by Richard P. Appelbaum and William I. Robinson, 11–18. London and New York: Routledge, 2005.

———. 'Critical Globalization Studies'. In *Critical Globalization Studies*. Edited by Richard P. Appelbaum and William I. Robinson, 11–18. London and New York: Routledge, 2005.

———. *Global Capitalism and the Crisis of Humanity*. Cambridge, UK: Cambridge University Press, 2014.

Rodrik, Dani. *Has Globalization Gone Too Far?* Washington, DC: Institute for International Economics, 1997.

Rosecrance, Richard. 'The Obsolescence of Territory'. *New Perspectives Quarterly* 12, no. 1 (1995): 44–50.

Rosenberg, Justin. *The Follies of Globalisation Theory: Polemical Essays*. London and New York: Verso, 2000.

———. 'Globalization Theory: A Post Mortem'. *International Politics* 42, no. 1 (2005): 2–74.

Rosow, Stephen J. 'Toward an Anti-Disciplinary Global Studies'. *International Studies Perspectives* 4, no. 1 (2003): 1–14.

Roy, Olivier. *Globalized Islam: The Search for a New Ummah*. New York: Columbia University Press, 2004.

Rugman, Alan M. *The End of Globalization*. New York: Random House, 2001.

Runciman, David. 'Destiny vs. Democracy'. *London Review of Books* 35, no. 8 (25 April 2013): 13–16.

Russell, Alice W. 'No Academic Borders?: Transdisciplinarity in University Teaching and Research'. *Australian Universities' Review* 48, no. 1 (2005): 35–41.

Saberi, Helen. *Tea: A Global History*. London: Reaktion Books, 2010.

Sachsenmaier, Dominic. *Global Perspectives on Global History: Theories and Approaches in a Connected World*. Cambridge, UK: Cambridge University Press, 2011.

Said, Edward W. *Orientalism*. New York: Vintage, 1979.

Santos, Boaventura de Sousa. *Epistemologies of the South: Justice against Epistemicide*. Boulder: Paradigm, 2014.

Sassen, Saskia. *The Mobility of Labor and Capital*, Cambridge, UK: Cambridge University Press, 1988.

———. *The Global City: New York, London, Tokyo*. Princeton, NJ: Princeton University Press, 1991.

———. *The Global City: New York, London, Tokyo*. 2nd ed. Princeton, NJ: Princeton University Press, 2001.

———. 'Globalization or Denationalization?' *Review of International Political Economy* 10, no. 1 (2003): 1–22.

———. *Territory, Authority, Rights: From Medieval to Global Assemblages*. Princeton, NJ: Princeton University Press, 2006.

———. 'The Places and Spaces of the Global: An Expanded Analytic Terrain'. In *Globalization Theory: Approaches and Controversies*. Edited by David Held and Anthony G. McGrew, 79–105. Cambridge, UK: Polity Press, 2007.

———. *A Sociology of Globalization*. New York: Norton, 2007.

———. *Expulsions: Brutality and Complexity in the Global Economy*. Cambridge, MA: Belknap Press of The Harvard University Press, 2014.

Schattle, Hans. *Globalization and Citizenship*. Lanham, MD: Rowman & Littlefield, 2012.

——. *The Practices of Global Citizenship*. Lanham, MD: Rowman & Littlefield, 2008.

Scholte, Jan Aart. *Globalization: A Critical Introduction*. Houndmills, UK: Palgrave Macmillan, 2000.

——. *Globalization: A Critical Introduction*. 2nd ed. Houndmills, UK: Palgrave Macmillan, 2005.

Shaw, Martin. *Theory of the Global State: Globality as an Unfinished Revolution*. Cambridge, UK: Cambridge University Press, 2000.

Singh, David Grewal. *Network Power: The Social Dynamics of Globalization*. New Haven: Yale University Press, 2008.

Singh, Supriya. *Globalization and Money: A Global South Perspective*. Lanham, MD: Rowman & Littlefield, 2013.

Sklair, Leslie. *Globalization: Capitalism and Its Alternatives*. 3rd ed. Oxford: Oxford University Press, 2002.

——. *The Transnational Capitalist Class*. Oxford: Blackwell, 2001.

Smith, Jackie. *Global Democracy and the World Social Forums*. Boulder: Paradigm, 2007.

——. *Social Movements for Global Democracy*. Baltimore, MD: Johns Hopkins University Press, 2008.

Snyder, Richard C. *Thinking, Teaching, Politicking About Globalization of the World: Toward a Synthesis and Possible Future Strategy*. Washington, DC: ERIC Clearinghouse, 1990. Accessed 1 January 2016. http://catalogue.nla.gov.au/record/5538423.

Stearns, Peter N. *Globalization in World History*. London and New York: Routledge, 2010.

Steger, Manfred B. *Globalism: The New Market Ideology*. Lanham, MD: Rowman & Littlefield, 2002.

——. ed. *Rethinking Globalism*. Lanham, MD: Rowman & Littlefield, 2004.

——. *The Rise of the Global Imaginary: Political Ideologies from the French Revolution to the Global War on Terror*. Oxford: Oxford University Press, 2008.

——. *Globalisms: The Great Ideological Struggle of the Twenty-First Century*. 3rd ed. Lanham, MD: Rowman & Littlefield, 2009.

——. *Globalization: A Very Short Introduction*. 3rd ed. Oxford: Oxford University Press, 2013.

——. *The Global Studies Reader*. Oxford: Oxford University Press, 2014.

Steger, Manfred B., James Goodman, and Erin K. Wilson. *Justice Globalism: Ideology, Crises, Policy*. London and Thousand Oaks: SAGE, 2013.

Steger, Manfred B., and Paul James. *Globalization: The Career of a Concept*. Rethinking Globalizations. London and New York: Routledge, 2015.

——. 'Levels of Subjective Globalization: Ideologies, Imaginaries, Ontologies'. *Perspectives on Global Development & Technology* 12, no. 1–2 (2013): 17–40.

Steger, Manfred B., and Ravi K. Roy. *Neoliberalism: A Very Short Introduction*. Oxford: Oxford University Press, 2010.

Stichweh, Rudolf. 'Differentiation of Scientific Disciplines: Causes and Consequences'. In *Encyclopedia of Life Support Systems*, 1–8. Paris: UNESCO, 2003.

Strange, Susan. *The Retreat of the State: The Diffusion of Power in the World Economy*. Cambridge, UK: Cambridge University Press, 1996.

Suarez, Michael F., and H. R. Woudhuysen. *The Book: A Global History*. Oxford: Oxford University Press, 2014.

Teune, Henry 'The International Studies Association'. International Studies Association, 1982. Accessed 20 January 2015. http://www.isanet.org/Portals/0/Documents/Institutional/Henry_Teune_The_ISA_1982.pdf.

Thakur, Ramesh, and Thomas G. Weiss. 'Framing Global Governance, Five Gaps'. In *Thinking About Global Governance: Why People and Ideas Matter.* 145–67. London and New York: Routledge, 2011.

Tomlinson, John. *Globalization and Culture.* Chicago: University of Chicago Press, 1999.

Toynbee, Arnold. *A Study of History.* 12 vols. Oxford: Oxford University Press, 1934–61.

Urry, John. *Global Complexity.* Cambridge, UK: Polity Press, 2003.

Veseth, Michael. *Globaloney 2.0: The Crash of 2008 and the Future of Globalization.* 2nd ed. Lanham, MD: Rowman & Littlefield, 2010.

Wade, Robert. 'Globalization and Its Limits: Reports on the Death of the National Economy Are Greatly Exaggerated'. In *National Diversity and Global Capitalism.* Edited by Suzanne Berger and Ronald Philip Dore, 60–88. Ithaca, NY: Cornell University Press, 1996.

Wallerstein, Immanuel. *The Capitalist World-Economy.* Cambridge, UK: Cambridge University Press, 1979.

———. *The Politics of the World-Economy: The States, the Movements, and the Civilizations.* Cambridge, UK: Cambridge University Press, 1984.

———. 'Culture as the Ideological Battleground of the Modern World System'. In *Global Culture: Nationalism, Globalization, and Modernity.* Edited by Mike Featherstone, 31–55. London and Thousand Oaks: SAGE, 1990.

———. *World-Systems Analysis: An Introduction.* Durham and London: Duke University Press, 2004.

Waters, Malcolm. *Globalization.* 2nd ed. London and New York: Routledge, 2001 [1995].

Weiss, Linda. *The Myth of the Powerless State: Governing the Economy in a Global Era* Ithaca, NY: Cornell University Press, 1998.

Weiss, Thomas G. *Thinking About Global Governance: Why People and Ideas Matter.* London and New York: Routledge, 2011.

Wildavsky, Ben. *The Great Brain Race: How Global Universities Are Reshaping the World.* Princeton, NJ: Princeton University Press, 2010.

Williams, Raymond. *Keywords: A Vocabulary of Culture and Society.* Oxford: Oxford University Press, 2014 [1983].

Willingham, Daniel T. 'Critical Thinking: Why Is It So Hard to Teach?' *Arts Education Policy Review* 109, no. 4 (2008): 21–32.

Wills, John E., Jr. *1688: A Global History.* New York: W. W. Norton, 2002.

Young, Robert J. C. *Postcolonialism: A Very Short Introduction.* Oxford: Oxford University Press, 2003.

Yúdice, George. *The Expediency of Culture: Uses of Culture in the Global Era.* Durham and London: Duke University Press, 2003.

Zeleza, Paul Tiyambe. *Rethinking Africa's Globalization.* Trenton, NJ: Africa World Press, 2003.

INDEX

Note: Page numbers in **bold** type refer to **figures**
Page numbers in *italic* type refer to *tables*
Page numbers followed by 'n' refer to notes
Page numbers followed by 'I' refer to images

academic disciplines *see* transdisciplinarity
academic globalization debates: globalizers 66–7, 83n25; hyperglobalizers 69; intellectual camps **72**; modifiers 69–72; overview 65–6, 83n24; rejectionists 67; skeptics 67–9
academic institutions 14, *15*
academic landscape (European) 14
academic networks 188–9
academic programs 184–7
academic research 86
activism 22, 157–9
Age of Divergence 135
Agnew, John 130
Albrow, Martin 121–3, **123**
Allied war conferences 5
Alvargonzález, David 91
Amar, Paul 130–2
American Pacific Century 130
American socio-cultural views 28–9
Amin, Ash 71, 84n42
Annals of the American Academy of Political and Social Science 29–30
Another World Is Possible If . . . (WSF) 165

Apollo photograph (Earth) 6, 6I, 138–9, 139I
Appadurai, Arjun 33, 63–4, 117
Appelbaum, Richard 35–6, 38; and Robinson, William 152–5, 157–8
Arendt, Hannah 7
Aristotle 88
Asghar, Sajeed Titu 39
Axford, Barrie 9, 96

BA program 39, 46
Ban Ki-moon 159
Barber, Benjamin 36
Barney, Darin 104, 105
Battersby, Paul 46
Bauman, Zygmunt 105
big data 13
Bilbo, Theodore G. 29
Bilbos in uniform 29
Blue Marble Shot (Apollo photograph) 138–9, 139I
book outline 19–23
borderless world 125
Bourdieu, Pierre 154–5
Boyd, William 28
Braudel, Fernand 70

Brenner, Neil 129–30
Bronner, Stephen Eric 148
Bryan, Lowell 125
Buffett, Warren 14
business and economics 31–2

Capella, Martianus 88
capital-labor relations 153
capitalism 153
Castells, Manuel 57, 101–8, 113n32, 113n39, 127, 140
Chan, Sucheng 38
Chanda, Nayan 33
change or continuity (Gidden vs. Albrow) 121–3, **123**
Chicago Defender 28–9
Choi, Bernard: and Pak, Anita 92
Christian fundamentalists 79
cities 105
citizenship 3, 159–62
Claude, Inis 30
cognitive injustice 174
Cohen, Benjamin C. 36
Cold War 5, 7, 33
Columbia University: Committee on Area Studies 8
Communism 8, 32
Communist Manifesto 62
Condition of Postmodernity, The (Harvey) 60
conflict resolution 158
Consequences of Modernity, The (Giddens) 117–18
continuity or change (Gidden vs. Albrow) 121–3, **123**
corporate-led globalization from above 150, 151
Cosgrove, Denis 138
Critical Globalization Studies (Appelbaum and Robinson) 152–3, 157–8, 166, 175
critical theory 22, 35, **149**
critical thinking: analytical and ethico-political 146–8, **147**; characteristics and outcomes of CGS **156**; critiques of global studies 170–6; educating for citizenship 159–62; emancipatory knowledge for GJM 162–70; global activist thinking 157–9; old and new 148–52; overview 21–2, 145; responsibilities of intellectuals 152–6, 177n10; skills 147; transdisciplinarity mode 166

cultural globalization 97
cultural theorists 64, 83n20
culture and society 28–30
cyber-warfare 158
cyberspace 116

Daily News 4, 51
Daily Planet 4
Darian-Smith, Eve 17–18, 40, 175
Decroly, Ovide 28
deterritorialization: absolutists 125–6, **128**; relativists 126–32, **128**
Devji, Faisal 78
Dicken, Peter 111, 113n52, 123
digital technologies 13, 28, 50n9
disaster capitalism 168
disasters (natural and man-made) 97
disciplinary territory 89
discipline: definition 87–8

Earthrise (Apollo photograph) 61, 138
ecological degradation 169, 178n41
economic globalization 96
economic homogenization 32
economics and business 31–2
economy: global 56–7
educating for global citizenship 159–62
education: European higher 88; and psychology 27–8
Elver, Hilal 41
emancipatory knowledge 162–70
English language (dominance) 175
Enquiry into the Origins of Cultural Change, An (Harvey) 61
environmental globalization 97
epistemological justice 174
Erasmus Mundus program 49
Eurocentrism 120

Faessel, Victor 47
Fahey, Johannah: and Kenway, Jane 108
fair trade 77
Falk, Richard 40–1
Falun Gong 79
Farrell, Diana 125
Foucault, Michel 88
four meaning branches 26–32, **32**
four pillars 18, **19**, 20
Frankfurt School of Social Research 35, 167
French strikes 150
Friedman, Milton 10
Friedman, Thomas 31, 33, 72–3

G&IS (Global & International Studies
Program) 37
George, Susan 164–6
GFs (global fluids) 107
Giddens, Anthony 23n4, 98, 117–18,
119–21, 122–3
Gills, Barry K. 71, 137
Gilpin, Robert 69
GINs (globally integrated networks)
106–7
GJM (global justice movement) 76–7,
84n45, 154, 158, 162–70, 162I, 175
Global & International Studies Program
(G&IS) 37
global activist thinking 22, 157–9
Global Age, The (Albrow) 121
global cities 105
global citizenship 3, 159, 160I; educating
for 159–62
global city model 64
global community 57
Global Complexity (Urry) 106
global consciousness 2
global economy 56–7
Global Education First Initiative 22
global enterprises 106
global epoch 136
global flow landscapes 63
global fluids (GFs) 107
global imaginary 2, 3–7, 23n3
global and international studies program
(USCB) 35–41
global justice movement (GJM) 76–7,
84n45, 154, 158, 162–70, 162I, 175
Global Learning Value Rubric 161
global literacy 161
global media 56
global personhood 57
global society 7
global South 62, 82n18
global studies: approaches and rationales
17–18; contours of the field 13–17;
overview 1–3; what name 7–13, **11**
Global Studies Association (GSA)
167, 172
Global Studies Consortium (GSC)
47, 172
Global Studies Department (UCSB) 93
Global Studies Initiative at Whitman
College (Walla Walla, WA) 93
Global Studies Knowledge Community
172
Global Transformations (Held) 98–100, 101

global village 7, 114, 138
Global War on Terror 158
globalism: Islamist (radical form) 77–9,
79I; justice 76–7, 84n45; market
10, 165
Globalism Institute (RMIT University)
41–7; religious 78–9; textbooks 18,
24n29
globality: social condition 55
*Globalization: Social Theory and Global
Culture* (Robertson) 59
globalization 3; articles and publication
54, 57, **58**; conflation of process and
condition 55; as continuity or change
123; corporate-led from above 150,
151; cultural 97; defining 53–7;
economic 96; environmental 97;
ideological 97; people-led from below
150; pioneers (1990s) 57–65, 82n16;
political 96–7; processes 59–60; public
debates 72–81, **80**; as a spatial concept
115–17; studies (1990s) 33–4, *see also*
academic globalization debates
Globalization (journal) 15–16, 17, 137
globalization (term): definition 119;
usage 26, 50n3
globalizing modernity 23n4
globally integrated networks (GINs)
106–7
globaloney 67, 81, 83n31
glocalization 56, 60, 95, 131I
Goldblatt, David 98–9, 101
Golden Globe Awards 4
Gramsci, Antonio 153, 154
Great Convergence 136
Great Recession (2008–9) 76
Grenfell, Damian 43, 46–7
Grosfoguel, Ramón 174
GSA (Global Studies Association)
167, 172
GSC (Global Studies Consortium)
47, 172
Gunn, Giles 36, 37–8, 40, 51n30

Hardt, Michael: and Negri, Antonio
127–8
Harper, Lucius 28–9
Harris, Jerry 167
Harvard Business Review 31
Harvey, David 60–2, 100, 117
Hayek, Friedrich 10
Hecht, Richard 36
Held, David 98–100, 101, 102, 108

Herodotus 133
higher education 88
Hirst-Thompson thesis 68
historical research 133, 142n42
History of Western Education, The
    (Boyd) 28
Hollywood Foreign Correspondents
    Association 4
Hollywood movie studios 4
Holton, Robert 95
hominids 27
homogenization 60
Hopkins, A.G. 133
hyperglobalists 99
hyperglobalizers 67, 69, 81

Ibn Khaldun 133
ICT (Information and Communication
    Technology) Revolution 102, 140
ideological claims 75
Ideological Dimensions of Globalization
    (conference) 44–5
ideological globalization 97
ideological perspectives 72–81, **80**
ideologies: imaginaries and ontologies
    74
Information Age 103
Information Age, The (Castells) 102
Information and Communication
    Technology (ICT) Revolution
    102, 140
INoSA (International Network of
    Scholar Activists) 167
Institute for Social Research in Frankfurt
    148
intellectual networks 188–9
intellectual scope 170
intellectuals: public 154–5, 163, 164, 169,
inter (Latin prefix) 91
inter-national (term) 4
interconnectivity 13
interdisciplinarity 86
interdisciplinary global studies 48–9
interdisciplinary programs 16
International Network of Scholar
    Activists (INoSA) 167
international relations (IR) 7–8, 30–1
International Studies Association (ISA)
    8, 12
international studies (IS) 7
IR (international relations) 7–8, 30–1
Iraq War 168
IS (international studies) 7

ISA (International Studies Association)
    8, 12
Islam: deterritorialization 78
Islamist globalism (radical form)
    77–9, 79l
James, Paul 34, 42, 43–4, 60; and Steger,
    Manfred 27, 130
Jameson, Fredric 2
Jewish organizations 79
jihad 78
Jones, Andrew 101
journals 181–3
JSTOR 57, **58**
Juergensmeyer, Mark 33, 36, 37, 38, 40,
    47, 161
justice 174, *see also* global justice
    movement (GJM)
justice globalism 76–7, 84n45

Kalantzis, Mary 43
Kaldor, Mary 158
Kamola, Isaac 9, 23n8
Kenway, Jane: and Fahey, Johannah
    108
Keohane, Robert 9
Keucheyan, Razmig 148–9, 151, 175
Keynesian-type taxation and
    redistribution 76–7
Keynesianism (nation-state centered)
    10
keyword meaning trajectories 19
keywords 57
Klein, Naomi 164, 167–9
knowledge: division of 2; emancipatory
    162–70; forms of 88; imperative to
    globalize 176; production 93
KOF Index of Globalization 53
Krishnan, Armin 89, 110
Krugman, Paul 69
Kuhn, Thomas 89

Le Pen, Marine 78
Lefebvre, Henri 116–17
Levitt, Theodore 31–2, 65
Lexus and the Olive Tree, The (Friedman)
    33, 72–3
liberalism 74
Lie, John 8
literacy: global 161
Local-Global (journal) 43
localization 60
Lyotard, Jean-François 118

McCarty, Philip 16
McGrew, Anthony 98, 101
McLuhan, Marshall 7, 114, 117, 138
McNevin, Anne 47
market globalism 10, 165
market-globalist propaganda 169
marketization 59
Marxism 61, 69, 148, 153, 165
mass social movements 169, *see also* global
    justice movement (GJM); Occupy
    Movement
master concepts 1
Mazlish, Bruce 134–7
Meadows, Paul 29–30, 59
media 56; social platforms 140, 151
Mein Kampf (Hitler) 29
Middell, Matthias 12–13
migrants: Syrian 132
Mines, Mattison 38
Mittelman, James 11, 155–6, 171
Modelski, George 30–1, 95
modernity: and globalization 3;
    globalizing 23n4; inner logic of 122;
    vital impulses 119
Modernity at Large (Appadurai) 63
Monash University 42–3
mondialisation de certains marches (Perroux)
    31, 51n19
Morais, Duarte: and Ogden, Anthony C.
    160–1
Mulligan, Martin 43
multidisciplinarity: definition 90

Nadarajah, Yaso 43
Nairn, Tom 42, 43–4
nation formation theory 42
Negri, Antonio: and Hardt, Michael
    127–8
negroes: American socio-cultural views
    28–9
neo-Marxist scholars 69
neoliberalism 10, 75, 151, 163
network society 102, 103
networks: academic and intellectual
    188–9; globally integrated
    networks (GINS) 106–7; social 56;
    terminology 101; Zapatista solidarity
    163
Neubauer, Deane 44
New Left 166
new spaces 140
newspapers 4
Ngram 54

No Logo: Taking Aim at Brand Bullies
    (Klein) 167
Northrup, David 135–6

Occupy Movement 162I, 163, 167,
    177n29
Occupy Wall Street Camp 162I
Ogden, Anthony C.: and Morais, Duarte
    160–1
Ohmae, Kenichi 125, 126
Oliver, Melvin 40
online resources 183–4
ontologies: imaginaries, and ideologies
    74
Orfalea Center for Global and
    International Studies 40, 47
Orfalea Family Foundation 40
Orfalea, Paul 39–40
Orientalism 173

Pak, Anita: and Choi, Bernard 92
Pan American World Airways 4
para-keepers 11–12
Paramount Pictures 4
Pentecostalism 79
people-led globalization from below 150
Perraton, Jonathan 99, 101
Perroux, François 31, 51n19
Phipps, Peter 47
Pieterse, Jan Nederveen 12, 18, 48, 109,
    121, 170–1, 172
Pohl, Christian 95
political activism 157
political belief systems 73
political globalization 96–7
political practice: social theory 42
political religions 77
politics: and IR 30–1; religious 77
Polybius 133
postcolonial theory 173
professional global studies associations
    187–8
psychology and education 27–8
public globalization debates:
    hyperglobalizers 81; ideological
    perspectives 72–81, **80**; rejectionists 81
public intellectuals 154–5, 163, 164, 169,
    see also critical thinking

readers and textbooks 18, 24n29
redistribution: Keynesian-type 76–7
reflexivity 155
rejectionists 67, 81, 83n31

religious belief system 77
religious globalisms 78–9
religious politics 77
Repko, Allen 90, 91, 109
resources: academic and intellectual networks 188–9; academic programs 184–7; journals 181–3; online resources 183–4; professional associations 187–8
RMIT (Royal Melbourne Institute of Technology) 34, 43, 45
Robert Buffett Institute for Global Studies 14
Robertson, Roland 58–60, 117, 135, 141m5
Robinson, William 22, 56, 68, 123; and Appelbaum, Richard 152–5, 157–8
Rosenberg, Justin 171
Roy, Olivier 78
Royal Melbourne Institute of Technology (RMIT) 34, 43, 45

Sachsenmaier, Dominic 38
Said, Edward 173
Santos, Boaventura de Sousa 174
Sassen, Saskia 33, 64–5, 128, 129
Schattle, Hans: typology of global engagement **161**
scholarly literature 15
Scholte, Jan Aart 126–7
School of International and Community Studies (RMIT) 45
securitization projects 132
self-criticism 170
Shaw, Martin 66
Shock Doctrine, The (Klein) 168
shopping malls 56
silo mentality 41, 87
Sima, Qian 133
Sklair, Leslie 71, 153–4
Smith, Jackie 167
social interactions 4
social media platforms 140, 151
social networks 56
social processes 55, 66
Social Science Research Council (SSRC) 8
social theory 42
social whole 7, 13
society and culture 28–30
Socrates 146
Soka Gakkai International Buddhist network 79

sovereignty 127, 130
space of flows 105
space and time: concluding remarks 137–41; global history, challenge of periodization 132–7; globalization as a spatial concept 115–17; modernity or postmodernity 117–24; overview 21, 114–15; territoriality, sovereignty and spatial scales 124–32
space-time distanciation 119
spatial law 117
spatial and temporal dynamics 60
spatial turn 12–13
SSRC (Social Science Research Council) 8
Steger, Manfred 44, 45, 46; and James, Paul 27, 130
Stiglitz, Joseph 33
strikes in France 150
structural adjustment programs 126
student mobility 28, 50n9
studies (lesser status of) 89
Syrian migrants 132

Al-Tabari 133
tawhid 78, 85n49, 85n50
taxation: Keynesian-type 76–7
teaching: interdisciplinarity 87
technologies: advancement 5–6, 13, 28, 50n9
terminology issues 71
territoriality concept 124
terrorism 77–9, 79I, 158
Teune, Henry 23n10
textbooks and readers 18, 24n29
This Changes Everything (Klein) 169
Thompson, Hirst 67–8
time see space and time
time-space distanciation 119
Timor-Leste Research Program 46–7
Tobin Tax 77
Tomlinson, John 95
trans (Latin prefix) 91–2
transdisciplinarity: domains and dimensions 96–101, **98**; dynamics of 109; evolution of disciplines 87–90; and global complexity 94–6; globalizing the research imagination 108–11; interdisciplinarity or multidisciplinarity 90–4, **94**, 112n9; networks, flows, fluids, and hybrids 102–8; overview 86–7
transdisciplinary framing 20

transnationalization 123
transregional studies 12
Trump, Donald 78
typology of global engagement (Schattle)
 161

UCSB (University of California Santa
 Barbara) 34; global and international
 studies program 35–41; Provost's Ad
 Hoc Planning Committee 35, 37
umma 78
United Nations (UN) 30
Universal Pictures 4
University of California Santa Barbara
 (UCSB) 34
University of Hawai'i- Mānoa 36, 44, 48
Urry, John 105–8
US National Science Foundation 31

virtual reality 116
Voltaire 133

Wallerstein, Immanuel 70–1
Washington Consensus 76, 125–6

Waters, Malcolm 59
Westernization Theory 120
White, James 45
whole worldness 28
Williams, Raymond 57
World Economic Forum (Davos)
 73, **75**
World Is Flat, The (Friedman) 31
World Social Forum (WSF) 62, 163–4,
 165, 167, 177n36
World Trade Organization (WTO):
 demonstrations against 150, 150I
World War II (1939–45) 4–5, 8
World Wide Web 57, 151
world-space 137
world-system theorists 69–70, 84n37
world-systems 70–1

Young, Robert 173

Zapatista solidarity network 163
Zapatista uprising (Mexico) 150, 151,
 163, 164I, 175
Zola, Émile 154